BRIDGING INTENTION TO IMPACT

Transform Digital Product Development
Through Evidence-Based Decision-Making

T0292825

CONNOR JOYCE

Bridging Intention to Impact

Transform Digital Product Development Through Evidence-Based Decision-Making

Connor Joyce

New Riders
www.peachpit.com
Copyright © 2025 by Pearson Education, Inc. or its affiliates. All Rights Reserved.

New Riders is an imprint of Pearson Education, Inc.
To report errors, please send a note to errata@peachpit.com

Executive Editor: Laura Norman
Development Editor: Robyn G. Thomas
Associate/Sponsoring Editor: Anshul Sharma
Senior Production Editor: Tracey Croom
Technical Editor: Anushkaa Gupta
Copy Editor: Scout Festa
Compositor: Kim Scott, Bumpy Design
Proofreader: Kim Wimpsett
Indexer: James Minkin
Cover Design: Chuti Prasertsith
Cover Illustration: bizvector/Shutterstock and hamylove/Shutterstock
Interior Design: Kim Scott, Bumpy Design
Art credits: Figure 1.1: Grammarly Inc., Figure 4.2: Apple Inc.

ISBN-13: 978-0-13-836046-7
ISBN-10: 0-13-836046-4

1 2024

About the Author

My career has been filled with unique experiences, each contributing to the ideas in this book. I found a home at Microsoft, where I am a Senior User Researcher and am happily building the next generation of AI products. I am also the CEO of Desired Outcome Labs, where I consult on the adoption of the philosophy outlined in this book along with approaches for encouraging AI adoption.

I see myself primarily in three roles: as a mixed-methods researcher focused on obtaining the right data to empower product teams to make informed decisions; as a product builder who relishes the opportunity to create new solutions, from paper prototypes through digital products; and as a behavioral scientist, my special sauce, which enabled me to take the novel approach, introduced in this book, of creating products with a focus on the specific behaviors impacted.

I derive great satisfaction from guiding others to new perspectives, which I achieve through contributions to various publications, podcasts, and conferences. This passion has led me to lecture at the University of Pennsylvania, where I help students learn to grow with artificial intelligence advances. It was also the drive that led me to co-founding the Applied Behavioral Science Association to build a growth pipeline for anyone interested in the field.

Outside my professional life, I enjoy spending time over meals and activities with many outstanding people who I am so lucky to have in my life. I live in Seattle and have found the outdoors my refuge, especially when accompanied by Chai, a dynamic and genial Australian Labradoodle. My most peaceful moments are in the mountains, where I can connect with the scale and ephemeral nature of life.

Acknowledgments

To the three people whom I can guarantee I would not be here without, thank you for your love and support: Mom for being a role model of kindess and strength, Dad for your advice when I needed it the most, and Alita for your believing in me to the point that I believed in myself.

To the many mentors who have inspired and guided me throughout my career, thank you. A special thanks to those who guided me through my toughest periods: Matt Wallaert, Chris Gideon, Jason Marshall, and John Davenport.

Writing any book is not easy; writing during significant life changes makes it even more challenging. Countless individuals supported me throughout this endeavor—thank you each and all.

Thank you to my editors, especially Robyn Thomas, Anushkaa Gupta, and Laura Norman, who each played a unique role in getting me to the finish line. I enjoyed this enough that I think I will do it again.

I live by the saying that if I am content in my current situation, I cannot change anything from my past. Publishing this, I am at peace with the idea that I have contributed to a field that means so much to me…and thus I am grateful to every interaction that in some way served as a learning and growth opportunity on the path here.

Table of Contents

Introduction

Technology holds the power to reshape our world, and it is those who wield this power—builders, designers, and strategists—who determine its impact. Recently, the trend has skewed negatively, a concerning shift that many in the industry are hesitant to acknowledge. Over the last decade and a half, public sentiment toward major tech firms has soured, their products increasingly perceived as having a detrimental effect.[1] This is not the future we in the tech industry envisioned. Instead, we find ourselves navigating a landscape shaped by corruptive forces that prioritize growth and usage above all else. The industry did not set out to be here; instead, it is a variety of corrupting forces that have led to the maximization of usage and growth over all else. Advances in AI are catalyzing a transition to a new way to design and build products, providing an ideal chance to transform products. Throughout this book, I emphasize building products that satisfy user outcomes through creating specific behavioral change. I do this by reinforcing three primary points:

1. Usage alone does equate to a product having its intended effect on the end user.

   Many factors have converged to normalize this assumption in product development, which, regrettably, often misleads companies. It's all too common for users to emerge from intensive product interaction—what might be called a *usage trance*—only to discover that their desires, which led them to engage, remain unmet. Although product teams enthusiastically adopt growth-hacking strategies from leading texts—embracing concepts like habit formation, gamification, and behavioral design—they frequently neglect to integrate these with solutions that genuinely address user needs. The result is addictive products that don't satisfy the users' needs.

---

1 Pew Research, www.pewresearch.org/short-reads/2019/07/29/americans-have-become-much-less-positive-about-tech-companies-impact-on-the-u-s/

2. Building products that create positive outcomes for the user and the business requires focusing on specific behaviors.

    After witnessing the same patterns across various sectors—from nascent startups to multinational enterprises—I identified the missing piece from most product teams' development approaches: measuring and maximizing behavioral change. True technological value derives not merely from usage but from how it alters specific user behaviors and the consequential outcomes for both the user and the business. Until this change in focus occurs, we are bound to continue down the path of addicting products that don't deliver on their promises. In return, product teams will continue to face leaky buckets and high customer acquisition costs.

3. Ensuring that all features create their intended behavioral change requires establishing an evidence-based decision-making culture.

    Embracing this philosophy individually can yield substantial value, but replicating such success organization-wide necessitates a cultural transformation. This shift should inspire every team member to take ownership of the evidence that informs their decisions. It is crucial for product teams to foster a robust demand for researching, creating, and using insights in their product development strategies. Implementing this on a larger scale involves establishing a central repository for insights that is readily accessible and promotes a culture of experimentation. The goal is to cultivate an environment in which teams are reluctant to make decisions without solid supporting evidence.

Painting a narrative that connects these three points, this book builds on established product management strategies, drawing from Marty Cagan's foundational book *Inspired* and Melissa Perri's insights in *Escaping the Build Trap*, the focus on behavior change introduced by Matt Wallaert in *Start at the End and by Joshua Seiden in Outcomes Over Outputs*, and the experimentation mindset of Stefan H. Thomke's *Experimentation Works*. It presents a transformative approach known as the *Impact Mindset*. This philosophy, designed to complement agile development and design thinking, emphasizes validating the links between each feature's influence on behavior and its ultimate impact on user outcomes and business performance. Presented through a combination of frameworks, processes, and philosophical guidance, adopting the Impact Mindset begins with you, the reader, as a catalyst for grassroots change.

How I Created the Impact Mindset

My fascination with technology began in childhood, when unboxing a new gadget meant hours exploring every setting to uncover its capabilities. In school, this passion evolved; I shifted from the technical details to the human side—how people interact with technology and how it transforms their behavior. It was disheartening to hear complaints about technology failing to meet expectations, often fostering negative behaviors instead of creating a genuine positive impact.

Starting my career as a consultant implementing large human capital systems, I saw the mismatch between promised value and reality at a large scale. Brought in to help organizations adopt these new systems, I quickly learned how even significant investment in traditional change management could not fill the void that these technologies created. In search of something better, I found the field of applied behavioral sciences, which I saw as an agile approach compared to the waterfall of large-scale change programs. I decided to pursue a master's degree to explore its potential.

During my studies, I discovered behavioral science's broad applicability—from simple nudges to complex interventions designed to forge new habits. The insights in the field could be used to drive people to act according to their values and long-term desires. Yet one thing seemed irrefutable: technology would be needed for these solutions to scale. I decided to pursue a tech career, expecting a welcoming environment for these principles.

However, the transition revealed a stark reality: little consideration was given to the actual behavioral changes driven by products. If anything, I found that techniques from behavioral sciences were often misused to boost engagement without regard to consequences. Even companies that built their brands around helping people change behaviors did minimal research to ensure their products generated desired outcomes.

I am not alone in noticing this trend, and being vocal about my disappointment led to the opportunity to talk and work with many who were building out solutions in hopes of driving behavioral change. Seeing both the best case and the common shortcomings led me to question what was preventing the team from focusing on what mattered. Teams focused on driving abstract outcomes with no way of measuring them, and thus defaulted to more accessible metrics such as usage and satisfaction. Compounding this was incentive structures that demanded output over outcomes and made it easier not to ask questions.

My research into this issue clarified the core problem: the missing link between usage and impactful outcomes was the behavior changed by the product. If a company wants its users to lose weight, it must encourage less calorie consumption or more exercise. Increased productivity? Less engaging in distractions and more task-tracking. Better data infrastructure? More upfront organization and following processes. It all came back to the original reason I wanted to get into the field: the promise of technology to scale behavioral interventions that companies can build more sustainable solutions on.

This realization led me to develop the User Outcome Connection, a framework for evaluating how specific behaviors altered by a product influence user outcomes and business impacts. My first opportunity to test this concept came through a feature designed with a clear purpose yet unproven effectiveness. I collaborated with engineers and product managers, and we defined new metrics to measure behavioral changes post-interaction. The positive results validated the approach and sparked broader organizational interest in adopting this methodology, which became the primary process introduced by this book, the Feature Impact Analysis (FIA).

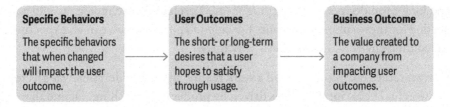

USER OUTCOME CONNECTION

Specific Behaviors	User Outcomes	Business Outcome
The specific behaviors that when changed will impact the user outcome.	The short- or long-term desires that a user hopes to satisfy through usage.	The value created to a company from impacting user outcomes.

As I shared these insights across organizations, I refined the philosophy into a comprehensive approach centered on building products grounded in validated User Outcome Connections: the *Impact Mindset*. I have found that adopting this framework is good for business, as it equips companies to develop products that retain users and promote organic growth, optimizing both customer lifetime value and acquisition costs.

Implementing a cultural shift and embracing a new philosophical approach to product development are monumental tasks. I have not written this book with the illusion that you alone should be responsible for creating the entire change. Instead, inspired by transformative works like Eric Reis's *The Lean Startup*, which advocates for a grassroots movement in organizations, it positions you to be the catalyst of the movement. Using the User Outcome Connection framework to illustrate the importance of rethinking features and sharing these insights, you will form the foundation of this culture change.

Defining the Impact Mindset

The Impact Mindset describes a novel product development philosophy that focuses on measuring and maximizing the behaviors that features cause users to do. My aim in writing this book is to encourage product teams of all sizes and throughout industries to adopt the Impact Mindset, as it yields more effective products that in turn increase business outcomes. The philosophy consists of four components that are explored in greater detail throughout this book.

TABLE A Four components of the Impact Mindset	
COMPONENT	**DESCRIPTION**
User Outcome Connections	Establishing a User Outcome Connection for each core feature helps teams understand the feature's purpose, validate behavioral changes, and ensure these changes positively influence user outcomes and business impacts.
Experimentation	Validating User Outcome Connections through experimentation involves collecting and analyzing data to generate insights, requiring systems that support the technical and administrative aspects of conducting experiments.
Insights Hub	Creating an Insights Hub centralizes all User Outcome Connections, research findings, and experimental results, fostering transparency and a shared understanding among team members to inform evidence-based decisions.
Evidence-based decision-making culture	Adopting an Impact Mindset requires cultivating a culture in product teams that prioritizes evidence-based decision-making, ensuring that every member understands their role in driving meaningful user actions aligned with user needs.

At the heart of the Impact Mindset is the validation of User Outcome Connections for all core features. Teams must develop these frameworks for each feature and find or create evidence that supports or refutes the connection between the behaviors changed by a feature, the satisfaction of user outcomes, and the resulting business impact. When new insights are needed to determine if a link exists between these variables, experimentation is required. Thus, having the infrastructure and team capabilities to conduct this work forms the second component.

As more demand for evidence is created due to the User Outcome Connections that need to be validated, a centralized location for all insights must be created. The third component of the Impact Mindset is the creation of an Insights Hub to store all feature definitions and the associated evidence that supports that they are achieving their intended purpose. A byproduct of having a unified hub for data that is organized in an intuitive way is that teams will have access to it to make decisions. Building a culture of evidence-based decision-making where teams are not just able to but truly empowered to seek, create, and rely on data for decision-making is the final component of the Impact Mindset.

You don't need to understand the intricacies at this point. Each step we take in this book will bring us toward the ideal end state. Whenever you're lost, recall the concept of the Impact Mindset and you will be sure to find a connection to one of these four concepts.

How to Use This Book

Bridging Intentions to Impact is tailored for product managers and user researchers, offering accessible concepts that are immediately actionable. However, the content is universally relevant, providing valuable insights for anyone involved in product development. The book is structured to support segmented reading—allowing you to engage with the material, apply the concepts, and return as needed—or to be a comprehensive guide.

Each chapter is designed to stand alone, delivering unique value on transitioning to the Impact Mindset, and concluding with key takeaways for quick reference. Read sequentially, the book presents a cohesive narrative through three sections. It begins with user outcome analysis, advances to Feature Impact Analysis (FIA), and culminates in the adoption of the Impact Mindset.

Part 1 deconstructs the User Outcome Connection, drawing on examples from the media industry to underscore the pitfalls of focusing solely on consumption metrics. You will see why measuring usage and usability alone leads companies astray. With this foundation, the remaining information solidifies the power of ensuring that behaviors that are changed by a product connect to user outcomes and, ultimately, to business impact. You will also learn the necessity of validating these connections to ensure that feature investments are genuinely fruitful.

Part 2 delves into the methodology of validating User Outcome Connections through FIA. This comprehensive five-phase process covers experimentation, the development of new metrics, and generating actionable insights. It lays out all the components needed to begin developing an Impact Mindset, and you will leave it equipped to start building your first User Outcome Connections and setting the stage for broader application.

Part 3 discusses how to expand from a single analysis into a cultural change. It includes detailed guidance on evaluating current capabilities and developing a strategic roadmap to bridge gaps, aiming to foster a culture conducive to sustained growth. You will leave this book ready to assess the systems and cultural change you will need to build, along with a vision to ensure that progress is made.

The narrative style varies across the book: Part 1 is theoretical, designed to build confidence and understanding; Part 2 is practical, focusing on detailed methodologies; and Part 3 is strategic, aimed at applying these insights on a larger scale. As you navigate the book, remember to start small, celebrate successes, and continually build on them.

Regardless of your approach to reading this book, two things are essential: familiarize yourself with the commonly used terms detailed in the glossary, which is included in the online resources, and use the complementary materials provided. These resources are designed to help you quickly transition from theory to practice, preparing you to grasp the concepts and champion them in your organization.

Theory to Action: Resources Offered Online

To support you through the implementation of the Impact Mindset a collection of resources is offered to you as part of your purchase of the book. The documents were constructed based on consulting I've done with companies to help them adopt these principles. Throughout the book I reference certain resources, but it can be beneficial to take a minute now to access the materials and familiarize yourself with what is available.

You must register your purchase on peachpit.com to access the lesson files:

1. Go to *peachpit.com/bridging*.

2. Sign in or create a new account.

3. Click **Submit**.

4. Click the **Access Bonus Content** link to download the bonus content from the Registered Products tab on your Account page.

If you purchased a digital product directly from peachpit.com, your product will already be registered.

Once in, you will see a collection of resources. Templates are ready for you to download and begin filling in. While the book holds the detailed steps and recommendations for how to approach completing a User Outcome Connection or to develop new metrics, these templates offer targeted guidance, ensuring you don't start from scratch. You will also find quick reference materials that enable the easy sharing of core concepts from the book. The book positions you as the leader of the Impact Mindset adoption, and equipped with these resources you will be ready to play that role. Additionally, you will find a glossary that defines the terms frequently used throughout the book.

Although you do not need to access these materials to benefit from this book, they are recommended to assist you in beginning to act on the book's recommendations. The vision of this collection of materials is to enable you to follow along with the book using a real example at your company. Ideally, you will complete the materials concurrently with the reading of each chapter, yielding you assets that are ready to share with your team. Concluding the book, you will be ready to kick-start an Impact Mindset shift at your organization. If you find yourself using and sharing these materials with your team, please reach out and let me know!

A Note on AI

I would be remiss if I did not address the artificial intelligence (AI) revolution that unfolded in 2023. Initially, I worried that the principles outlined in this book might become outdated in the rapidly evolving landscape of AI-enhanced products. However, as I delved deeper into the field, mainly through a set of projects that I led at a large start-up company, I discovered that the need for these teachings is more pressing than ever.

Artificial intelligence, especially generative AI, is just a tool, albeit a mighty one. Yet its capability does not automatically imply it should be used indiscriminately. Although AI can enhance product engagement, this does not translate to satisfying user needs or driving positive user outcomes. For instance, TikTok's sophisticated algorithm does not prevent user fatigue and frustration from overuse. Similarly, although a powerful chatbot, Google's Gemini does not ensure more efficient or satisfactory answers. Will these tools get better? Yes, but for genuinely satisfying outcomes, they must ensure they are changing the right behaviors.

On the development front, AI is likely to accelerate feature production significantly. However, this ability does not ensure the effectiveness of these features. If anything, it may exacerbate the existing problem of feature bloat. Personalizing the product experience to deliver precise solutions becomes crucial as the capacity to create features expands. This necessitates a deep understanding of why customers seek out specific solutions—essentially, a profound comprehension of their needs.

Although we cannot guarantee what the future of AI will bring, what is sure is that people will continue to use products with the desire to satisfy some need. Regardless of the development methods, investment in understanding these needs and the behaviors influencing them is essential. In a world where creating features becomes increasingly effortless, the competitive edge will belong to those who offer the most valuable solutions. Adopting the Impact Mindset prepares organizations to thrive amid technological advancements by ensuring a solid grasp of user needs, fitting in new solutions based purely on its impact on desired outcomes.

This book is the culmination of years of ideation and experimentation. It began with a commitment to invest in features with proven efficacy and has evolved into a comprehensive approach to feature development that ensures products grow in a positive direction for their users and the business. Whether you adopt a new framework for defining features, embrace a process to build on success metrics and foster experimentation, or fully integrate the Impact Mindset philosophy, I hope this book provides you with a fresh perspective. Let's get into it.

PART 1

FOCUSING ON BEHAVIORS TO BUILD VALUABLE PRODUCTS

Welcome to the first step of building products that work for your users. Building successful products starts with focusing on specific behaviors changed by a feature. We will delve into the foundation of building products that impact users and, in turn, the business—what I call the *Impact Mindset*. Breaking free from the standard product success definition to measure and maximize user impact is core to this approach.

You will leave this section

- Understanding why measuring usage and usability provides only part of the picture

- Knowledgeable on why it is important to measure the impact that features create

- Prepared to construct and use a User Outcome Connection

- Equipped with the knowledge and motivation to champion the adoption of an Impact Mindset

CHAPTER 1

Measuring Usage Is Only the Beginning

Take a deep breath. We are going to start our exploration of measuring the success of a product . . . with the heavy stuff. Imagine you are in a situation where customer churn is growing, and you cannot understand why. Even worse, the customer acquisition costs outweigh the money they bring in over their lifetime with the company. You look to your product analytics dashboards—you are hitting your application usage goals, and your net promoter score (NPS) is in the green, but customers are still leaving to your competitors. What do you do?

If you have been here, you are among the 71 percent of product builders who are unsure of how to understand the behaviors of users; you know the feeling of "flying a plane without all the instruments"—in other words, not having the correct data to resolve your biggest problems. This book reimagines the definition of product success by focusing on the behaviors that a product changes and the subsequent impact the product has on user and business outcomes. By offering a process to measure the impact a feature makes on user behaviors and outcomes, this book aims to put you on the path to positive customer experiences and a proven method to boost long-term business outcomes. You will be empowered to evangelize the measurement of impact that your features create for users, what we will call having an *Impact Mindset*.

That is all to come, but for now this chapter begins by detailing why situations in which product teams feel unequipped to diagnose and rectify product challenges are all too common. Then it covers how to avoid such situations. Starting at the highest level and moving more tactically, this chapter shows how over-reliance on usage statistics leads teams astray.

Ambitious Mission Statements, Misaligned Execution

Are you a frequent social media user or a gamer? If you are, ask yourself what desire you are trying to satisfy when engaging. If not, think about someone you know who can't seem to take a break from it. What objectives, conscious or subconscious, might they strive to achieve through their constant usage? What initial allure or circumstance prompted them to begin their interaction?

You might be thinking something along the lines of community building, friendship development and maintenance, or entertainment. Even those who have a nuanced, perhaps ambivalent, relationship with these platforms often underscore their perceived social and personal advantages. This perception isn't by chance; it's meticulously crafted. Leading digital companies have astutely shaped their brand narratives around aspirational ideals, with mission statements that echo these sentiments. Consider, for instance, Facebook's mission:

> To give people the power to build community and bring the world closer together.

And the beginning of Electronic Arts' (EA) purpose statement?

> At EA, we thrive on outrageous thinking. It's the fuel that inspires the best games in the world. We are a community of artists, storytellers, technologists and innovators working in one of the most dynamic industries today. We're building a company that thinks about the player experience at every step . . .

These lofty declarations might elicit skepticism, given the public's perception of these corporations as being profit driven. The dichotomy lies in the evident chasm between their articulated visions and the onground realities. The prevailing trend, not limited to them but pervasive across the entire tech industry, is an unwavering emphasis on crafting products that prioritize user engagement—often at the expense of user-focused outcomes.

Overuse of Usage Metrics as Success Criteria

A pattern is seen time and time again by companies developing digital products of all kinds: their initial, noble aspirations undergo a metamorphosis, gravitating toward a singular focus on maximizing user engagement for immediate revenue benefits. Prioritizing the growth of effortlessly developed surface metrics, they sideline creating transformative experiences that could benefit both the individual user and the broader global community and instead focus on marginal additions. It has led to about half of product teams suggesting daily active users (DAU) and monthly active users (MAU) being the primary measurements for success. Employees recognize this turn but don't fight it as their incentives become aligned to these metrics, and leadership enjoys the ability to point toward growth—regardless of what it means. Usage, a simple metric of whether someone engaged with a product, becomes the primary means of determining success.

Consider the evolution of Facebook. Starting as a digital yearbook, it stayed true to its mission of building community within college campuses. However, as its reach expanded beyond the confines of educational institutions, so did its user base—bridging geographical divides and fostering connections across regions and nations. The introduction of advertising mechanisms marked a pivotal shift; a new imperative to retain users for prolonged durations, primarily to enhance ad visibility, became supreme. This shift replaced a focus of fulfilling user community needs to encourage loyalty with a content strategy often prioritizing emotionally charged narratives, sparking debates and ensuring repeated user engagement. Before long, the Facebook product team abandoned its pursuit of increased social well-being and instead adopted a new strategy of building a platform that would do everything possible to keep users glued to their screens while filling space with ads whenever possible to juice profit.

As 2024 rolled around, Facebook began to communicate a desire to return to its roots and in doing so move closer to pursuing their mission of building a healthy community that creates more positive relationships than divisions. It begs the question, where should they begin? A possible starting point could be a recalibration of their content algorithm, emphasizing narratives that foster positivity. From there, they could develop new features to facilitate authentic community interactions and create deeper connections that might require conversations outside the Facebook ecosystem. It would require developing tools that nudge users toward more prosocial behavior along with determining what users genuinely desire out of a social platform and ensuring their new releases contribute to improving those factors.

This narrative isn't exclusive to Facebook. Most successful social media enterprises set out to establish new ways to allow people to communicate with each other. Yet, influenced by the pursuit of never-ending profit growth, they have shifted their focus to building emotional and gamified experiences to keep users glued to their products. Addiction equates to continuous advertising revenue. Of course, this shift probably didn't happen all at once, after one boardroom decision. Instead, it was likely a slippery slope as these companies incentivized their product teams to focus on the creation of free products that, through people's usage, generate valuable data used for targeting ads. Our modern social media industry continues to grow while it is also known to be increasing the likelihood of adverse mental outcomes for its users.

What they left on the table is the ability to fulfill user needs by creating products that sell themselves and encourage sustained loyalty. The advertising model, though financially successful, has left these companies vulnerable to fluctuations in consumer spending. Pressed to sell their products, early examples of paid versions of these platforms have shown little promise. Users appear reluctant to pay for services that fail to meet their fundamental needs for social connection. Another ramification of this is shown by how TikTok was able to quickly capture a part of this attention economy and build a strong user base. Had Facebook adequately fulfilled the needs for connection and entertainment, TikTok's ascent might have been less meteoric.

Social media companies are the most straightforward case study for what it means to maximize usage above all else; they have been able to survive by building addictive yet not always effective products. Many companies don't have the option of advertisement revenue. When they over-rely on usage, it means building a customer base that is expensive to acquire and is ready to flee as soon as a better alternative is created. It also leads product teams to feel bad about their work, with a 2021 survey by Productboard[1] suggesting that 69 percent of teams say their products and features are not consistently well-received by customers.

The video game industry illustrates this, with its increasing focus on engagement to drive microtransactions. This strategy has sparked a backlash, driving players toward independent developers who prioritize the creation of genuinely enjoyable and engaging games. Such shifts in consumer allegiance are telltale signs of an industry's overemphasis on engagement at the expense of meaningful impact. Overreliance on surface-level engagement metrics brought upon by misaligned business objectives has yielded many missed opportunities to genuinely impact desired user outcomes.

How Grand Ambitions Became Usage Obsessions

The formative years of the internet brought a transformative shift in the accessibility of information. A by-product of this was that content that publishers had traditionally nestled behind paywalls in newspapers and magazines found its way online, freely accessible to the masses. In response, many established entities adopted a hybrid approach, offering a selection of free articles to entice readers, hoping to redirect them to their paid offerings. When this failed to boost sales, executives questioned subscription viability and let free content became the de facto standard in hopes of turning the subsequent traffic into revenue another way. As the populace increasingly turned to the web for news, stalwarts like the *Wall Street Journal* and newcomers like BuzzFeed found themselves vying for attention, with website usage emerging as the primary metric for communicating their success.

Developing a business model around this new digital frontier, media companies began to realize that the ability to monitor user engagement offered a compelling proposition to advertisers, suggesting a direct correlation between eyeballs and advertisement spending.[2] A self-perpetuating cycle emerged: heightened user engagement led to increased advertising budgets, facilitating the creation of

---

1 Product Excellence Report 2021 by Productboard
2 *Traffic: Genius, Rivalry, and Delusion in the Billion-Dollar Race to Go Viral* by Ben Smith

even more content. Advertisers embraced this model, convinced of its superior return on investment (ROI) compared to traditional avenues. Usage growth became the gold-standard metric communicated within and across boardrooms, intending to garner more advertiser dollars. This trajectory—while initially promising—harbored inherent flaws, which we'll examine soon. However, a deeper dive is essential into the three systemic forces at play: default to the simplest metric to capture, lack of trust, and the ascendency of the advertisement model.

Defaulting to the Most Straightforward

The first factor is the allure of the usage metric, which lies in its simplicity. At its core, it is a binary of whether someone is engaged. At scale, it shares how many people interacted, their engagement duration, and their frequency of usage. Measuring usage comes naturally to any product or service; teams require a clear picture of whether people are engaging to make fundamental business decisions. The digital realm made these metrics even more accessible. As digital products gained prominence, measuring adoption became synonymous with these readily available metrics.

Product analytics tools, from their early iterations to contemporary giants, have enshrined usage as a cornerstone. Again, this is due to the simplicity of the metric, along with these products' goal to get customers to use their tool. Most of these products onboard a user by having them complete a usage-based dashboard. Even as these tools have evolved, offering a variety of data streams, usage remains the default starting point in product discussions. This default makes deeper explorations into the nuances of user engagement feel like a tremendous effort compared to what is already available to explore.

Concurrently, two prevailing business philosophies emerged. The first is encapsulated by the adage coined by John Doerr, "measure what matters." Although this mantra underscores the importance of quantifiable metrics in tracking progress and predicting outcomes, it commonly promotes a path of least resistance in practice. The result? A disproportionate focus on easily attainable metrics, with usage being the prime candidate in the technology space.

In parallel, developing a North Star Metric, or single metric that when increased yields product growth, has become a common step in any product launch.

Teams choose a metric that they hope to see spike as they push out their new features, all with the hope it ties back to positive business outcomes. Yet, they commonly fall victim to the trap of defaulting toward the most straightforward metric even without asking whether the single metric captures something that moves the company closer to fulfilling its mission.

Together these philosophies, *when done right*, are significant progress toward measuring the impact that products create; the problem is they are commonly not executed effectively. Strategic planning sessions, often initiated with ambitious objectives such as improving the effectiveness of a product, tend to narrow their measurement scope when confronted with the limitations of available metrics; the ubiquity of usage metrics in analytics tools further reinforces this trend. Thus, the team scopes its vision around what can be measured rather than valid quantifications of its aspirational goals. In the cases when teams venture beyond usage, they typically gravitate toward usability metrics that are commonly constrained by available tools, often defaulting to rudimentary customer satisfaction (CSAT) measurements or the polarizing NPS.

Measuring what really matters means finding the variables that connect to customer value, help form new habits of usage, inspire the team, and indicate long-term business success. This is even more important when selecting a single North Star Metric for the team to rally around. Airbnb might want people to be on its app searching for more time, but the real value it wants to maximize comes from nights booked. Tinder would like to see the number of swipes increase, but the real value comes from the number of matches or conversations it sees on its platform. These metrics really do matter for its product outcomes.

Unfortunately, when companies focus on the wrong metrics, the leadership still emerges from planning sessions harboring misplaced confidence in the faulty North Start Metrics and subsequent established goals, equating high usage or usability scores with fulfilling customer desires. But what success have they scoped? When leadership sets usage-based goals, it communicates to teams that they should focus on outputs over all else. Employees are mandated to prioritize improvements that enhance engagement, ultimately perpetuating the myth that usage equates to solving a user problem.

Lacking Trust Means Increased Dependence on Leading Indicators

When investors lack trust that a product team they have financed will accomplish their ambitious long-term goals, they tend to overemphasize growth to leading indicators. Due to its straightforwardness, usage stands as a quintessential leading indicator. Alterations to a product swiftly manifest in the initial data points, such as changes in user progression within an engagement funnel and the aggregate user interaction. The pervasiveness of usage metrics is such that they're often tracked daily, with week-over-week growth figures serving as a testament to their prompt availability.

In contrast, lagging indicators emerge over a more extended period. These metrics are discerned only after user interaction, providing insights into the subsequent effects on individuals or their surroundings. For instance, a budgeting app may immediately indicate the number of new budgets created, but it takes time to evaluate whether users are adhering to these budgets or whether specific interventions increase budget maintenance likelihood.

Leading indicators, while expedient for detecting immediate changes, tend to scratch only the surface. Product managers quickly identify they reveal engagement but fall short of indicating whether that engagement has achieved the objective—respecting that level of understanding requires patience. Yet they face a strong force preventing them from prioritizing the maximization of lagging indicators.

Our current economic framework, which favors the rapid ascent of metrics, often neglects the time necessary to determine if a product genuinely impacts a user. Trust in a product's ability to achieve its grand vision is scarce, with investors and markets alike fixating on upward trends. This trust deficit is often addressed by emphasizing the growth of leading indicators while hoping they will eventually influence the more consequential lagging indicators.

Consequently, companies are incentivized to prioritize the enhancement of these leading indicators, sidelining the actual impact on users. Similarly, public market investors focus on superficial data that promises immediate returns, often at the expense of considering the enduring effects on a company's customer base. Trickling down, this lack of trust influences leadership to demand their teams make product changes that grow the leading indicators over all else, further disempowering product managers from pursuing features that will truly transform the customer's life.

Ascendancy of the Advertisement Business Model: Maximize Engagement to Maximize Profit

Business leaders' focus on usage as the end-all metric is reinforced by our third primary factor: the ascendancy of the advertising business model. As was discussed with media companies, the intertwined histories of the internet and the advertising industry have shaped our digital landscape. The early days of the app ecosystem, embodied by the beginning of the iPhone App Store, witnessed a traditional software model. Popular apps such as Day One Journal and Scanner Pro became priced commodities like Microsoft Office or Adobe Creative Suite. Advertisers were an afterthought for those who could find a place for ads in the interface.

However, the meteoric rise of platforms like Facebook, offering expansive services at no cost, revolutionized this approach. These platforms positioned themselves as advertising hubs, leveraging user engagement to drive ad revenue. This approach's success didn't go unnoticed. In a short span, it became the preferred business model for app developers. The proposition was enticing: why convince users of an app's monetary value when gaining their time and attention sufficed? Soon, two of the most popular mobile apps were Evernote and Shazam, offered for free due to the backing of advertisers, who were happy to pay to have their content embedded in these products. Popular apps—emboldened by advertiser support—flourished on the basis that maximizing usage and retention would yield increased investment and profit. Building companies around the pursuit of engagement for ad revenue meant usage metrics were organically prioritized, and this belief spread without much question about the value being delivered to actual users.

Championed by industry titans like Facebook and Google, this trend grew with the advent of targeted advertising campaigns, promising enhanced ROI. The underlying premise was simple: increased user engagement equated to richer data profiles, translating to higher ad revenues. This model—dominant through the late 2010s—began showing cracks amid rising data–privacy concerns and questions about the actual value derived from incessant advertising. Yet its influence was profound, shaping the ethos of a generation of tech executives who assume product success can be evaluated using only usage and retention metrics.

The elevation of usage as the primary success metric is thanks to the confluence of its inherent simplicity and the advertising model's dominance. This focus was further amplified by the tech industry's growth-centric mindset, often fueled by venture capital. The funding structure these investors chose for many startups during the zero-interest-rate-phenomenon era viewed the pursuit of growth as the end-all metric to maximize. It meant choosing a North Start Metric that would showcase a graph going up and to the right without much concern for what was happening to the users within that graph. Users might love the product or hate it; it works for them, or it might decrease the likelihood they accomplish their desired outcome. In this paradigm, usage aligned with the primary metric that investors cared about without caring that it is indicative of engagement but offers little insight into genuine impact.

The Pitfalls of Solely Prioritizing Usage

Measuring usage is not a harmful practice entirely; only when it is the sole metric that companies focus on does it lead them astray. Engagement is paramount to building successful products; many life-changing prototypes are collecting dust on academic and R&D (research and development) lab bookshelves. Usage metrics, such as daily active users, duration, and retention, are valuable leading indicators for building an easy and enjoyable interface. The missed opportunity to build long-term viable solutions emerges when the pursuit of expanding user

---

Zero-Interest-Rate Phenomena

The "zero-interest-rate phenomenon" describes a period when central banks set short-term interest rates at or near zero, primarily to stimulate economic growth after significant downturns, like the 2008 financial crisis. This policy made borrowing cheaper, prompting businesses and consumers to spend and invest more. As a result, with an influx of capital seeking higher yields, venture capital (VC) firms began emphasizing rapid growth over immediate profitability for startups. This "growth at all costs" approach meant investors often pushed startups to prioritize user acquisition, leading to an industry-wide focus on usage metrics. In this environment, the number of users a startup could attract became a primary indicator of success, sometimes overshadowing other meaningful metrics related to usability, impact, and long-term viability.

numbers overshadows all other objectives, creating an environment in which problems arise without explanation.

The media sector confronted this reality in the early 2020s as audiences began disengaging.[3] While part of this shift is attributed to the allure of newer, more captivating platforms like TikTok, the saturation of low-quality content and *listicles* (for example, "20 pictures you must see before you die") had also peaked. As detailed in the book *Traffic,* by Ben Smith, for years, media giants, notably Buzzfeed, had shifted their content creation toward that which would become viral at as low a cost as possible, yielding engagement for cheap. Although each article might momentarily boost engagement, it rarely conferred lasting value to the reader.

These corporations lost sight of the fundamental reasons people sought content: information, understanding, and entertainment. Instead, these low-cost content pieces were devoid of depth or substance, offering only something to look at and maybe share with one's social media community. As the cycle continued, user after user became uninterested in the piece, no longer choosing to go toward a solution that was not satisfying their desire. The gradual decline accelerated, and by 2023, once-dominant media entities like Vice and Vox faced bankruptcy, while Buzzfeed languished, a mere shadow of its former glory.

The media industry was among the first to see the pitfalls of an unwavering focus on user acquisition. When an organization's focus is trained purely on adding more users, the outcomes that their users face become irrelevant. Growth comes at the cost of usability and use-case fulfillment. On a granular level, this might manifest as users abandoning a platform or hesitating to upgrade. On a broader scale, it distances companies from their visionary mission statements and, in more severe cases, contributes to societal challenges such as mental health issues, as touched on with social media, along with the reduction of privacy and increased social polarization.

These adverse outcomes caused by neglecting user-focused outcome metrics might take time. However, a pattern emerges over time: users are initially enticed, remain for a while, but eventually depart after realizing the platform doesn't meet their needs. In product jargon, this is called a *leaky bucket*. Even products that inherently create switching costs for users, like social media with

---

3 2023 Digital News Report by Reuters Institute

its vast network effect caused by a user's connections being on the same platform, aren't immune. As users discern the misalignment between their needs and the platform's offerings, even these giants face attrition.

The stakes for products in competitive markets are even higher without such built-in retention mechanisms. Without solving problems for users, users can easily switch to another solution as soon as a competitor launches a better solution into the market. Only when products are doing something for the user can a switching cost begin to form where customers will stay because they don't want to risk missing out on something valuable to them. And research shows that a 5 percent improvement in retention leads to an increase of at least 25 percent in profits.

Beyond retention issues, teams can commonly attribute operational challenges to an incomplete picture of product success caused by missing user outcome measurements. Groups operating in the dark about the real-world impact of their features are likely to grapple with product planning ambiguities. They must judge a feature's success based on engagement alone and make improvement and depreciation decisions with benchmarks that share only *what* happened rather than *why*. Decisions become rooted in intuition rather than empirical evidence. Looking at their metrics, such as daily active users and NPS, might highlight a problem. However, without a thorough understanding, correlations remain elusive, and teams are once again left chasing a number that doesn't matter to end users.

For product teams grappling with dwindling retention or significant challenges in planning, the initial inquiry should center on the product's tangible value to users. This approach transcends mere user engagement or usability. It delves into whether a solution transformed a user's behavior or perspectives through interaction. A product's success is genuinely affirmed only when tangible, real-world outcomes shift. Otherwise, it's hardly surprising when users swiftly transition to alternative solutions, lured by promises of faster, more affordable, or more innovative benefits.

Building new metrics requires time and effort, which most product people find scarce; it also requires the functional knowledge of creating new variables. By reading this book you are taking a step closer to expanding your metric portfolio. This chapter makes the case for adopting new metrics to equip you to sell the vision.

Measurements of Success Beyond Usage and Usability

One company, the *New York Times*, has successfully bucked the trend of declining usage faced by the media industry. Their leadership resisted the digital tide for years, appearing as a laggard in the early internet era. However, when they finally embraced the digital frontier, they eschewed the prevailing trend of offering vast amounts of free content. Instead, they leaned into their century-old strength: producing premium content worthy of a paid subscription.

The *Times*'s editorial board remained unwavering in its commitment to delivering articles that resonated with readers, satisfying their needs for information, understanding, and entertainment. As the digital realm became saturated with fleeting, free content, readers gravitated back to the trusted source they had relied on pre-internet. Subscriptions to the *Times* continued to climb as people enjoyed the experience of accessing their expansive library of resources while finding that it fulfilled their desires. By 2023, the *New York Times* boasted the most extensive subscription base of any U.S. media entity, a testament to their dedication to quality over mere engagement.

It is no surprise that the company, coming out of the "growth at all costs" era of media, also stuck to its lofty mission of "We seek the truth and help people understand the world." This ethos compelled them to look beyond superficial metrics, focusing instead on whether they were satisfying their readers' thirst for knowledge and entertainment. Describing their success, the consulting company McKinsey highlighted how the *Times*'s product team works alongside their reporters to find the best display format for each article to maximize the content delivery. This approach has proven beneficial at encouraging app returns, subsequently improving subscription retention.

User and Behavioral Outcomes

Measuring impact based on outcome metrics, in addition to usage and usability, is the core tenet of this book. This lens is called the *Impact Mindset* and focuses on measuring success based on whether a product made an impact on the outcome a user is attempting to create. Throughout the subsequent chapters, we will discuss the five levels of metrics shown in **TABLE 1.1**, each providing a piece of the puzzle to identify whether a feature is successful. With an Impact Mindset, success means an enjoyable experience that is widely used while also accomplishing its desired impact. We've already covered the first level of success

TABLE 1.1 Success Levels

LEVEL	DETAILS	EXAMPLES	BENEFITS	DRAWBACKS
Usage	Whether a user engaged with a feature	• Daily active usage • Usage growth	• Data is easy to capture. • Product teams are familiar with it.	• It offers little evidence toward the outcome the feature is creating. • Its simplicity makes it easy for teams to fall into the trap of overfocusing on it.
Usability	Rating of how well a user interacted with the feature	• Satisfaction score • Ease of use	• Lots of resources and frameworks are available to help capture and understand user interactions. • It can be easy as one question.	• The results are biased by users who respond at the moment and do not necessarily reflect long-term outcomes. • Obtaining nuanced data on user interactions requires thoughtful effort and user input.
Behavioral Outcomes	What actions a user took during and after interacting with a feature	• Frequency of daily journal entry completion • Length of conversations • Number of workouts completed	• These offer an understanding of what the feature is causing a user to do during and after usage. • These begin to explain whether a feature is having an intended effect on users.	• It does not explain the benefit a user experienced. • It is challenging to collect outside of digital environments.
User Outcomes	Impact to a user that occurred due to their usage of a feature	• Change in confidence • Data synced to warehouse • Gain or loss of weight	• The primary metric for determining if a product is impacting users in the desired way. • Powerful for communicating the effects of features.	• It is the hardest to measure. • It may require soliciting user feedback.
Business Outcomes	Impact to the business that occurs when user outcomes are fulfilled	• Revenue • Custom acquisition cost	• The most important metrics for the business's survival.	• Over focus on short-term outcomes can cause long-term value loss.

metrics in detail: **usage**. It is the easiest to measure and is good for understanding how much a product grows, along with whether it is sticky when measuring retention.

Usability, the second level, captures a user's sentiment toward their product experience. At its most straightforward, usability is measured as satisfaction and a single question such as, *On a scale of 1–10, what level of satisfaction did you have with this experience?* Another frequent approach is the net promotor score, commonly asked as *How likely is it that you would recommend this company to a friend or colleague?* Although both questions offer a glimpse into user sentiment, they remain surface-level indicators. For instance, a dip in NPS might signal a problem but doesn't pinpoint the root cause.

Making usability a more valuable measurement requires breaking the overall experience into defined chunks. More granular usability metrics, such as *Rate the level of difficulty that you had finding the Complete Purchase button*, provide more actionable insights. The question targets a specific element of the product interaction. If the difficulty-finding-a-button metric spiked, it is likely due to a bug or a recent design change, and with that information, the team could remediate it more swiftly. Quantifying usability is a newer approach that teams are adopting and has much to offer on building satisfying products. It is a powerful tool for measuring whether people like and will continue using a product, which is essential for growth, but it still doesn't determine if it fully satisfies user desires.

The third metric—the first novel one—in Table 1.1 introduces the **behavioral outcome**. This metric captures a user's tangible actions within the product environment and in their real-world activities post-engagement. Consider a meditation app with a user aiming for stress reduction. Behavioral outcomes might encompass the number of guided mediations in-app that they completed or more emotional check-ins they performed throughout the week—specific actions linked to their overarching goal. Behavioral outcomes focus on what activities a user performs during and after usage.

The fourth metric—another novel one—is **user outcomes**, which assesses whether a product has catalyzed the desired change or impact for the user. If that sentence confuses you, don't worry; the next chapter provides more detail. Following the previous example of a meditation app, the user outcome could be reduced stress, gauged by heart rate variability, or perceived stress levels. A team could measure both outcomes across time and in combination with the user's behaviors to determine if the product is making an impact.

The fifth and final metric is one that is all too familiar to the financial side of the business but is often overlooked by research and even sometimes product teams, the **business outcomes**. These are the variables that are used to track the success of the company at selling products. Used to determine whether a product is a viable source of funding to continue sustaining operations, these metrics are critical to the ultimate impact of a product to the firm. While generally determined by the leadership of the company, impacting these metrics with the release of new features is an essential component to a successful product.

A comprehensive assessment of these five metric levels paints a vivid picture of user engagement, sentiment, and the tangible benefits caused by specific actions prompted by the product. Adopting an Impact Mindset is underpinned by the ability to measure the behavioral and user outcomes, and the next chapter further details the value of collecting both. For now, let's explore two illustrative examples measuring all five success metric levels.

Case Studies: Grammarly and Ninjio

The first example focuses on a business-to-consumer (B2C) company, Grammarly, which offers a writing assistance tool. Consumers purchase the solution to have a significantly enhanced autocorrect that focuses not just on spelling but on the entire sentence structure. Grammarly doesn't stop working after fixing errors; it improves the user's writing by offering scores based on five metrics to measure a writer's success (**FIGURE 1.1**): grammatical correctness, clarity, engagement, and overall delivery. It has taken abstract constructs likely learned in grade school and turned them into beautiful visuals. As the tool learns more about the writer's style, it personalizes recommendations and the goals it attempts to improve through its recommendations. Grammarly's success, as per their marketing, is developing better writers, and their product does so as shown through anecdotal account and academic study alike.[4] **TABLE 1.2** shows how Grammarly could hypothetically measure the five levels of success of its app.

---

4 "Grammarly: An instructional intervention for writing enhancement in management education" hosted on Elsevier

FIGURE 1.1 Grammarly's five metrics to measure the effectiveness of a user's writing

TABLE 1.2 Grammarly Metric Level

LEVEL	EXAMPLE METRICS	DETAILS
Usage	App usage	Number of integrations activated (Gmail, keyboard, etc.)
Usability	App satisfaction score	Ratings of grammar suggestions
Behavioral Outcomes	Number of rewrites based on suggestions	Increased rewriting to maximize four main metrics for the writer
User Outcomes	Reduction of errors	Greater impact of writing
Business Outcome	Customer retention	As Grammarly improves writing, a customer will continue paying for it

Shifting to the business-to-business (B2B) space, Ninjio addresses the pressing issue of cybersecurity awareness. Recognizing that many cyber breaches are caused by human error, their solutions focus on training employees on best practices to reduce human-based cyber risk. They have developed a suite of programs intended to train employees on risk-reducing behaviors. One of their offerings, Ninjio Aware, comprises short, engaging videos that spotlight specific actions that employees can adopt to minimize errors. By creating memorable learning experiences, Ninjio aspires to reduce data breaches, a claim that a customer can test by using fake email phishing campaigns. **TABLE 1.3** shows how Ninjio could hypothetically measure the five levels of success of its training.

TABLE 1.3 Ninjio Metric Level

LEVEL	EXAMPLE METRICS	DETAILS
Usage	Video engagement rates	Completion of modules
Usability	Video ratings	Website NPS
Behavioral Outcomes	Increased reporting of potentially harmful emails	Decreased sharing of company information without protection
User Outcomes	Decreased data breaches	Increased knowledge of best practices
Business Outcomes	Seat expansion	As the business sees increased security awareness, they will continue purchasing more licenses

Comprehensive Approach to Metrics for Your Team

You might be pondering the feasibility of adopting the Impact Mindset and implementing such a comprehensive metric system within your team or organization. Doubts may arise regarding the practicality of crafting metrics across all levels. However, transitioning to this holistic approach is gradual, and the rewards explored throughout this book are profound.

The initial step is to galvanize your team around looking beyond mere usage metrics. Surprisingly, this shift often encounters less resistance than anticipated. Companies often attract talent with their ambitious missions, and employees are inherently driven by the prospect of crafting products that resonate deeply with end-users. Your role is to weave the narrative, highlighting how this multifaceted approach fosters a more intimate bond with customers.

Rest assured, you're not alone if you doubt the measurability of behavioral and outcome metrics. Addressing this very concern is a primary objective of this book. Chapter 2 touches upon, and Chapter 7 goes into extensive detail about, a methodical process for this, which commences with detailed observations of user interactions, distilling these into discernible behaviors and subsequently formulating proxy metrics. The reality is that wherever behavior occurs, a team can measure it, so it is not whether it exists but rather how difficult it is to measure and how to make the process of measuring it simpler.

Admittedly, this approach is more intricate than the straightforward task of gauging usage; otherwise, everyone would be doing it. However, its merits are undeniable and guarantee a competitive edge in satisfying user needs. A product's efficacy is contingent on its usage, but its transformative impact hinges on its effectiveness. Therefore, while usage metrics are indispensable, they should complement other indicators that elucidate the broader impact. The ensuing chapter will delve deeper, illuminating the possibilities that unfold when teams grasp the full spectrum of their product's success.

CHAPTER RECAP

- **The Impact Mindset:** A new lens for determining product success, focused on whether usage achieved the outcomes that a user desires.

- **The usage metric pitfall:** Solely relying on usage metrics can lead to a narrow view of success, potentially sidelining the actual value delivered to users.

- **Historical context:** Our modern emphasis on usage metrics stems from the philosophy of "what is measured, matters," combined with its ease of measuring engagement and the influential ascent of the advertising-driven business model.

- **Staying true to core values:** The *New York Times'* resurgence, driven by its commitment to quality, highlights the long-term benefits of an outcome-centric approach.

- **A holistic measurement framework:** Evaluating product success requires a layered approach, considering not just usage but also usability, behaviors, and ultimate outcomes.

- **Implementing the approach:** Transitioning to a multi-metric approach is a gradual process, but with commitment and a straightforward narrative, teams can better align with their product's true impact on users.

CHAPTER 2

Exploring the Value of Measuring User Outcomes

Picture your favorite digital tool. Visualize yourself using it, connecting with the emotions that are evoked. Now, reflect on the aftermath of your interaction. What elements make it so special to you? My favorite digital tool is an app named Delightful, a simple gratitude journal. Merely mentioning it makes me smile as I'm transported to the comforting sensation I get after every entry. My interaction with Delightful is as simple as reminding me each day at 8 p.m. to record three things I am grateful for. Yet the emotional depth I traverse with it is profound. Every interaction grounds me, infusing a sense of gratitude even on challenging days. This modest tool aids my quest to pause and meditate on all the good in my life.

If Delightful were to analyze my daily activity, they'd see a moderately active user. A usability survey might hint at my appreciation, albeit with some interface gripes. With this data, they might presume I'm on the brink of churning. But if they gauged the surge in my happiness, the dip in stress levels, or the frequency of my daily gratitude pauses, they'd realize the monumental shift their app has instigated in my life. Adopting an Impact Mindset and the complete picture of product success it offers would provide them with the reality that I am a highly committed superfan who is ripe to be targeted for a premium version—if they ever create one.

Solely tracking usage and usability can mislead teams to inaccurate assumptions about their products' value to users. True value is when companies can definitively solve user problems, which then sets the stage for favorable business outcomes. Products that successfully achieve the outcomes that users seek not only enhance customer experience but also boost retention and increase customer lifetime value. Moreover, they cultivate a reputation for efficacy, which can reduce marketing expenses and complement the increasingly prevalent product-led growth strategy. This chapter explores these benefits and others associated with developing products that positively influence all four tiers of success metrics.

Tools That Change Behavior to Satisfy User Needs

Virtually every digital product enterprise boasts a grand mission statement reminiscent of those championed by giants like Facebook and EA. Yes, it is partly because these companies start with noble aspirations to revolutionize the world. In the early days, a lofty mission represents not only a compelling narrative for fundraising but also an ever-expanding vision that can continue to be used to pursue more capital in private and public markets.

Such ambitious mission statements resonate with customers, signaling a company's commitment to enhancing their lives. Take Grammarly, which was touched on in Chapter 1. Their mission, "To improve lives by improving communication," might have seemed a tad ambitious in its early days. However, their current product lineup genuinely embodies this vision. They have used this guiding mission to raise over $400 million and continue to grow even in a market that is filled with powerful competitors. All this is driven by their CEO's focus on their customer needs and following through with building solutions that work for them.

Grammarly's aspiration to make a significant impact isn't an anomaly. Customers have been conditioned to expect companies to cater to their every whim in today's consumer-centric landscape. Supermarkets consolidated diverse grocery offerings in one place, which was then eclipsed by superstores offering even more. Ready-made meals, car washes, and beauty offerings once reserved for the elite have become more commoditized and accessible. For most, a myriad of desires can be fulfilled within a short drive. Organizations now recognize that to satiate the heightened expectations of modern consumers, they must deliver immediate value along with a promise for a brighter future. With the rise of the digital economy, it is easy to question why there isn't a digital solution for every conceivable challenge. And once a solution emerges, a superior alternative is invariably around the corner.

At the heart of this trend lies a simple truth: consumers spend their time and money on products and services that address their needs. Technology either accelerates real-world tasks or unlocks experiences beyond physical constraints. Digital products are—at their core—tools, and tools are used to solve problems. This includes tools like Grammarly, which refines writing; Audible, which offers a vast library of audiobooks; and Hinge, which facilitates connections ranging from fleeting encounters to lifelong partnerships.

Perceiving products as tools naturally leads to an urge to evaluate their efficacy in fulfilling user objectives. The once-revered usage metric is dethroned, revealing its limited scope: mere engagement, devoid of any insight into actual utility. Embracing this view will lead to abandoning what is currently an assumption based on convenience—that increases in usage indicate that a product is achieving its intent.

Tracking and measuring the outcomes created by-products is not entirely novel. Two predominant philosophies, outcome-driven innovation (ODI) and human-centered design (HCD), have already garnered widespread usage and acclaim. A review of what has made these philosophies so pervasive in the product development space can illuminate the power of focusing on user needs. However, their limitations also highlight the potential enhancements that are introduced when adopting an Impact Mindset and zeroing in on the effects that the product generates.

> **NOTE** For those well versed in these frameworks, feel free to forgo this section. However, understanding their historical context can be invaluable, especially when discussing the concepts of this book with stakeholders familiar with these philosophies. It also underscores how an impact-centric approach augments these already robust methodologies.

Outcome-Driven Innovation and Jobs to Be Done

In 1991, Anthony Ulwick, who coined ODI, advocated for understanding a customer's core objective and desired outcome. Collaborating with giants of the Fortune 500, including Apple and Intuit, he developed a five-tiered blueprint, as shown in **FIGURE 2.1**, to decode customer needs and devise strategies to meet them.

FIGURE 2.1 The 5-step outcome-driven innovation framework

Step 1: The journey begins by defining the market landscape. Doing so requires identifying what group of potential customers a company is catering to, combined with their jobs to be done (JTBD). Think of JTBD as the role a product plays in a customer's life; it is a framework for identifying what a customer is hiring a product to do for them. With a solid job defined, the group of customers are those who would ultimately do the "hiring."

Kitchen appliances offer a straightforward way to evaluate jobs. For instance, consider a JTBD focused on reheating food with the steps of preparation for reheating, the process of reheating, and cleaning after reheating. Ovens can do it, but they require waiting for preheating and can seem overkill for something small. Microwaves are also capable but carry a risk of drying out food. Frying pans can enhance the flavor of reheated food but require significant cleanup. Rapidly growing in popularity over the 2020s, air fryers have found success by completing the reheating job the most effectively. With this defined JTBD, identifying the primary purchaser comes more naturally. In our kitchen scenario, it's likely the household's primary cook or the main breadwinner.

Step 2: Next in the ODI process is uncovering customer needs. This is about dissecting the JTBD into steps and identifying tangible, quantifiable outcomes at every turn. Using our reheating analogy, consider the first phase, preparation. Key outcomes include time, additional equipment (plates, pans, etc.), and the number of actions required to initiate the process. A potential solution would aim to maximize each of these needs. The air fryer takes no time to preheat, requires no additional plates, and requires the user to turn only a few knobs to begin. Defining customer needs in this way ensures that they are quantifiable, allowing a company to compare solutions effectively.

Step 3: With quantifiable outcomes identified, the third step of the ODI process involves identifying opportunities where needs are not met or solutions are over-engineered. In the former, current solutions are underserving customers when they do not create a high enough outcome to satisfy the need. New solutions could be created to better perform at the most important outcomes. In the latter, current solutions are overserving when they deliver too many aspects that are not of the highest importance to customers. New solutions here could forgo the extra elements to match users' expectations and do so with a cheaper approach. Truly identifying outcomes requires determining their measurements and hierarchy of importance.

Step 4: As the exploration of jobs and outcomes progresses, patterns emerge. Distinct customer segments with unique preferences become evident. When this occurs, the fourth step of the ODI flow comes into play: designing tailor-made solutions for each subpopulation. Instead of a generic approach, the emphasis shifts to bespoke solutions catering to specific customer clusters with distinct needs.

Step 5: The final step of the ODI process involves aligning current products to market needs while creating new products to solve underserved outcomes. With a comprehensive outcome list at hand, marketing becomes intuitive, spotlighting standout features. If existing products don't hit the mark, it's an opportunity to innovate, focusing on the most impactful outcomes. Following this process ensures a company stays in an innovative loop, continuously understanding their customers' greatest needs and positioning solutions to solve them.

Although ODI's holistic approach boasts a stellar success rate, it demands significant time and resources. Hence, many firms lean toward the more streamlined JTBD methodology. Digital product managers often reference JTBD during brainstorming sessions or marketing pitches. Regardless of where a company falls on the ODI process, ranging from full adherence to casually using the JTBD spectrum, this philosophy is a useful launching point to understand why a person "hires a product" and how to measure the outcomes that it creates.

To further illuminate the JTBD concept, let's explore a few illustrative examples in **TABLE 2.1**.

TABLE 2.1 Examples of Jobs To Be Done			
COMPANY	**DESCRIPTION**	**JTBD**	**ALTERNATIVES**
Ring	At-home security system that has grown into a large business, ultimately being acquired by Amazon	Protect a property from trespassers and intruders.	• Private security • Living in a high-rise
Zillow	A property listing site that collocates residences for sale and rent across a variety of sources	Find property listings quickly and easily.	• Real estate agents • Home listing magazines
DocuSign	A digital product that turns contracts into documents with easy signature capabilities	Sign documents easily.	• Pen and paper • PDF documents

Human-Centered Design and Design Thinking

Human-centered design (HCD) has deep roots predating the digital product era. The Stanford Design program, under the guidance of Professor John Arnold, is believed to be the pioneer in emphasizing human-centricity in design. In their seminal work "Designing for Everyday Things," Don Norman and Jacob Nielsen shed light on this approach, making it a must-read for digital designers. IDEO, a renowned design agency, championed HCD in its projects, with the creation of the original Apple mouse, a well-known achievement.

Around the same time, *design thinking* emerged as a philosophy. Though its origins predate the digital age, its prominence soared when IDEO harnessed it for groundbreaking innovations. Recognized as a dynamic approach to product design, design thinking is a structured six-step process. It emphasizes swift ideation, leading to the evolution of user-centric solutions. This methodology has been instrumental in crafting numerous standout products, ranging from Willow, a wearable breast pump, to an updated approach to voting in Los Angeles County.

The relationship between HCD and design thinking isn't as clear as that between ODI and JTBD. HCD and design thinking can be used as both philosophies and processes. They have been widely discussed, championed by industry leaders, and adopted by top-tier design and consulting firms. For the purposes of this book, we will consider HCD a broader philosophy and design thinking a process to implement it, in the same way that JTBD is a necessary step to complete the ODI approach. The importance for both is the creation of solutions tailored to user needs.

Embracing HCD means prioritizing users and understanding their context. The Interaction Design Foundation, a leading voice in the domain, highlights four pivotal HCD tenets.

- It's about keeping users at the forefront and understanding their motivations, actions, and objectives.

- Ensuring that the devised solution addresses the right problem is crucial.

- Every solution exists within a broader ecosystem; this context is vital.

- Iterative, incremental feature development is preferred over massive, singular updates.

Adhering to these principles paves the way for crafting products that resonate with users. But how is this operationalized? Although HCD offers a high-level roadmap—defining user needs, ideating solutions, testing and refining solutions, and implementing—design thinking provides a granular approach when a team wants more detailed guidance. As articulated by the Nielsen Norman Group (NN/g), a leading user experience agency, design thinking unfolds in six stages, as shown in **FIGURE 2.2**.

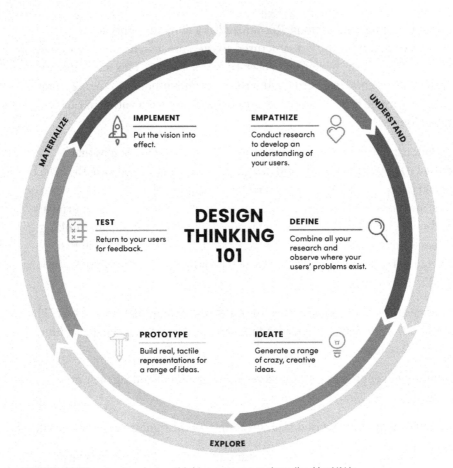

FIGURE 2.2 The six-step design thinking process as described by NN/g

Stage 1: The design thinking process starts with the Empathize stage, when users are researched to develop an understanding of who they are and the context they operate within.

Stage 2: Once the user is understood, the Define stage pinpoints specific user challenges.

Stage 3: The Ideation stage encourages inventive brainstorming, urging teams to venture beyond conventional boundaries.

Stage 4: Once a set of promising solutions emerges, the focus shifts to the Prototype stage, balancing testability and flexibility to make rapid changes.

Stage 5: Naturally, testing these prototypes is the subsequent stage.

Stage 6: Upon identifying a standout solution, the final stage is implementation.

Whether a team loosely adheres to HCD principles or rigorously follows design thinking, the crux remains the same: a deep-rooted understanding of users and their needs. This user-centric ethos ensures that solutions seamlessly integrate into users' lives, fostering genuine engagement. The goal is to create meaningful solutions that users gravitate toward rather than coercing usage.

TABLE 2.2 includes a few examples that further illustrate the definition of user needs.

TABLE 2.2 Examples of User Needs

COMPANY	DESCRIPTION	CONTEXT	USER NEED
Venmo	Focused on increasing the ease of making person-to-person payments	After going out to dinner with friends, collecting money from those without cash is challenging.	People need to easily send money to their friends after dinner or entertainment.
Snowflake	Cloud database company with many services to easily manage data	Companies are relying heavily on the creation of databases to store their user data and use it for many downstream applications.	Data engineers need to have clean, accessible data stored in the cloud.
Slack	A productivity and communication application that allows for multiple channels of sharing information	Employees are working across time zones and need to store information for future reference.	Employees need the ability to communicate with their team across time zones.

Commonalities Among These Frameworks

ODI and HCD are influential methodologies with a global following. Both have been proven to yield powerful business outcomes for companies that are able to build new, valuable solutions. These approaches champion the user, ensuring that solutions are tailored to their needs and aspirations. By doing so, they challenge teams to move beyond assumptions and genuinely understand user requirements. Both approaches focus on how solutions could truly change a user's life in a positive direction.

The identification and resolution of core user challenges are central to both ODI and HCD. Their processes encourage the creation of products that understand a user and the context they are operating within. ODI culminates before the design of an actual solution, leaving the team with a profound comprehension of the primary outcomes that a solution should address. Empowered with this, a streamlining of the design process should follow, along with the measurement of prototypes based on the degree they satisfy user outcomes. But it does require a design team familiar with ODI on top of their chosen design framework.

In contrast, HCD, particularly design thinking, encompasses a comprehensive design journey, detailing the solution's blueprint. Teams following the HCD philosophy have a path from scoping a potential feature through a well-tested design ready to launch. The completeness of the HCD approach means it is especially well equipped to help a company deliver a solution that fulfills user needs.

> **NOTE** While this book offers design insights, its primary focus is on evaluation. The novel frameworks introduced are intended to be used in conjunction with established frameworks, with a particular emphasis on design thinking, which the author has the most experience applying. Integrating an Impact Mindset ensures that teams have a deeper understanding of their features, increasing the likelihood that chosen solutions accurately address user challenges.

The Value in Measuring Specific Behaviors

ODI and HCD focus on needs, jobs, and the user, but they both have deficits when generating quantitative metrics to measure them. Although ODI introduces some quantifiable elements, it often becomes convoluted and predominantly focuses on tangible outcomes, overlooking emotional and long-term goals. On the other hand, HCD offers limited support in this measurement domain. As a result, many product teams possess a rich qualitative understanding of their users' needs but lack clear definitions of exactly what a feature is doing to help users fulfill their desire. When metrics are created, they focus on the usability of the feature, the insight ends at whether people are perceiving the experience as useful. Both methodologies acknowledge that users seek specific outcomes from solutions but fall short in the evaluation of whether outcomes are genuinely achieved.

One of the main drivers in the lack of useful metrics for defining true product success is that neither framework has a component focused on the identification of specific behaviors that a user must take to satisfy their need or achieve a certain outcome. For instance, while ODI and HCD will identify that a user desires to increase their daily mindfulness, neither is built to identify the specific actions required to facilitate that change. Only through adopting an Impact Mindset will a team pinpoint connected behaviors—such as taking moments for emotional reflection or increasing meditation sessions that would encourage the user's desired outcome. Defining these behaviors is critical for developing products that can truly make an impact.

Absent these behavior-focused metrics, teams often revert to tracking surface-level metrics. ODI and HCD practitioners, when advocating for user experience measurement, do exactly that, quantifying the experience itself rather than the transformation in outcomes. This approach can yield products that function well but don't fully meet the user's needs. It's only by examining the actions that users take that teams can gain a full understanding of a product's effectiveness.

Identification and measurement of specific behaviors is the standout difference between an Impact Mindset and these other frameworks. By mapping connected behaviors to the user outcome, a team can define success at all four levels, but especially with behavioral outcomes, which become a leading indicator much more powerful than usage. Empowered with the Impact Mindset, teams can confirm not only that their features are modifying the intended behaviors but also that these behavioral changes are impacting the desired outcomes.

By charting the course of user actions, the Impact Mindset enhances ODI and HCD, overcoming their measurement shortcomings and ensuring that solutions have a tangible effect on user outcomes. Integrating the Impact Mindset with design thinking enables teams not only to identify the user outcomes that need addressing but also to pinpoint and target the specific behaviors that a feature will influence, allowing for precise measurement during product testing. This amalgamation of methodologies paves the way for features that deliver lasting impact and fulfill user needs effectively.

Impact Mindset as a Business Strategy

Embracing an Impact Mindset goes beyond assessing product usability or gauging customer sentiment. It's about creating products that change user behaviors and, by doing so, consistently satisfy user desires and needs. When companies adopt an Impact Mindset, they are establishing a system of tracking and validating the impact each feature intends to create. When it's done right, teams can be confident their product is creating a positive customer experience by improving user outcomes after each use and throughout the user's entire journey.

Illustrating the benefits of adopting an Impact Mindset at its finest is the Fabulous app, which not only has an outstanding user experience, as shown by its multiple awards for exceptional design and functionality, but that has numerous stories showing that it helps users follow through with their desired change. Designed as a lifestyle tool, Fabulous aids users in adopting healthier habits. Its consistent top ranking on the Apple App Store is a further testament to the profound influence it has on its user base. The app's success is attributed to the team's unwavering commitment to a captivating design that not only resonates with users but also encourages repeat engagement. With its focus on habit formation, Fabulous assists users in realizing their behavioral change goals. By translating user goals into actionable strategies, Fabulous epitomizes the essence of user-focused design, solidifying its renowned position in the digital realm.

Short- and Long-Term Outcomes

In the competitive landscape of the fitness industry, Peloton confronts a universal challenge, but magnified. Users approach their platform with aspirations like shedding 15 pounds, enhancing stamina, or increasing muscle mass. Although these goals are attainable, they demand hard work and dedication. Peloton's array of offerings facilitates this journey. Their secret sauce is not in their physical fitness equipment—the only addition to a standard stationary bike is a giant tablet. It lies in the immersive experience and rewards they curate for users during each session.

Synonymous with a vibrant, health-conscious lifestyle, Peloton has mastered the art of fostering exercise habits. They have crafted every interaction with their equipment to be gratifying, propelling users to prioritize their next session. Created through gamification elements along with reflection on the positive sentiment experienced by completing a workout, each workout leaves a user with a positive short-term outcome. Over time, these consistent, positive interactions evolve into habits, putting users on track toward achieving their long-term fitness objectives. **TABLE 2.3** illustrates how short-term goals accomplish long-term goals.

TABLE 2.3 A Collection of Short-Term Versus Long-Term Outcomes

SHORT-TERM OUTCOMES	LONG-TERM OUTCOMES
Single interaction/at most one day	Across interactions/more than one day
Satisfying some want or need from a user after a single interaction with the product or service	Satisfying a want or need that occurs over time in a user's life
Improving one's thoughts or feelings	Increasing aspects of one's wellbeing
Providing useful Information	Improving productivity
Saving time or action	Learning new knowledge or ability

Rarely do users interact with digital platforms solely for the act of engagement. Instead, users are interacting with a product or service to satisfy a need that can be short-term, long-term, or both. Short-term outcomes manifest within a single interaction, altering the user's immediate lived experience. It can mean creating a positive emotion, such as the boost of dopamine from completing a video game level, or removing a negative feeling, as is done when escaping boredom by finding entertainment from media. Numerous services, like Doordash or Instacart, have emerged to cater to users' immediate convenience needs. Essentially, products address a short-term outcome when they cater to an immediate user requirement.

Satisfying short-term outcomes can occur at two levels in the case of business-to-business products. Take, for example, delivering relevant context to call center employees in as simple a way as possible. At the individual level, this would manifest in call center employees spending less time and mental resources reading previous call logs, allowing for a more meaningful connection with the customer. At the organizational level, this would yield higher-performing customer support calls, as shown in outcomes such as faster time to resolution and higher satisfaction rates, ideally leading to the longer-term desire of customer retention.

Shifting the focus to long-term aspirations, the spectrum of desires broadens. For individuals, a widely understood desired outcome is well-being improvements. Two facets of this are mental and financial well-being. The former occurs when someone can relieve stress and feel happier. The latter generally means improving emergency and retirement savings. Another long-term outcome commonly sought is developing new knowledge and skills, such as how Duolingo assists with learning a new language or how LinkedIn Learning enables new skill development.

Organizations, too, invest in solutions targeting long-term benefits, often underpinned by substantial data. Productivity enhancements remain a primary objective. This could manifest as detailed metrics like reduced sales cycle durations or more abstract indicators like improved mental well-being. Long-term outcomes don't end at productivity, though, and products can aim to reduce the cost of customer health insurance or decrease employee turnover.

Discerning short- and long-term outcomes is pivotal for crafting products that captivate users and drive behavioral shifts that lead to impact. Creating a sticky or habit-forming product starts with ensuring that every time a user visits the solution, they are fulfilling a short-term outcome. Doing so makes the experience fun and a destination they want to visit repeatedly. Then, the art lies in ensuring that short-term gratification is aligned with actions that contribute to long-term goals. Users might not witness immediate progress toward their overarching objectives, but the consistent short-term rewards keep them engaged, cumulatively leading to long-term achievements. For a deeper dive into this design philosophy, I recommend *Engaged: Designing for Behavior Change,* by Amy Bucher (Rosenfeld Media LLC), or *Design for Behavioral Change: Applying Psychology and Behavioral Economics,* by Stephen Wendell (O'Reilly Media). For the context of this book, it's imperative to understand and measure both short- and long-term outcomes for product success.

A quintessential illustration of this balance is the financial app Acorns. Every interaction with Acorns shows users their progress toward building an emergency fund. Acorns' unique proposition is its feature that rounds up users' transactions, incrementally boosting their savings. This approach has not only cemented Acorns' position in the financial sector but also empowered countless individuals toward financial resilience. Acorns bridges the gap between the intent to save and actual savings, not by mere user engagement metrics but by tangible growth in users' savings.

Quantified Self Movement

The "quantified self" concept first emerged in the 1970s, only to fade within a decade.[1] It then experienced a resurgence in the early 2010s with a deluge of devices designed to metricize various facets of personal life. Wearables like the Apple Watch and Fitbit became cultural phenomena, offering personal data and a social platform on which to share these metrics. However, the mere quantification of one's daily life holds little value outside of the pursuits of academics; the true allure lies in the potential health and wellness improvements these devices promise. Over the past decade, the quantified self industry has spawned hundreds of companies, each angling to improve users' lives. The victors in this space have been those who embraced an Impact Mindset, expertly delivering on both short- and long-term outcomes.

The initial wave of "quantified self" companies excelled in integrating sophisticated sensor technology, once exclusive to medical facilities, into consumer gadgets. People could now monitor their number of steps, determine their resting heart rate, and even record their performance in sports and exercise. This influx of information was initially thrilling, but enthusiasm waned as users realized that raw data wasn't sufficient to spur behavioral change.

Rather than merely counting steps, they sought understanding—how did these behaviors contribute to overarching goals like weight loss? Sustained success demanded a transition from smart devices to comprehensive platforms that could catalyze action based on insights. In this hypercompetitive space, only those products that show a real impact on a user's life through the altering of specific behaviors will have a long-term growth potential.

Whoop has become a leading company in this movement toward a device–software relationship yielding short- and long-term outcomes with the creation of its Band. Launched in 2015, the Whoop Band melded the positive aspects and learning lessons of other wearables into a sleek, functional device. Despite its advanced human performance metrics, the platform didn't achieve immediate acclaim. The insight of new metrics failed to catch a wide audience, and users craved something more substantive.

---

1 "Learning Tomorrow: Visualising Student And Staff's Daily Activities and Reflect On It" by M. Riphagen, M. V. Hout, D. Krijnen, and G. Gootjes, published 2013 by Education, Environmental Science

Recognizing the need to build something that didn't just provide insights, Whoop began to invest in building out a platform that allowed users to act on the metrics. Two features added over the years since its launch have made the device–software symbiosis a reality. The first is a journaling feature that allows users to track habits and, over time, correlate them with their physiological data. Equipped with this data alongside the patterns of millions of other users, the second feature is the delivery of personalized recommendations for improvements. Whoop can tell the user what actions they can take to improve their metrics when a deficit occurs, likely leading to a change in their lived experience.

Each glance at the Whoop app offers a snapshot of their current state represented by three simple metrics: strain, recovery, and sleep. To ensure users satisfy a short-term outcome every time they visit the app, Whoop provides recommendations for the user to fulfill their daily goals for each of the tracked metrics. Most importantly, this captivating experience is progressing users toward their long-term goals. While the user might not notice they were losing some weight after each interaction, the consistent encouragement and sense of progress were leading them to significant health improvements.

Today, Whoop is heralded as one of the most advanced wearables on the market and is backed up by numerous studies that show that users who adhere to its recommendations achieve positive long-term health outcomes. More recently, other smart devices, such as the Oura Ring and Garmin Watch, echo the principle of daily engagement and long-term rewards leading to positive outcomes. These emerging companies, now valued in the billions, embody the profound value of adopting an Impact Mindset and genuinely fulfilling users' desired outcomes.

Benefits of Outcome Focus

By now, the imperative of impact measurement should resonate. On a practical level, it offers a holistic assessment of a product's efficacy. At a greater scope, it synchronizes a product's evolution with a company's core mission, exemplified by Oura, whose mission statement, "Our mission is to make health a daily practice," is not just rhetoric but a reality backed by their marketing strategies and scholarly research. This commitment to their mission has propelled them to notable achievements, including the sale of over a million rings and a valuation of $2.5 billion as of 2022.

This alignment fosters a sense of ethical integrity and purpose among employees, instilling a belief that their efforts genuinely improve their stakeholders' welfare. All this might excite you, but you also recognize that a change like this requires a solid business case. This concluding section delineates the specific business metrics that stand to benefit from the adoption of an Impact Mindset.

Decreasing Customer Acquisition Costs and Increasing Life-Time Value

The financial outlay for advertising and sales initiatives, pivotal in persuading a customer to commit to a purchase, is substantial. Customer acquisition cost (CAC) has become widely used to quantify this. It represents the aggregate cost of marketing and sales activities needed to secure each new customer within a specified timeframe. Teams use this metric to identify how much it costs to add one additional customer. When constructed correctly, CAC is a strategic tool for optimizing marketing and sales channels.

Post-purchase, the focus shifts to a customer's lifetime value (LTV). By analyzing historical data on subscription duration, add-on purchases, and other relevant indicators, companies forecast the total revenue a customer will likely generate before their eventual departure. Maximizing LTV involves strategies to prolong user engagement, promote frequent interaction, and encourage upgrades, among others. For instance, an increase of 5 percent in retention leads to at least 25 percent in profits due to gaining more revenue without having to spend more on attracting new customers.

Lifetime value is an important counterpart to CAC, as it helps define whether that investment in gaining a new customer is worth it. An optimal LTV-to-CAC ratio hovers around 4, indicating that the revenue from a customer is four times the cost incurred in their acquisition. This ratio also suggests a healthy business state when the LTV offsets the CAC within a year. In cases where CAC is higher than LTV, it is a significant concern, as it means new customers are a net loss for the business.

Companies prioritizing these metrics significantly benefit from quantifying the impact their products engender. High CAC often stems from a lack of brand awareness and clarity about a product's benefits. Increasing a company's virality is a natural way to seed recognition across many potential customers. Recognizing this, companies increasingly use social media and other platforms to engage influencers. A cheaper way to do this is to launch a product that solves user problems from the start. The app Fabulous demonstrated this when it carved a unique space in a crowded market by building a solution that worked at developing new habits.

Lowering CAC can also be achieved through more impactful marketing narratives. Articulating the tangible impact of a product on its users elevates public messaging. Rather than vague promises of transformation, companies can present authentic data illustrating the positive changes users have experienced. Noom, a leading weight management platform, is an excellent example. Their "science-backed" marketing, coupled with a weight-loss guarantee, underscores a commitment to achieving user goals.

Building a product that works won't just help with marketing but will aid in retaining current customers, consequently increasing LTV. When users perceive tangible benefits, it raises the switching costs associated with transitioning to a competitor. Some products, like the UpRight posture corrector, have an immediate, profound impact. In most cases, though, changes are gradual, necessitating mechanisms to highlight incremental progress. Tonal, the strength training fitness device, shows this through the increases a user sees in their strength score after most sessions.

Solving user problems over time and feeding back progress toward their journey will also increase overall loyalty to a brand, positioning them as ideal customers for new products and services. Oura had established a solid reputation for effectively enhancing sleep quality, leading them to continue their substantial growth even after transitioning from a free to a paid subscription model. Rarely are customers accepting of such a switch, but Oura proved they were worth it, significantly increasing the LTV of its customer base.

Decreasing Time to Market and Reducing Rework

With clarity on how a product impacts users across all key success metrics, a company is poised to craft effective solutions. Starting at an organizational level, alignment around these metrics simplifies decision-making. As advocated by the "measure what matters" philosophy, rallying a team around a few metrics is a clear path to ensuring those metrics are maximized. Clarity of what a product is supposed to do for customers enables leaders to steer efforts toward maximizing user impact.

At the team level, understanding the link between a group's work and user impact leads to more efficient planning. The design phase starts with a clear grasp of the user need and the specific behavioral changes desired through use to impact short- and long-term outcomes, streamlining both design and development. This efficiency allows time for the creation of tests to confirm that solutions meet their objectives. Equipped with leading indicators on customer impact, quick identification of issues ensures rapid adjustments.

At the employee level, having a clear, direct view of how work contributes to a product that changes behaviors means a greater recognition of impact. Seeing their work contribute to meaningful user changes enhances engagement and productivity. This clear picture of what needs to be improved to enhance the impact on the end user also provides a framework for prioritizing tasks.

These factors collectively expedite the launch of new products and services. From strategic guidance to tactical execution and individual efficiencies, new products should be designed, developed, and launched faster. Moreover, alignment with user outcomes minimizes errors, reducing costly future corrections and thereby enhancing overall operational efficiency. Although estimates vary, research suggests that 30 to 50 percent of engineering work is dedicated to rework, indicating that investment in research can prevent thousands of dollars in expenses otherwise spent on rectifying avoidable errors.

As epitomized by successful "quantified self" companies like Oura, Whoop, and Noom, embracing an Impact Mindset and outcome focus lays the foundation for a business that genuinely addresses user desires and needs. In the evolving economic landscape post the zero-interest-rate phenomenon, these companies serve as beacons of the immense potential awaiting businesses that adopt this approach. Doing so establishes a focus on measurable behaviors that can be altered by the features a team creates. The final piece of this is ensuring that when user outcomes are fulfilled it yields positive business outcomes. The next chapter will introduce a framework to further clarify the link between connected behaviors, user outcomes, and business outcomes, empowering you to advocate compellingly for adopting an Impact Mindset.

CHAPTER RECAP

- **Digital products are tools:** Digital products should be viewed as tools to be used and as functional instruments designed to facilitate specific impact on users' lives.

- **Other frameworks focus on needs and outcomes:** Traditional philosophies, such as outcome-driven innovation and human-centered design, prioritize identifying and fulfilling user needs and desired outcomes.

- **Impact Mindset focuses on behaviors:** The Impact Mindset diverges from conventional approaches by emphasizing the modification of user behaviors as a primary way to satisfy user desires, thereby enhancing the overall effectiveness of digital products.

- **Short-term versus long-term:** Balancing short-term wins with long-term goals highlights that immediate successes fuel user engagement and retention, while sustained achievements ensure lasting value and user satisfaction.

- **Quantified self and the need for impact:** The "quantified self" movement shows the evolution from mere data collection to the necessity for meaningful impact, where digital tools must gather information and drive substantial improvements in health and wellness.

- **Business benefits of an Impact Mindset:** Adopting an Impact Mindset is not solely altruistic; it results in tangible business advantages, including reduced CAC, increased LVT, and enhanced operational efficiency, all contributing to a robust and ethical business model.

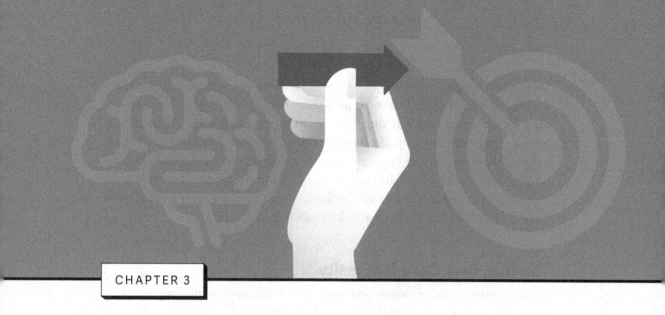

CHAPTER 3

Connecting User Behavior to Business Outcomes

Imagine a brand that's become a staple in your life, one that's woven itself into your daily routine over the years. This could be anything—a gadget you can't live without, a service that's your go-to solution, or even a simple household item that's head and shoulders above the rest. Pause for a moment and consider this: has that led your lifetime value to increase with this company? What has led you to stay retained and not switch to their competitor?

The marketplace of guided meditation apps is vast with a few large players and a long tail of products tailored to specific audiences. Between trials and free media, you can find quality content without having to pay. After experimenting with a collection of offerings, I have become a superfan of the Waking Up app. Although on the pricier side of services, the content connects with me: high usability and high impact—the more I use it the better I feel. Each morning, I wake up excited to listen to the daily mediation, embedding this app into my daily routine.

My positive interactions with the service have led me to purchase yearly memberships and other content that the publisher offers, increasing my life-time value for the company. Switching from the service would require a tremendous increase in the price or a significant reduction in the quality of content. Without either of these, the service continues to satisfy my needs in a way that no other offering has been able to replicate. For Waking Up and any other digital product on a mission to impact their users, the final piece to adopting an Impact Mindset is connecting user outcomes created by usage to business impact.

The Business Case Necessity

Crafting products that resonate and make a mark is rooted in fulfilling user needs. When done right, it also serves as the foundation for innovation and establishes high switching costs. Regardless of what combination of Impact Mindset, outcome-driven innovation, human-centered design, and any other framework focused on charting and resolving user problems a team is using, the key is to do it in a way that drives positive business and user outcomes. Doing so ignites a virtuous cycle, encouraging companies to funnel a portion of their gains back into superior product development, confident in future returns.

This chapter is dedicated to solidifying the assurance that when products pivot around precise behavioral changes, they don't just meet outcomes—they propel business growth. Numerous frameworks and processes promise the creation of superior products. Yet they often miss a direct link to fiscal business impacts, such as improved retention, deceased customer acquisition costs, and increased collaboration efficiency that ultimately drives boosted revenue or trimmed costs. But let's face it: in our profit-oriented world, advocating for a fresh mindset needs more than just noble intentions; it demands a compelling narrative of lucrative returns. Establishing this financial foresight wards off the risk of your Impact Mindset endeavors being dismissed as mere academic exercises or, worse, as unnecessary frills. As you navigate through this content, anchor yourself in the ultimate objective: to be armed with a convincing response when queried, "What's the business payoff for this investment?"

SaaS Competes on the Promise of Improving Company Outcomes

In the realm of business outcomes, the software-as-a-service (SaaS) industry stands in a league of its own, compelled to identify and prioritize the measurement of business outcomes like no other. The SaaS saga began in 1999 with the debut of Salesforce.com's Customer Relationship Management platform, revolutionizing how business solutions were delivered. Selling software as a monthly subscription rather than a single purchase has not only skyrocketed potential earnings but also transformed customer service—the sporadic software update became a relic, replaced by the dynamism of monthly enhancements. It has also lowered the entry barrier, with SaaS becoming the dominant way of delivering business solutions. Each product offers a slightly different way to address an employee's user needs. Businesses, in turn, purchase these products with the belief that gains accrued from adoption will increase their bottom lines.

SaaS enterprises are tasked with a dual mandate: keep a pulse on their own fiscal vitality and concurrently monitor the ripple effect of their solutions on client businesses. They must show how their product drives efficiency and improves effectiveness, yielding better earnings for their customers. This is emblematic of the universal challenge for all digital offerings, pinpointing how satisfying user outcomes translate to upticks in pivotal business metrics. While business-to-consumer (B2C) firms only need to juggle this for their own ledger, business-to-business (B2B) entities must focus on the end user, the business customer, and their own business, mastering the art of quantifying business impact for their clientele and themselves.

Consider Zendesk, a beacon in customer service solutions. Its sustainable growth hinges on clients witnessing tangible benefits from its suite of support tools. Their support tools are intended to help customer service agents by providing the collocation of support tickets, access to relevant information to satisfy these requests, and monitoring of recurring issues. Advertising their potential to precisely do this, Zendesk's landing page touts their average successes of "23% increase in average e-commerce order value" and "40% cost savings per ticket."

Organizations that purchase Zendesk intend to increase customer service efficiency and satisfaction with the end goal of inflating their bottom line. Success stories see clients' profits swell, cementing their loyalty to the tool. Failures, regardless of the cause, breed doubt about the usefulness of the software, encouraging users to consider alternatives.

The SaaS landscape has exploded over the past few years, with each entrant touting a novel fix for age-old business headaches. Seduced by persuasive sales narratives, firms have been amassing these "efficiency multipliers," leading to an average portfolio of more than 100 SaaS tools per company as of 2022.[1] Yet this product inflation is quickly questioned whenever a downturn looks possible. The specter of a recession in 2022 had firms reevaluating their toolkits, seeking justification for each dollar allocated.

SaaS growth has long followed a script: tailor solutions for a few marquee clients; then parlay these successes into wider adoption backed by glossy testimonials, painting a dreamy picture of the future that would occur after implementation. Titans like Workday and Salesforce emerged, dominating their niches through savvy branding and robust consulting ecosystems, reinforcing the perception of their prowess in fulfilling user needs and bolstering business results. Yet the tide is turning. Jaded by hefty setup costs and elusive benefits, clients now demand concrete evidence linking tool usage to business gains at renewal time.

Caught off guard, many SaaS firms find themselves in a challenging situation. After years of building marginal features that would satisfy their largest and loudest customers, their products are overloaded with disparate features and lack legitimate usefulness. Consequently, they are often left brandishing shallow stats that reveal little about true impact.

Pivoting to outcome measurement necessitates a paradigm shift, echoing themes from previous chapters. It calls for clarity in feature purpose, identifying specific behavioral shifts expected upon tool adoption by client teams. These behaviors must then be tied to individual and business outcomes. Take Asana, a project management application. It's committed to boosting project delivery efficiency. Showing a pairing between the user behaviors they alter and changes to the desired outcomes that actually exist, they have released a report that confirms product usage yields a rate of execution that is 54 percent faster, which is the user outcome. With these improved operations, users of the product also found a 57 percent increase of on-time project completion, the business outcome. Both are clear indicators of enhanced performance and, implicitly, a healthier balance sheet. Armed with such impactful insights, Asana enters renewal discussions with conviction. Unfortunately, many SaaS counterparts will find themselves less equipped.

---

1 "Average number of software as a service (SaaS) applications used by organizations worldwide from 2015 to 2022" by Statista

User Outcomes as a Differentiator

Responding to the myriad of SaaS providers with noble ambitions and lackluster execution, especially those requiring a significant up-front cost, a new business model has arisen in the past few years. Flipping the script, rather than wooing business customers with glossy pitches to secure hefty contracts, these companies plant their offerings directly within the workforce, letting the seeds of adoption grow organically. Bringing the freemium model to business products means that a SaaS company must engineer solutions that satisfy short- and long-term outcomes and thus seamlessly weave into daily operations. In successful cases, employee endorsement reaches a critical mass, arming the SaaS vendor with a trove of real-time data to demonstrate the tangible benefits they're already delivering as they step into negotiation talks.

Slack, a communication platform, is one of the best examples of this *bottom-up SaaS* business model. By reimagining workplace communication, they offered a platform that any team member could deploy without the usual bureaucratic red tape, free of charge. They did this by building a blend of productivity enhancements and innovative collaboration features that fueled a natural propagation across workspaces, eventually capturing the corporate IT radar and prompting deliberations over enterprise-grade offerings.

Disruption of the market-leading SaaS products is happening in almost every industry. By 2020, 30 percent of the leading SaaS companies were taking a bottom-up approach,[2] and this trend has continued to grow because these new bottom-up products are being built in a way that ensures they make an impact for end users and businesses alike.

Consider HubSpot, a contender in the customer relationship management space, who's been chipping away at Salesforce's stronghold, particularly within the small-to-mid-tier market. Their strategy? A constellation of functionalities that are not just valuable but also a breeze to deploy, all while slashing up-front expenses and presenting a no-cost entry point. New ventures latching onto HubSpot grow symbiotically with the platform, reaching a point where the free ride ends and the pay-to-play chapter commences. But HubSpot comes to this crossroads armed with compelling narratives, rich with insights on how their toolkit has reshaped workplace dynamics and bolstered the bottom line. Such

---

2 "Bottom-up SaaS: A framework for mapping pricing to customer value" by TechCrunch

triumphs hinge on crafting tools that transcend mere usage, resonating deeply enough to trigger real impact.

The bottom-up approach isn't without its pitfalls, harboring an inherent bias toward hyper-growth and stickiness, often manifesting in a gamified user journey. These elements, while effective in keeping users hooked, can blur the line between genuine problem solving and superficial engagement. However, when the hour arrives to justify an enterprise upgrade, the spotlight shifts to the hardcore facts—user outcomes and, crucially, business results. The victors in the bottom-up SaaS arena are those who tune in to their user chorus, addressing pervasive needs (not just the noisiest) and catalyzing meaningful behavioral evolution.

Outcomes in Business to Business vs. Business to Consumer

As illustrated by the SaaS industry, understanding business outcomes connected to satisfying user outcomes is imperative. Once established, companies can confidently invest in improving the user impact, knowing that it will pay off. For B2C companies, satisfying desires yields end users who are more likely to stay retained and are ripe for upselling. For those selling to businesses, such as SaaS products, increasing user outcomes means that the company is less likely to churn and may expand its purchases.

Illustrated by two examples in the healthcare field (**TABLE 3.1**), you can see how, regardless of who a company is selling to, a similar path emerges. HealthJoy is a B2B benefit co-locator that intends to help employees access their benefits with more ease. By increasing the likelihood that an employee utilizes a benefit their employer offers, the employee should pay less in healthcare expenses. When HealthJoy is working, it should yield employees who are more likely to have a positive sentiment toward their employer, thereby increasing retention. HealthJoy should aim to validate that a connection does exist among these steps, and if it does, they can work toward maximizing the employee behavior of benefit usage.

In parallel, One Medical is a B2C primary care service that also serves to help people maximize their insurance utilization. Through increasing in-network claims, they also aim to decrease customers' healthcare costs. If they do this well, showing users how they saved them money, One Medical should see increased retention to their service. Both companies have a similar operating model, just different stakeholders who must see value through usage.

TABLE 3.1 B2B vs. B2C Healthcare Companies

	COMPANY	
IMPACT	B2B: HEALTHJOY	B2C: ONE MEDICAL
Specific behaviors	Increased access to benefits	Increased access to in-network providers
User outcomes	Increased utilization of benefits	Lower healthcare costs
Business customer outcomes	Decreased insurance claims	N/A
Business outcomes	Increased retention	Increased retention

Reviewing the differences between One Medical and HealthJoy showcases the additional complexity faced by products that are intended for business customers. They must build something that works for end users, generally employees, but that also impacts the company's desired outcomes. Whether a company is B2B or B2C, the maximization of outcomes should be connected to the product creator's bottom line. An ideal situation is one where the use of a product causes certain behaviors that positively impact the user, their organization (if applicable), and the company providing the solution.

Measurable Behaviors to Measurable Business Outcomes

Achieving user outcomes occurs only with intentional design; they occur through building experiences that encourage new user actions. These precise behaviors, intended to evolve through feature interaction, stand as the proxy for measuring the influence a feature generates. Therefore, behaviors that can be measured are the bedrock for determining the impact that features create. Skepticism often creeps in, casting doubt over whether a feature or product genuinely alters behavior. The concern arises when someone compares products like fitness trackers or financial applications with obvious behaviors—like exercise minutes and monthly savings contributions, respectively—to their product, which isn't straightforward. Imagine your product is a customer data platform (CDP), which can be viewed as just a digital interface for a data pipeline. The behavioral shift in a technical product like this is nebulous in comparison to those with straightforward metrics like fitness and finance.

However, all applications, overt or subtle, pivot user behavior, but they vary in degree of measurement complexity. In the CDP example, identifying behaviors that change is as easy as thinking about what someone would do without it. Devoid of a CDP's mastery in consolidating diverse visitor event data, data scientists would be embroiled in a time-draining slog through disparate data sources. Without a CDP, a cascade of clicks, incessant app toggling, and mental juggling of procedures occur, all of which the CDP curtails, and the CPT becomes the data scientist's new data haven and a massive time-saver.

Reducing clicks isn't the only behavioral change. The platform's presence could kindle an ambition to integrate more data sources, dive deeper into analyses, or scout for novel applications downstream. These tasks, integral to the data scientist's role, are all touched by what might pass as a rudimentary SaaS offering. If this still seems convoluted, do not fret; we discuss the identification of behaviors in more detail in later chapters.

Flow Between Specific Behaviors and Business Outcomes— Interlinks with a Framework

The first two chapters of this book underscored the imperative of gauging user outcomes and pinpointing specific connected behaviors. This chapter illuminates the pathway to tethering these insights to business outcomes. Collectively, these chapters form the triad that will underpin our future efforts to quantify the impact generated by products.

The User Outcome Connection framework (**FIGURE 3.1**) is our compass, charting the links among specific behaviors, user outcomes, and business repercussions. It is the foundational framework that adopting an Impact Mindset relies upon. Building out this blueprint, your team will be empowered with a clear-eyed

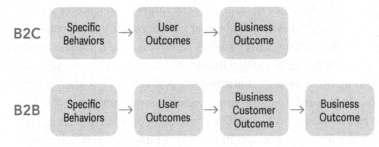

FIGURE 3.1 User Outcome Connection framework

understanding of the behavioral shifts your features seek to instigate, the user outcomes to be augmented, and the favorable business results intended to follow.

- **Specific Behaviors:** The actions that are altered through interaction with a feature.

- **User Outcomes:** The short- and long-term desires that a user hopes to fulfill through usage.

- **[B2B Only] Business Customer Outcomes:** The business impact that a company hopes to fulfill through their employees' usage.

- **Business Outcomes:** Impact on product developer for building something that fulfills user outcomes.

You can start a User Outcome Connection framework on any of your features today. You can do this at its simplest purely from intuition, documenting what you have seen and heard about a feature. As you increase the quality of data backing the framework, you can seek data to further define each part of a feature and validate whether relationships between each exist. Ultimately, a "completed" User Outcome Connection framework has data that supports each of the connections.

Throughout this book, whenever you feel lost, ask yourself how whatever you are reading connects back to the User Outcome Connection. As you build out the framework, more questions and potential avenues to chase will continue to bloom. Your aim will be to remain steadfast on completing User Outcome Connections for the feature you select to analyze. Once on the other end, you will have a documented feature purpose and data to support that it is effective at accomplishing the desired user behavioral change.

To vividly demonstrate the transformative potential that the User Outcome Connection framework can unleash, let's analyze two distinct products: one catering to end consumers (B2C) and another designed for businesses (B2B). Through these examples, we will explore what makes them especially valuable and conclude with a user connection example to illustrate the lens we will use throughout this journey.

Business-to-Consumer User Outcome Connection—Noom

In the realm of health and wellness, Noom has etched its mark amid the numerous weight management apps. When individuals seek tools to streamline their calorie intake or amplify their physical activity, they search for tangible results. With its straightforward yet potent outcome metrics, the health sector offers users a clear lens through which to discern the efficacy of various products. Daily calorie intake is a reliable proxy for potential weight fluctuations, while the tally of daily exercise minutes offers another layer to the weight transformation equation.

Drawing from years of behavioral science studies, Noom has crafted strategies to fuel motivation and bolster commitment to intentions. A user's journey with Noom begins with a survey to curate their experience based on their specific goals. Beyond a conventional food-logging feature, Noom infuses timely bursts of pertinent health insights into the user experience. But that's not all; the platform delves deeper, pinpointing user motivators and rolling out targeted strategies when goals go astray.

The brilliance of Noom lies in its approach. Unlike its counterparts, Noom doesn't merely release features, measure their usage, and label high engagement a success. They are steadfast in their mission to ensure that their offerings genuinely steer users toward their weight aspirations. This involves rigorous evaluation to confirm their sustained usage culminates in health milestones. And it works, with a staggering 80 percent of users reporting shedding pounds after an average span of 267 days.

Noom's ambition is to steer users toward nutritionally rich food choices. This is manifested through a color-coded system that ranks foods based on their nutritional essence. This framework then bridges specific behaviors to the desired outcome (**FIGURE 3.2**). In the Noom narrative, this translates to curating meal plans rich in wholesome ingredients, gravitating toward fruits and veggies

FIGURE 3.2 How Noom bridges specific behaviors to user and business outcomes

during grocery trips, and unearthing triggers for unhealthy snacking patterns. The business linkage is the final piece. Although no formal study corroborates this directly, Noom's soaring success suggests that users reaping the benefits of healthier dietary choices are more likely to remain loyal to the platform.

Business-to-Business User Outcome Connection—Mailchimp

As previously discussed, building a tailored approach to corporate clientele comes with a distinct set of challenges and nuances. Ultimately, the product or service is intended to make the end user become more effective at whatever task they are completing but also improve the business customer's bottom line. Although the trajectory to behavioral transformation might not be as linear as that of endeavors like weight reduction or financial savings, there undeniably exists a pathway leading to a specific behavior that culminates in the sought-after result. Enter Mailchimp, a globally renowned email-marketing juggernaut instrumental in channeling valuable and captivating communications.

For Mailchimp, the surface-level test of success is gauged by the extent of feature utilization within its ecosystem. Initial monetary gains from business patrons stem from heightened platform engagement. However, the true hallmark of enduring success is when clients, through usage of Mailchimp, amplify their communication's business value. Sustained customer loyalty is achieved when customers discern tangible benefits, such as augmented email open rates and a surge in click-through conversions.

With its sights set on the long game, Mailchimp meticulously curates an experience that propels business users to harness features that will increase the likelihood of generating value, which in turn creates an impact on business outcomes (**FIGURE 3.3**). This is exemplified by intuitive, in-app nudges inquiring about the user's engagement with Mailchimp's email template offerings.

Specific Behaviors	User Outcomes	Business Customer Outcome	Business Outcome
Start new campaigns using templates that have been proven successful.	Spend less time to create more effective email campaigns.	Improved effectiveness of marketers that yield higher rates of return on ad spend.	Increased sales through marketers who rely on Mailchimp's templates for campaigns.

FIGURE 3.3 How Mailchimp bridges specific behaviors to user and business outcomes

By encouraging users to immerse themselves holistically in the platform—via guides, templates, and in-app prompts—even for features that don't directly bolster revenue, Mailchimp is strategically ushering its clientele along the digital marketing evolution spectrum. This not only fosters the adoption of its revenue-generating platform but also cultivates a clientele base that's more adept and successful. A quick perusal of the Mailchimp website reveals a tapestry of success narratives, spotlighting business customers who initiated their marketing journey with the platform and evolved into formidable marketers. These tales underscore the transformative power of Mailchimp in reshaping marketing behaviors, ultimately steering businesses toward favorable outcomes.

The User Outcome Connection—Assessing the Connections

The first draft of a User Outcome Connection framework should be rough but enough to start a conversation. Crafting a valuable one necessitates a collaborative endeavor, drawing insights from all teams that played a role in the feature's conceptualization, design, and execution. The treasure trove of knowledge these teams possess can be gleaned either through direct engagements, such as stakeholder dialogues, or by delving into research and planning artifacts they previously crafted. The linchpin to this exploration is the immersion into the psyche of the individuals who created the feature.

As a picture of the feature's intention begins to form, the next phase involves discerning the nexus between each facet of the framework. Although it's one thing to harbor an intuitive belief about a behavior influencing an outcome, it's an entirely different approach to be armed with empirical data corroborating the linkage. Unearthing such pivotal data might begin by poring over product analytics dossiers and user research synopses and collating insights from customer-centric teams regarding the interplay between behaviors and outcomes. Meanwhile, bridging the gap between user outcomes and business ramifications requires investigating sales enablement insights, business development analytics, and strategic financial dispatches.

> **NOTE** Chapters 5 and 6 go into more detail on uncovering data sources that will generate evidence of whether a connection exists and what to do when it does not.

This data quest might yield a void, indicating the lack of a discernible connection. This might seem disheartening in the context of creating a user outcome connection framework, but it is far from rendering the endeavor without merit. Instead, it underscores a chance to showcase the power of the Impact Mindset and generate fresh data to bolster confidence that investments to amplify user outcomes will yield a return. Wherever data gaps exist within the User Outcome Connection framework, there is an opportunity to conduct a feature impact analysis (detailed in Chapter 4) to create new evidence of whether the connection between measurable behaviors and business outcomes exists.

In some cases, there might be an instance where evidence points toward a disconnect between two pivotal variables. In such junctures, it's paramount to rigorously vet the validity of the counter-narrative research. When, after scrutiny, a connection does not exist, then what led the team to their initial, incorrect belief must be reviewed. After this post-mortem, a recalibration of the team's foundational beliefs around the newfound understanding of a feature's purpose is necessary. This might entail revising the targeted user and business outcomes based on newfound insights or redefining the behaviors a feature seeks to alter a much more challenging endeavor. It's pivotal to remember that although all features invariably influence behaviors, they might not always align with the intended ones or catalyze the desired user outcomes.

Building a User Outcome Connection framework should come with relative ease, but there will be instances marred by incongruities across behaviors, user outcomes, and business results. Charting these connections in a framework enhances the likelihood of identifying these disparities and planning a course of action to rectify them. Irrespective of the effort required, documenting this tripartite connection is the cornerstone to embracing an Impact Mindset. The User Outcome Connection framework identifies ways to gauge and augment the true value of features.

Standalone Value of Creating a User Outcome Connection Framework

A complete User Outcome Connection framework is the first step in adopting an Impact Mindset and also serves as a valuable deliverable. A definition of how a feature will change user behavior, creating positive outcomes for both the user and the business, serves as a powerful tool for alignment. This clarity ensures that every stakeholder, be it a seasoned team member or a nascent partner, can eloquently articulate the feature's overarching objective and its pivotal role in fulfilling user needs. Having a solid definition of what is being observed also serves as a powerful basis for the creation of new metrics.

A solidified understanding of a feature's intent across the organization augments transparency into the endeavors of diverse teams, enabling teams to partner and build upon each other's contributions. For teams operating across the organizational spectrum, this clarity translates into minimized time spent on definitions and maximized focus on unearthing efficiencies and deriving value across initiatives. Lastly, leadership will have a nuanced understanding of the challenges products address and opportunities they open for innovative solutions catering to unfulfilled needs.

During feature improvement or the creation of new features and products, having a clear picture of how the outcomes are pursued accelerates the design and testing phases. User experience (UX) designers, armed with this clarity, can judiciously make trade-offs, prioritizing those that promise the most profound impact on pivotal metrics tied to these outcomes of importance. Meanwhile, testing becomes a streamlined endeavor, given that the metrics warranting scrutiny are predefined, facilitating the swift identification of the most efficacious version.

For teams championing the adoption of an Impact Mindset, the journey of sculpting a User Outcome Connection framework offers a sneak peek into the intricacies of a comprehensive impact assessment. When there is palpable resistance in pinpointing specific behaviors influenced by a feature, it's a harbinger of potential challenges when transitioning to tangible metric assessments. Similarly, if the organization exhibits reluctance to invest in efforts to establish a connection between user outcomes and business ramifications, future endeavors to secure support might be fraught with challenges.

Such impediments shouldn't prevent a team's effort. Instead, they should be perceived as experiments in change management, spotlighting areas of resistance and strategies to mollify detractors. With this arsenal of insights, your working group will be better equipped to chart a realistic roadmap for promoting the adoption of an Impact Mindset tailored to your organization's distinctive culture and product landscape. Conversely, it's a golden opportunity to identify change champions who resonate with this revamped definition of product success. The next chapter promises to unveil the methodology to embark on your first impact measurement endeavor.

CHAPTER RECAP

- **Business case for Impact Mindset:** Teams need to establish a clear link between the fulfillment of user outcomes through changing user behavior and increased business outcomes to champion the adoption of an Impact Mindset.

- **SaaS firms are pioneers in business outcome realization:** SaaS entities exemplify the art of demonstrating their product's worth by correlating user engagement with tangible benefits for their business clientele. This model serves as a blueprint for all enterprises, urging them to internalize this approach.

- **User Outcome Connection framework:** A tool to chart the connections between specific user behavior changes by a feature, user outcomes, and business outcomes; completed ones are the basis on which an organization can adopt an Impact Mindset. When lacking evidence that a connection exists, there is an opportunity to create new data using the feature Impact Analysis.

- **Divergence in B2B and B2C outcome connections:** Companies operating in the B2B realm, as illustrated by SaaS entities, have an added layer to navigate: discerning the value proposition for business clients stemming from product interactions.

- **Detecting disconnects:** Instances where there's an apparent disconnect within the User Outcome Connection framework signal a need to generate data to provide evidence of whether a connection exists or raise red flags about a feature's intended purpose and efficacy.

- **Intrinsic merits of the User Outcome Connection:** Crafting a comprehensive User Outcome Connection not only demystifies a feature's core objectives but also serves as a unifying beacon across the organization, fostering a shared understanding and collaborative endeavors.

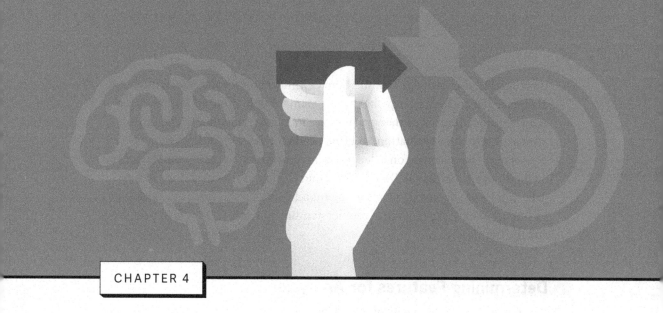

CHAPTER 4

Ensuring Features Make an Impact

Reflect on a product you're currently developing, or, if you're not actively involved in product creation, envision yourself as part of the team for an application you use frequently. What level of confidence do you have that user engagement with this product leads to behavioral changes, more closely aligning users to their desired outcomes? If you were able to validate that your feature successfully satisfies user outcomes, what would you do with that data? This reality is not as distant as it may seem; it's attainable now.

In Chapter 1, the Impact Mindset was introduced as a philosophy of determining feature success based on behavioral change yielding positive user outcome. Chapter 2 emphasized the salience of pinpointing and measuring behaviors tied to these impacts. Chapter 3 highlighted the need to link a feature's influence to business key performance indicators. These insights converge in the three core components of the User Outcome Connection: connected behaviors, user outcomes, and business outcomes. The lack of evidence for these connections signals a need for data creation, which will be done through a process called the *Feature Impact Analysis* (FIA).

It's crucial to acknowledge that the Impact Mindset philosophy is not intended to replace the creative energy that fuels a team's design process. Rather, it serves as an amplification, a lens that provides greater clarity and focus. The Impact Mindset is a tool for evaluation, steering product teams toward developing experiences that resonate on a deeper, more meaningful level. It complements methodologies such as the Double-Diamond Design process, refining feature definitions and shaping products with tangible, measurable impacts. Adopting an Impact Mindset means clearly understanding how a feature will impact users and the business.

Determining Features for Analysis

When measuring the success of digital features, it's vital first to unravel the concept of a *feature* in the context of the tech industry. This term, borrowed from the realm of physical products, takes on various forms in the digital world, often referring to anything from a simple design element to a complex array of functionalities. A clearly defined feature guides teams to evaluate and articulate the purpose and impact of different product components.

The approach to organizing and defining features often reflects the unique culture of a product team's leadership. Although a meticulously structured hierarchy of features isn't a prerequisite for success, the ability to discern and focus on key features that significantly enhance a product's value is crucial. This skill not only aids in effective measurement but also lays the groundwork for a more insightful analysis. In the context of this book, rather than pinning down a rigid definition, we'll navigate through a series of parameters to help you identify the most impactful features worthy of measurement. To illustrate these criteria, we will use a hypothetical example based on Spotify.

When determining a feature for analysis, start by assessing its scale. Features range from subtle additions, like a new button, to comprehensive experiences, such as an entire onboarding journey. Although small details are important, they often don't significantly affect user outcomes. On the other hand, overly complex features can obfuscate analysis, making it difficult to identify effective elements. Aim for a middle ground, where a feature encompasses more than a singular design element but doesn't exceed a set of interactions revolving around one action. In Spotify, for instance, features like "top recommendations" or the "explore this playlist" option, allowing users to sample tracks, would be ideal for measurement.

The next step involves distinguishing between functional features (like composing a message or adjusting audio settings), which directly engage users, and non-functional features (like security enhancements), which subtly support the user experience. Although the latter can be quantified, it is more difficult to home in on the specific effect they create. It is also more challenging to differentiate users of non-functional features from non-users, which is a pivotal aspect of measuring impact. The recommendation and playlist exploration features in Spotify are functional, engaging users interactively. In contrast, Spotify's global availability and consistent uptime represent non-functional features.

Lastly, evaluate a feature's uniqueness and its alignment with the product's core mission. The ubiquitous elements of digital design—the menus, the back buttons, the settings pages—are the unsung standards of any app. They're expected to be unremarkable unless they introduce innovative functionality. The features that truly define a product are those that are inextricably linked to its purpose and deliver unmistakable value to the user. Spotify has set itself as the leader in music streaming services with a few unique and valuable features, such as *Spotify Wrapped,* which recaps a user's music habits from the year and becomes a common meme at the end of each year.

To identify features that are ready for measurement, you must navigate a triad of considerations: the feature's scope, functionality, and indispensability. If I were consulting for Spotify, I would recommend they start by measuring the "group session" feature because it is a unique feature that is tightly scoped to a few user actions. The feature makes creating shared playlists easier and encourages more social interaction around music.

The team could begin filling out a User Outcome Connection, suggesting that the group session feature increases the behaviors of sharing music and playlists with contacts. Viewing it through this framework reveals that there are likely two primary user outcomes connected: improved connection through music and increased discovery of "loved" songs. The aim would be that by satisfying these outcomes, Spotify is building a compelling case for users to stay on their platform, rather than leaving for alternatives, while drawing new users through organic channels. This flow is captured in the Spotify User Outcome Connection shown in **FIGURE 4.1.**

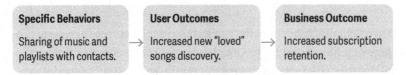

SPOTIFIY USER OUTCOME CONNECTION

Specific Behaviors	User Outcomes	Business Outcome
Sharing of music and playlists with contacts.	Increased new "loved" songs discovery.	Increased subscription retention.

FIGURE 4.1 How Spotify bridges specific behaviors to user and business outcomes

For the sake of this chapter and its supplementary material, we will analyze the success of Apple Watch's three rings fitness feature. This analysis exemplifies a balanced approach, neither too detailed (like focusing on a single metric within the Apple exercise app) nor too broad (like evaluating the entire Activity app). Present on both the iPhone and the Apple Watch, the three rings feature is a central aspect of the user's fitness journey and serves as an exemplary case for a FIA, demonstrating the effectiveness of the Impact Mindset.

Validating Feature Impact— A Complete Hypothetical Walkthrough

Transforming a product team's evaluative methods to embrace an Impact Mindset is not an overnight process. As with most large changes, some team members will immediately recognize its value and champion its implementation, while others may cling to familiar, time-tested methods. The majority will likely adopt a wait-and-see approach, observing from the sidelines to assess the effectiveness of this new philosophy. Swaying this silent majority toward your side requires moving beyond theory into the realm of reality, best shown by a real example. The guiding principle is simple: show, don't tell.

Completing a User Outcome Connection will be your first step. In an ideal scenario, you'll have sufficient data to confidently demonstrate a link between all three variables: connected behaviors, user outcomes, and business outcomes. However, you'll often find yourself equipped with enough data to identify ideal behaviors and outcomes for a feature but lacking evidence of a direct connection. The difference between stopping at this stage and validating these connections can transform this book from an "interesting read" into a catalyst for real change in product development.

When faced with connections that lack sufficient data for validation, you need a structured process. Begin by identifying the gaps in your User Outcome

Connection. The clarity created by this initial effort lets you craft metrics that reflect the intended behavioral shifts, which, in turn, influence the user and business outcomes. With these variables ready for measurement, the next phase involves conducting an experiment to compare the experiences of users and non-users. By analyzing the variance in outcomes, the final step involves quantifying the impact of the feature and sharing these insights with relevant stakeholders.

Completing this process takes effort but is not as daunting as it may seem. The granularity of the analysis can be tailored to the resources at your disposal—data on hand and technical acumen. The first attempt is less about precision or statistical significance and more about illustrating the potential of this new perspective. It allows your extended team to peer through the lens of outcome measurement to witness the transformative clarity it can bring to product development.

Many real companies apply this process to measure their impact. But for now, I will use a detailed hypothetical example of my favorite feature from a digital product, demonstrating how this process can be effectively applied in a real-world scenario.

The Impact of the Apple Fitness Three Rings

Apple's ascent to the zenith of the tech world is a testament to its marriage of impeccable design and unparalleled quality. Apple is a titan in the industry with a valuation over a trillion dollars, so its foray into any category often heralds a seismic shift. Launched in 2015, the Apple Watch has followed this trend. It melded the positive aspects and learning lessons of other smartwatches into a sleek, functional wearable. Despite its aesthetic appeal, the platform didn't achieve immediate acclaim. Initial excitement over having notifications on one's wrist waned, leaving users yearning for a more meaningful engagement with the device.

FIGURE 4.2 Apple Watch's three rings of the Activity app. © 2024 Apple Inc.

In response, Apple reoriented the watch to focus on solving a specific user problem, emphasizing its fitness-tracking features. Among these, the three rings activity tracker, as shown in **FIGURE 4.2**, emerged as a particularly innovative aspect. This design translated abstract fitness metrics into an intuitive, goal-driven visual. Instead of puzzling over what it meant to burn 300 calories, users now had a simple visual displaying their daily target to achieve. It did the same for the number of minutes engaged in exercise and the number of hours the user stood for at least one minute. These were no longer intangible data points but integral components of a daily quest, encapsulated in a trio of rings that users could effortlessly monitor.

Each interaction with the Apple Watch became a micro-journey toward wellness, offering users a snapshot of their day's fitness narrative. Apple didn't stop at mere tracking; it wove in motivational nudges for the less active moments and exuberant celebrations for milestones reached, ensuring that users felt a sense of accomplishment with each glance. Most importantly, this captivating experience was progressing users toward their long-term goals. While the user might not notice they were losing some weight after each interaction, the consistent encouragement and sense of progress were steering them to significant health milestones.

The fitness capabilities of the Apple Watch have ascended to become its crown jewel, convincing roughly one-third of iPhone users to pair it with an Apple Watch.[1] Its stickiness is evident, and while direct public data linking the three rings to retention is elusive, the fact that a third of Apple Watch purchasers are repeat buyers speaks for itself.[2] Similarly, the Apple Watch's effectiveness is not a metric that Apple shares, but with a 97 percent satisfaction rate and most customers reporting it is a "good value," there is reason to suspect (but not enough to validate) that something is working. All this leads to a belief that the Apple team might not have a structured process for measuring the nuanced behavioral changes induced by this feature.

Impact Measurement

Envision a scenario where Apple, inspired by the early chapters of this book, decides to launch a marketing campaign highlighting the tangible fitness benefits of Apple Fitness, particularly for Apple Watch users. The first step would be to clearly articulate the impact of the Apple Watch on users' fitness objectives. Presuming Apple has already charted the outcomes they seek to create through usage, that would be the starting point—defining the precise fitness aspirations customers seek to fulfill with their Apple Watch. With these ambitions in hand,

---

1 Survey reported by Patently Apple
2 "Two-Thirds of Customers Purchasing the Apple Watch in Q1 2023 Were First-Time Buyers" by Wccftech

the next phase would involve crafting a User Outcome Connection, focusing on the three rings feature.

Given Apple Watch's reputation as a fitness tracker and the research backing its clinical efficacy, the anticipated user outcomes likely revolve around enhanced physical health, which can be distilled into feeling healthier and improved health metrics. Elevating these outcomes, the watch's goal is to increase users' activity by encouraging regular standing, more general movement, and fostering workouts. It creates behavioral change by nudging specific behaviors—more frequent standing, increased calorie burn, and amplified physical exertion. The ultimate goal for Apple is that these behavioral shifts not only improve health outcomes but also fuel continued engagement with the product, leading to upgrades and investments in the premium tiers of their fitness ecosystem.

Revisiting this example, Apple's goal is to enhance users' health outcomes, which they hope will encourage upgrades to both the physical product and the associated software, ideally by promoting healthier behaviors. Each link in this chain, from health outcomes to product upgrades, remains hypothetical until it is backed by concrete data. For a company of Apple's stature, it's conceivable that they have the analytics capabilities to support the theory that users who realize positive health benefits are more likely to increase their investment in Apple's fitness ecosystem, thereby raising their lifetime value. These connections are embodied in **FIGURE 4.3**, the Apple User Outcome Connection. If this data is trustworthy, they could validate the assumption that a connection exists between the business and user outcomes.

However, establishing a direct link between using the three rings feature and achieving health outcomes may be more challenging. If it were not, Apple would likely already be championing this story. Thus, more groundwork is required to fortify the evidence for this assumed connection. A hypothesis would be

APPLE USER OUTCOME CONNECTION

Specific Behaviors		User Outcomes		Business Outcome
Increased exercise, standing, and overall movement.	→	Improved health metrics.	→	Increased LTV through device upgrades and premium software.

FIGURE 4.3 How Apple bridges specific behaviors to user and business outcomes

created, and an experiment would be conducted to validate it; the same process would be required to validate the assumption that the feature itself does increase healthy behaviors.

Metrics for Charting Impact

To turn hypotheses into validated truths, we need to establish metrics that act as navigational tools, guiding us through the user's interaction with the product. The Apple Watch, by design, already tracks various activity and health-related behaviors, but the team could introduce additional, more nuanced metrics to gain deeper insights. Additional behavioral outcomes could include measuring the diversity of exercise types that users engage in, providing more detailed information on standing minutes per hour beyond a simple yes-or-no metric, and monitoring the speed at which users complete their rings.

Simultaneously, metrics that assess the feature's adoption and user engagement are essential. Potential metrics include daily active users (DAU), the frequency users check their progress toward daily goals, and the average number of inter-actions with the fitness features. These metrics would shed light on the extent of the feature's integration into users' daily routines and its overall appeal.

Regarding user outcomes, improved health metrics can be tracked using indica-tors such as resting heart rate and average oxygen levels, which the Apple Watch can monitor seamlessly. Adding data from the Apple Health app, like body mass index (BMI) calculations, could further enrich this information. A proxy metric might be needed to gauge users' perceived health, such as the frequency of achieving set fitness goals. This approach is based on the idea that regularly meeting goals promotes a sense of improved health. Alternatively, user feedback could be collected through a questionnaire or by using the daily feelings feature in the Apple Health app to assess their sense of wellness.

Usability scores could be utilized better to understand users' experiences with the three rings design by deploying a survey. These would provide insights into how intuitive and effective users find the feature. Business metrics, such as the average time between product upgrades and the rate of adoption of premium services—while not the focus of this discussion and presuming they have been previously established—still serve as indicators of the feature's impact on the business side. In summary, by expanding and refining the metrics used to track the Apple Watch's fitness features (**TABLE 4.1**), the team would gain a comprehen-sive understanding of both user engagement and the feature's effectiveness.

TABLE 4.1 Success Metrics for Apple's Three Rings Feature	
LEVEL	METRICS
Usage	• Daily active users • Percentage of time wearing watch • Frequency of checking progress • Average clicks on app pages
Usability	• General satisfaction score • Usability ratings
Behavioral Outcomes	• Stand hours • Calories burned • Exercise minutes • Diversity of exercise • Speed to complete rings
User Outcomes	• Number of days goals completed • Resting heart rate • Average O^2 levels • BMI • Daily feelings • Feelings of health
Business Outcomes	• Time between device upgrades • Premium service upgrades • Apple ecosystem retention

The Quest for Evidence

With a suite of metrics ready, the most intricate phase of the process is complete. The team now begins to experiment with their hypothesis, with the first task being to distinguish between users and non-users. An ideal criterion might be to define a user as someone who engages with the app, checking their metrics at least once a month, while a non-user has set up the app but remains passive. This distinction aims to separate two cohorts interested in fitness capabilities but differing engagement levels.

Alternatively, users could be defined as individuals who have personalized their goal settings instead of those who stick to the default targets. However, this approach might be less effective if most active users prefer the default settings.

Such strategies aim to gain a nuanced understanding of user engagement, ensuring that any observed impact can be confidently attributed to the feature rather than external, unrelated factors. Should all these methods prove impractical, a broader comparison might be drawn between those who actively use the fitness app and those who do not engage with it. Although this approach is straightforward, it risks missing key insights if some users have yet to initiate the feature's tracking capabilities.

In this hypothetical example, let's assume we categorize a user as someone who reviews their metrics at least monthly and a non-user as someone who reviews their metrics less frequently or not at all. With the app passively collecting most metrics, the team can proceed with an experiment without needing active participant recruitment. Instead, they can employ a statistical technique known as *coerced exact matching* to pair similar individuals—one user and one non-user—based on health indicators like weight and height, demographic details, and past fitness behaviors. With a cohort of over a thousand matched pairs, the team can scrutinize the relevant metrics over a six-month span to ascertain the impact of feature engagement. To complement this quantitative data, an in-product survey could be deployed to these participants, inviting them to self-assess their healthiness and enriching the quantitative findings with attitudinal insights.

> **NOTE** This section mentions an advanced statistical technique, *coerced exact matching*. While a deep understanding of data science isn't a prerequisite for applying the concepts in this book, advanced analytics skills can prove valuable when measuring impact. If you encounter methodologies like this and feel uncertain, remember that it's not necessary to grasp every technical detail for the purposes of this book. However, collaborating with your data team will be beneficial when you undertake your own impact measurement projects. We delve deeper into experimentation methods and data analysis techniques in Chapters 9 and 10.

Data-Backed Decisions

Once the data gathering and analysis are completed, the team can critically evaluate their initial hypotheses. The first step involves assessing whether engagement with the three rings feature correlates with increased targeted behaviors. A positive result would validate the hypothesis that the three rings feature effectively influences physical activity. The team must then ascertain whether these altered behaviors improve user outcomes. Should the results confirm this, it would substantiate the hypothesis that increased physical activities positively affect users' physical health. Conversely, if the data indicates no significant change in users' perceived healthiness, the team must come to terms with the possibility that the link to this specific outcome has not been established.

Armed with results indicating a relationship, the team's next task is effectively communicating these findings to stakeholders. The marketing department would be the primary recipient of this new, data-backed information, which could be integrated into campaign narratives to demonstrate the effectiveness of the three rings design. The product development team, too, would benefit from these insights, potentially leading to new features or identifying areas needing further exploration. Additionally, if any unforeseen negative impacts were revealed, the research team could suggest modifications to the feature to address these issues.

However, the most significant result of this process is the potential ignition of an Impact Mindset across the organization. By embarking on a roadshow of sorts, the team could evangelize the methodology they employed—defining, measuring, and evaluating the true success of a feature and the value it delivers. This endeavor transcends the enhancement of a single product. It's about promoting a philosophy that can elevate the company's entire product portfolio, instilling a mindset prioritizing impactful, user-centric development.

Coining This Process to Measure the Impact

Having delved into the hypothetical case study of Apple's three rings feature, you might find yourself better informed yet brimming with questions on how to implement a similar approach. This reaction is natural, and the example is designed to illustrate an ideal scenario, offering a vision to model. The Apple three rings case study showcases a structured five-step process—the FIA, shown in **TABLE 4.2**—aimed at measuring the impact of features.

Define involves defining a feature by completing the User Outcome Connection framework, a concept we've extensively explored.

Validate is the step when the team tests the assumptions linking specific behaviors, user outcomes, and business outcomes. The process can conclude if data supports these connections, and the team can focus on maintaining the feature's effectiveness. However, additional hypotheses must be formed and tested in most cases due to insufficient data, as in the Apple three rings study.

TABLE 4.2 Feature Impact Analysis

STEP	ACTION	PROCESS	OUTCOME
1	Define	Identify the specific behaviors that a feature alters to impact user and business outcomes.	Completed User Outcome Connection(s) for the feature.
2	Validate	Validate User Outcome Connections assumptions and document evidence gaps.	Validated user outcomes connection and hypotheses to be answered.
3	Collect Data	Scope metrics at each level of the success metric framework and determine how to collect.	Identified metrics and strategy for how each will be collected.
4	Experiment and Analyze	Compare users versus non-users to generate data to support or deny hypotheses.	Determined whether a feature is creating its intended impact.
5	Take Action	Share the results of the analysis and determining the next steps based on findings.	Identified next steps based on the results of an analysis.

Collect Data is dedicated to the craft of metric creation. With behaviors and outcomes identified, the team must scope out a collection of measurements for each. As the Apple three rings example demonstrated, some metrics are inherent to the product, while others necessitate the invention of proxies that echo reality. Creating metrics involves first defining the variable, followed by building the systems required to collect and use it. We got a taste of this in the example when the team had to create a survey to capture user sentiment and connect to other services to gather complementary metrics. With metrics in hand, the stage is set for genuinely measuring impact.

Experiment and Analyze starts with differentiating users from non-users, a task that can prove challenging. In the Apple example, this differentiation was based on monthly metric reviews. This step also includes designing and conducting an experiment, which can be either passive, as in the Apple case, or active, involving direct data collection. The final part is analyzing the new data to determine if the feature impacts users differently than non-users.

Take Action is where the insights are applied. The data analysis either confirms or refutes the initial hypotheses, leading to an informed evaluation of the feature. This step is crucial for actionable outcomes, shaping future feature development or refinement based on the study's findings. In the Apple example, this resulted in the marketing team crafting a campaign around the feature's success. For teams new to this process, it's also about promoting the methodology used and encouraging its adoption across the organization.

By adhering to the five outlined steps, a team arrives at a robust understanding of their feature and is equipped with newly minted metrics and tangible evidence to answer the pivotal question: Is the feature achieving its intended impact? The ambiguity surrounding a feature's purpose and effectiveness dissipates. In the most favorable scenarios, features are validated as effective, paving the way for targeted marketing campaigns and further analytical deep dives to enhance and replicate success. Conversely, when a feature falls short of its objectives, the team is positioned to make informed decisions about whether to refine or retire it. Either outcome illuminates the path forward, steering the team toward a more profound comprehension of their product in its entirety.

The FIA is a guiding framework, not a rigid set of rules. Every team's journey through this process is unique, with its own challenges and adjustments. Your initial attempt will likely not mirror the idealized narrative of the Apple example but will nonetheless be a significant advancement. My golden rule for all applied research is to ensure you are creating evidence that is at least better than intuition alone. With respect to the fact that each journey through this process will present its own decisions and necessary compromises, Part 2 of this book is dedicated to reviewing and preparing for many potential realities. You will finish that section confident to begin conducting your first FIA.

Retroactive vs. Proactive Approaches

When initiating the FIA, teams face a crucial decision: adopt a retrospective approach, as seen in the Apple Watch case study, or opt for a proactive strategy, integrating FIA into the feature's design and development. Drawing from my experience in large corporations, where development cycles are extensive but the impact reaches millions, I've observed that retrospective analysis often serves as an optimal starting point. In such settings, it's beneficial first to establish and apply the process independently, and then present the convincing results to the main team. This approach demonstrates the value of an Impact Mindset without the initial challenge of persuading skeptics.

However, this isolated, retroactive method may not suit all, particularly in smaller, more agile companies. Startup teams often ask why they must wait until a feature is launched to start FIA. The answer is they don't have to. If there's an established need for deeper measurements or the team is easily convinced of its necessity, then FIA can be implemented alongside a feature's development. This proactive approach is the ideal goal but is usually unrealistic to expect at the outset. Most companies need a few proven examples before adopting a new product development and evaluation philosophy.

A proactive FIA involves engaging with the *define* and *hypothesize* stages before the design process begins. As the feature is developed, data collection systems are set up in parallel. This method allows the *experiment and analyze* phase to start right from the feature's launch, or it can be incorporated into the feature testing phase, assuming the prototype is sufficiently detailed to evoke measurable behavioral changes. Chapter 16 will delve deeper into this methodology, advocating for its position as the ultimate manifestation of a fully embraced Impact Mindset. However, it's important to recognize the challenges of obtaining the necessary buy-in for simultaneous implementation with development. Consequently, the first FIA is often more feasibly conducted retrospectively.

Once a team decides between a proactive or retroactive approach, the next vital task is selecting the right feature for analysis. As discussed earlier, this choice is influenced by factors like the feature's alignment with the company's strategic goals and the complexity involved in measuring its outcomes. Organizational dynamics, such as team support and available resources, also significantly influence this decision. Chapter 12 provides a detailed guide on selecting the appropriate feature. The key is to choose a feature of sufficient importance, ensuring that its performance—whether successful or not—draws significant attention.

Catalyst for Adopting an Impact Mindset

The journey to measuring impact may begin with the User Outcome Connection, but it is the FIA that provides a team with a comprehensive pathway to discovering valuable insights about their feature. This process effectively connects the dots between altering user behaviors through feature engagement, achieving desired user outcomes, and ultimately realizing beneficial business results. Completing a FIA not only affirms the feature's influence on behavior but also broadens the team's viewpoint, positioning products as catalysts for behavioral change and advancing the practice of measurement and experimentation.

A single, well-executed FIA can act as a powerful impetus, demonstrating the effectiveness of a focused, behavior-centric evaluation. The tangible example you create, drawn from your company's experience and supplemented by the case studies in this book, becomes an influential tool for advocacy. This practical approach ensures that teams gain a refined understanding of their feature and acquire concrete metrics that delineate the positive influence on user outcomes.

Whether the FIA confirms the feature's success or highlights areas needing improvement, the methodology proves the significance of evaluating features as drivers of behavioral change. It showcases the power of adopting an evidence-based decision-making culture while advocating for the need to invest in creating insights to guide the way. At the same time, it reaffirms the potential to trace a direct line from these behaviors to the company's financial health, advocating for the strategic wisdom of investing in long-term outcomes over short-term indicators like click-through rates.

Teams are consistently striving to refine their measurement and experimentation methods. The FIA is pivotal in this quest, calling for a robust measurement and experimentation framework deployment. Even for organizations not fully prepared to adopt an Impact Mindset, the progress made through a FIA will likely attract attention from those seeking to improve their team's evaluation skills. Perfecting the skill of accurately assessing a feature's value is an invaluable asset, one that is honed through practical experience. Developing this expertise is almost guaranteed to increase your value within any team.

While executing a FIA can yield substantial rewards for a product team, it's the integration of this analysis into a broader strategic vision where its true transformative potential is unleashed. Embracing an Impact Mindset is not an overnight transformation; it's a deliberate process peppered with experimentation, learning, and adaptation to find the most fitting approach for your team's unique context. The Apple Watch example is an illustration and a comprehensive blueprint of what a fully realized FIA embodies. It serves as a springboard for your ideation on tailoring and implementing a similar analysis within your organization. Part 2 of this book will guide you through each phase of the FIA. It aims to set you on a course toward conducting your own analysis while fostering an Impact Mindset that will gradually become part of your team's DNA.

CHAPTER RECAP

- **Defining a feature for analysis:** Product features that are identified for an analysis should be scoped to be neither too big nor too small while ideally being functional and aligned with the unique value offered by the product.

- **Apple's three rings example:** The Apple Watch's three rings hypothetical example exemplifies how a team can conduct an analysis to determine whether a feature is creating its intended impact.

- **Introducing Feature Impact Analysis:** FIA is a structured approach to measure the real-world impact of a product feature on user behavior and outcomes.

- **Retroactive versus proactive approaches:** Deciding between retroactive and proactive FIA approaches hinges on the team's readiness and the strategic timing of measurement integration.

- **FIA is a catalyst for the Impact Mindset:** Implementing FIA can ignite a transformative Impact Mindset, fostering a culture of evidence-based decision-making and long-term product success.

PART 2

STARTING AN IMPACT MINDSET CULTURE CHANGE WITH A SINGLE PROJECT

Having made it through Part 1 of *Bridging Intention to Impact*, you are now acquainted with the transformative concept of the Impact Mindset. In Part 2, the focus shifts to actualizing this philosophy with a Feature Impact Analysis (FIA). This process is pivotal in forging a fully validated User Outcome Connection. Each chapter in this part covers a specific phase of the FIA, sometimes spanning two chapters for a single phase.

You will leave this section:

- With a deep understanding of each phase of FIA

- Ready to take the necessary steps to complete a FIA of your own

- Understanding where to start your FIA planning and who to contact

- Equipped with the knowledge to own functional metric development on your team

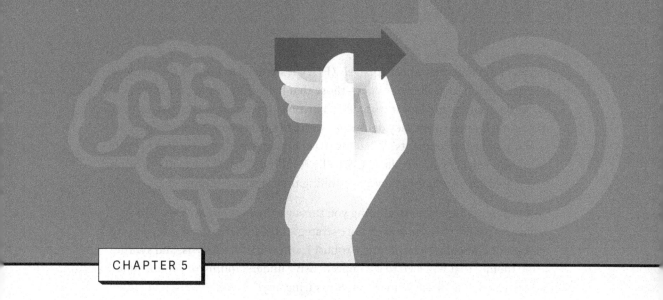

CHAPTER 5

Defining the Feature's Purpose (FIA Step 1)

In the realm of highly competitive markets, differentiation often hinges on unique features that elevate a product beyond its standard offerings. Consider the dating app landscape, where basic functionalities like profile creation, browsing potential matches, and communication channels are ubiquitous. To stand out, apps like Bumble and the League introduced distinctive features—Bumble empowered women to initiate conversations, and the League fostered in-person interactions through event organization. These innovations not only distinguished them in the market but also significantly contributed to their success. Features, in essence, become the lifeblood of a product, carving out niches and fostering dedicated user bases.

As you begin Feature Impact Analysis (FIA), it's crucial to ponder the elements that truly distinguish your product—those that help drive your company toward its mission statement. This introspection involves questioning the basis of your standout features—were they deliberate strategies to set your product apart or serendipitous developments? What instills confidence in these features as critical components of your product? Critically thinking about these features begins the exploration of whether they are fulfilling their true intentions.

This chapter is dedicated to guiding you through the first phase of the FIA: define. As part of this, we will explore strategies for gathering and categorizing relevant documents, constructing a robust framework for analysis, and synthesizing themes that will lead to a comprehensive understanding of your product's intent. The define phase is not about measuring anything; it's focused on understanding what led to the creation of a feature and then formalizing a definition of why it was created. The chapter concludes with advice on filling out the User Outcome Connection, equipping you to begin your journey in impact measurement with confidence and clarity.

Arriving at a Clear Definition of a Feature's Purpose

The digital landscape of the 21st century has erased the once-clear line between a company's digital products and its other offerings. Today, an online presence—whether through a website or social media—is indispensable for any business. This digital footprint becomes even more crucial as a company grows, with the expansion of online services, collection of customer data, and development of mobile applications becoming natural progressions.

In the early 2000s, the responsibility for new digital products often fell on disparate teams. However, as we progress into the third decade of the century, a clear trend has emerged, mirroring the path initially carved out by pioneering technology companies. The rise of chief product officers and an increased emphasis on product managers (PMs) across various industries is a testament to this shift.[1] While diverse in structure, these product teams share a common mission: to oversee and deliver the company's digital solutions. They are the architects of digital experiences, coordinating cross-functional teams and making pivotal decisions that shape the final product.

---

1 "2023 CPO Insights Report" by Products That Count

These teams shouldn't just develop features; they should also chart the "why" behind each feature, mapping out its creation to address specific user problems and ensuring alignment with the company's vision. This is not always the case, but it is beginning to change, with a majority of product teams sharing a desire to shift their measurements from outputs to outcomes.[2] Some teams strictly adhere to documentation and organization best practices, while others fly by pure intuition. Not everyone reading this book needs to be a PM, but influencing your product team to adopt an Impact Mindset is crucial for a significant cultural shift in feature development. No matter your role, embracing the principles laid out in this book and sharing them with your product team are pivotal to seeing features as behavior-changing tools (which is embodied by the User Outcome Connection filled out in the define stage in **TABLE 5.1**). Doing so will enhance your understanding of product development and contribute to a broader organizational transformation toward creating impactful digital experiences.

TABLE 5.1 Feature Impact Analysis, the Define Stage

STEP	ACTION	PROCESS	OUTCOME
1	Define	Identify the specific behaviors that a feature alters to impact user and business outcomes.	Completed User Outcome Connection(s) for the feature.
2	Validate	Validate User Outcome Connections assumptions and document evidence gaps.	Validated user outcomes connection and hypotheses to be answered.
3	Collect Data	Scope metrics at each level of the success metric framework and determine how to collect.	Identified metrics and strategy for how each will be collected.
4	Experiment and Analyze	Compare users versus non-users to generate data to support or deny hypotheses.	Determined whether a feature is creating its intended impact.
5	Take Action	Share the results of the analysis and determine the next steps based on findings.	Identified next steps based on the results of an analysis.

---

2 "The 2024 State of Product Management Report" by ProductPlan

Becoming the Knowledge Hub of a Feature

Embracing an Impact Mindset involves a deep commitment to understanding and quantifying the influence of a feature within a product. This task requires you to become the central source on a feature's purpose, evolution, and current functionality. In essence, you will need to adopt the roles of both detective and adjudicator, diligently gathering information from the creators while analyzing the unity between what was supposed to be and the actual development trajectory of the feature.

During this investigation, you will often find that the real-world application of a feature diverges from its initial intent. Consider a productivity app introducing a daily reflection feature to give users a sense of accomplishment. Post-launch, it may emerge that users predominantly use it for planning subsequent days. Such discoveries can reveal unanticipated user needs or new functionalities, but in either case, they necessitate a reassessment of the feature's original purpose.

The challenge lies in understanding not just the initial vision behind a feature but also how that vision has adapted over time. This dual understanding is crucial to accurately determining the user problems the feature addresses or, in some cases, that the feature has gone widely off its intended value course. Achieving this requires engaging in comprehensive discussions with the product team, delving into the insights that spurred the feature's creation, and meticulously reviewing the documentation that guided its development. When one of these avenues isn't available, it requires deeper exploration of the others, but obtaining this historical context is essential.

Most products are filled with dozens, and sometimes hundreds, of features. It is not realistic that a PM will be able to detail the purpose of each one in excruciating detail. This is particularly true for features that are not directly linked to the product's unique value proposition. A menu for easy navigation, a help button to quickly connect to customer support, and a login page that allows for third-party sign-ins are all standard. While these features may not have elaborate backstories, it would be surprising to hear any product person suggest that a product team built a feature "just because." The reality is that, whether a core aspect or a necessary addition, those who own products will generally have a rationale for every part of what is under their responsibility.

However, a PM's ownership of their product can sometimes cloud a feature's true origin and intent. Particularly when it comes to fundamental components,

PMs might have pursued a feature based more on their vision than on solid evidence. When researching a feature's history, you might encounter narratives shaped by its success or failure. A natural human tendency, this reality is not a deliberate attempt to deceive; it instead underscores the complexity involved in uncovering the genuine purpose of a feature. You may even be that feature owner or have been so in the past, and if so, ask yourself how you have allowed for updating your definition of success without updating the intent of how the feature is changing the user's desired outcomes.

The process is more straightforward in cases where robust documentation exists or where the narrative surrounding a feature has remained consistent. Regardless, the goal is to ensure that the FIA team has a lucid and comprehensive understanding of the feature's original purpose and the journey that led to its current positioning. This clarity is foundational to accurately assessing the feature's impact and aligning it with the broader objectives of the product.

Starting with a User Outcome Connection

Establishing a clear definition of a feature and its purpose is paramount, as this sets the stage for creating a User Outcome Connection—the initial phase in assessing a feature's impact. As a reminder, the User Outcome Connection consists of specific behaviors that when altered lead to user outcomes occurring, which then create positive business outcomes. At the end of a FIA, you will have a *completed* User Outcome Connection where you can be confident that the connections exist. For this first phase you are completing a *filled-out* User Outcome Connection, as shown in **FIGURE 5.1**, which means a description for each variable is completed but does not have data to validate that connections between each part exist.

DEFINE STEP

Specific Behaviors	User Outcomes	Business Outcome
The specific behaviors that when changed will impact the user outcome.	The short or long term desires that a user hopes to satisfy through usage.	The value created to a company from impacting user outcomes.

Connection not yet validated

FIGURE 5.1 User Outcome Connection at the define stage means that the connection between the variables has yet to be validated.

Filling out a User Outcome Connection begins with distilling the collective insights of everyone involved in the feature's development into a singular, coherent description. The approach used to complete the User Outcome Connection varies depending on what initiated the feature: user outcome, business objective, or modification of a specific behavior.

User outcome: Typically, the most effective starting point is pinpointing the user outcome the team aims to influence. Given that many product teams adopt approaches like human-centered design and outcome-driven innovation, which focus on understanding user needs, beginning with the user outcome is a logical choice. This approach allows you to use gathered evidence to determine which behaviors are altered to achieve this outcome and why these changes are significant to the customer. For the User Outcome Connection, you generally want to focus on the long-term outcome a feature is attempting to create, although subsequent frameworks can be filled out for short-term outcomes if relevant to the overall product.

Business objectives: There are instances where business objectives dictate feature creation. In such scenarios, defining a clear user outcome becomes crucial for measurement. For example, a company might introduce new gamification elements like badges to boost user engagement or develop a feature in response to a major client's request. When business needs are the driving force, starting the User Outcome Connection with these needs and then working backward to uncover the impacted user outcomes and behaviors is an appropriate strategy.

Specific behavior modification: Occasionally, product teams initiate feature development aimed at modifying a specific behavior without a clear understanding of the underlying purpose. An example of this might be an employee experience product team introducing a feature for tracking daily emotions, with the sole articulated goal of "allowing people to log their sentiments." In such cases, initiating the User Outcome Connection with the targeted behavior is advisable. However, it's important to recognize that when a business need or the desire to change a behavior is at the heart of a feature's genesis, it underscores the necessity of conducting a FIA. This evaluation ensures a genuine link between the modified behaviors and the desired business outcomes, validating the feature's efficacy and relevance.

As an illustration of this with a product I worked on, a chatbot was intended to help a user prepare for a difficult conversation. The User Outcome is somewhat obvious—after the engagement, a user should feel more confident that they will get their points across. Ideally, they will be more successful in the discussion. Through accomplishing this objective, the company hopes that it will drive more usage of their core product and thus increase retention.

Specific behaviors require consideration of what being prepared for a meeting entails. It starts with having a clear understanding of what one hopes to achieve and then how they will make that case. From there, practicing different scenarios or even running through mock conversations can aid in a feeling of preparedness. For the chatbot, it does both, and thus the team was hoping to see that people were finding more clarity through their conversation and becoming more refined in their ability to articulate their position in repeated usage.

Uncovering a Feature's Knowledge

Uncovering the history and rationale behind a feature's creation is akin to navigating a labyrinth of diverse and sometimes conflicting information sources. This task involves meticulously collecting, organizing, and analyzing a variety of documents and insights. To effectively uncover the details of the feature, a structured approach is necessary, coupled with a reliable method to assess the relevance and value of each piece of evidence. I recommend a process that combines direct conversations with the product team and a comprehensive review of supporting documentation. (The next section will delve into the framework for evaluating this evidence.)

Scouring the product team for any insight about the purpose and intent of a feature will involve a wide array of sources. These may include team members, other stakeholders, or anyone who might have had a hand in shaping the feature's development. Additionally, it involves scrutinizing documents and reports, ranging from technical specifications like product requirement documents (PRDs) to research-oriented materials such as research decks and findings. Generally, the closer the source is to the individuals who conceptualized and developed the feature, the more value it will offer.

Interviewing the Product Team

Several strategies can be effective when conducting interviews with sources around the product team. One approach is to adopt the role of a neutral reporter, inquiring about the feature's history and objectives without imposing any judgment. This approach might involve asking questions like "What was the primary goal of this feature?" or "How did the team decide to prioritize its development?" Alternatively, you could take on the role of an investigative journalist, targeting specific individuals for more pointed queries. This approach demands more time and effort, but it can be instrumental in cutting through the peripheral noise, particularly in larger teams. Investigative questions might include asking a product manager about the main user outcome affected by the feature or querying a designer on the specific actions they expect a user to take post-interaction.

I recommend starting with simple questions in an informal structure to gauge the level of collaboration you receive. Then, if there is resistance, reluctance, or just general aversion, you can begin to take a more structured and formal approach using investigative questions. Whatever your interviewing technique, it is crucial to engage with those directly involved with the feature, and then broaden the scope to include others who can offer additional perspectives and insights. These discussions will provide clarity on the research underpinning the feature and reveal the creators' current views and intentions. Interviews often lead to specific evidence or direct you to pivotal documents detailing the feature's purpose.

When approaching discussions with product teams, remember two important factors: you will be discussing *their* features, and whenever something is not documented, it is accessible only through someone else's mind. Since you will be soliciting interviews to better understand another's perspective on their feature, remember to be friendly and do not be put off by any defensiveness you may experience. Ownership, especially in a business context, commonly means someone's performance and incentives are tied to outcomes. Your questioning may appear threatening at first. At the same time, you need this information to make effective decisions in the FIA, so be sure to avoid "burning any bridges." Without documentation to follow, you must default to asking the people who made the decisions; if you cannot access them, the entire process becomes much more challenging.

Reviewing Design and Development Documents

Regarding resources, there are two primary categories of document to seek out. The first category includes documents that describe a feature in detail, defining how it should be constructed. These documents, like production requirement documents (PRDs) and technical specifications, shed light on the intended user actions following feature interaction, thus informing both the expected behaviors and outcomes. They also often contain links to the research that justified the feature's creation. The second category includes research artifacts illuminating the data and rationale behind a feature's inception. These artifacts reveal how the feature is expected to change specific behaviors, impacting user and business outcomes. Examples of such research, which we will discuss in the next section, include user research reports and data science analyses.

Throughout this process, your goal is to gather materials that clarify a feature's intended function. Additionally, you'll identify whether these materials suggest a link between the feature and the outcomes—an essential consideration for the subsequent stages of the FIA. Your aim is to gather and review as much as possible. At first, it may feel like a lot, but you will quickly learn to assess what is worth further detailing and what you can confidently scan and put aside. The more data that you can glean from documents, the less you have to worry about obtaining it through conversation, saving that time to do the valuable process of connecting the dots.

Defining the Feature's Purpose Using Three Main Types of Evidence

When sifting through the plethora of materials related to the creation of a feature, it's advantageous to categorize the evidence into three distinct types.

Primary research encompasses data directly collected by the company or closely linked to its unique context. This type of research is often highly specific, addressing particular queries pertinent to the organization.

Secondary research refers to data supporting the feature's intent but not originally generated for the organization's specific use. It's essentially second-hand evidence.

Intuition plays a crucial role in product development. Instead of being rooted in evidence-based research, intuition is the collective experience and instinct of the product team and thus can be very powerful but also significantly misleading.

Properly categorizing the gathered information in this manner aids in a comprehensive analysis. Most features are shaped by a blend of secondary research and intuition, with larger companies likely incorporating all three types. Post-categorization, the subsequent task is to discern which type of research predominantly influenced the feature's development, as this will provide insight into the likelihood of a genuine correlation between the feature and its intended outcomes.

Beyond these three categories is the reality that features do not exist in isolation; they often form part of broader roadmaps and product visions. Companies like GitHub and Front, which publicly share their product roadmaps, demonstrate commendable transparency and a readiness to embrace feedback—traits indicative of a customer-centric culture. Nevertheless, the commitment to a predefined roadmap can sometimes lead to developing features irrespective of new findings. Ideally, these companies would incorporate feedback to refine and optimize their features within the scope of their roadmap commitments. However, if the roadmap isn't aligned with effective outcomes, it may predispose subsequent features to ineffective driving of meaningful change. In such scenarios, expanding your document search to include materials that influenced the prioritization of certain features becomes necessary.

In other cases, companies, particularly startups, may operate under a strong product vision without a concrete roadmap. This scenario typically involves one or a few leaders steering the team in a specific direction. While not inherently doomed to failure, this approach further necessitates scrutinizing the data underpinning the vision.

For the User Outcome Connection, focus primarily on the evidence that led to creating a feature. Yet you should also consider the broader factors that shaped the company's strategic direction. You don't want to mistake the trees for the forest, but understanding the border context can be greatly beneficial. Linking the discovery of feature intents to strategic documents may foster greater interest and enthusiasm for the analysis process. As was discussed with lofty mission statements, many companies desire to make products with a purpose, and only through measuring impact can a team truly know it is successful.

Primary Research

Primary research, conducted firsthand by a company or its commissioned agents, offers a potent tool for understanding specific contexts and addressing unique queries. Tailored to a company's unique needs, this type of research can precisely pinpoint user problems or potential outcomes to address. When well executed, primary research often uncovers patterns and preferences specific to a company's customer base. Typically, primary research is the domain of applied research teams within an organization, encompassing areas like user research, market research, and data science. The insights these teams generate are invaluable, providing foundational data that product teams can use throughout the product development lifecycle. Common projects from these teams include user interviews for defining specific user problems and needs, usability studies with prototypes to evaluate functionality, and retention analyses to understand factors influencing long-term user engagement or churn.

Consider Zillow, a comprehensive marketplace for homebuyers offering various resources to simplify the home-buying process. Zillow stands out as a research-driven company, particularly with its advanced behavioral science team that excels in using user behavior data to identify new product opportunities. Their user research team is often featured at industry conferences, showcasing their use of mixed methods to unravel users' motivations and needs. An exemplary case study from Zillow's research team, presented at the EPIC conference, detailed their approach to benchmarking the user experience across the customer journey.[3] Although the specifics of how Zillow's research translates into product development is not public, their continued dominance as a top home marketplace suggests successful application. For a Zillow team member to build a User Outcome Connection, examining this research and consulting with the research team are imperative.

In essence, primary research is a critical asset in affirming the existence of genuine user problems and the potential of your features to drive new behaviors. It comes in various forms, always originating from work done by or for your organization and tailored to your specific context. Although invaluable for defining feature purposes, primary research is not infallible. It's naturally limited in scope to answer certain questions, potentially overlooking other factors or broader contexts. Thus, it's crucial to understand the findings and how your team interprets and applies them in the product development process.

---

3 "Scaling Experience Measurement: Capturing and Quantifying User Experiences across the Real Estate Journey," EPIC Conference "Scaling Experience Measurement: Capturing and Quantifying User Experiences Across the Real Estate Journey," article by EPIC

Secondary Research

Secondary research, sourced externally from an organization, offers insights that, while relevant, may not capture the unique nuances of a specific firm's customers.

Industry reports are the best examples of secondary research. I commonly see industry reports offered by software-as-a-service (SaaS) companies. These reports, often based on extensive surveys with substantial participant numbers, shed light on trends and needs within a particular sector. Such research can be instrumental in identifying market patterns and substantiating the necessity for specific products or features. However, its broad audience focus means that its findings may not directly apply to the peculiarities of a particular company's product. The presence of a need within a market doesn't automatically imply that a specific company's product is aptly positioned to address it.

Academic articles are another prevalent form of secondary research. These scholarly works can be valuable in pinpointing possible solutions to user issues, though they are typically conducted in settings that don't mirror the practicalities of product environments such as paying customers, frequent distractions, and pressure from peers and managers. Replicating approaches successful in academic research may indicate a potential for influencing user behavior, but this doesn't ensure effective solutions or guarantee a change in user outcomes. This holds true for any form of applied research conducted outside an organization—it may guide you in the right direction, but its conclusions shouldn't automatically be presumed applicable to your specific context.

Competitive analyses and exploring how other organizations penetrate new markets through examining their website, applications, and public-facing materials is another form of secondary research. Facebook, for instance, is known for its keen eye on emerging technologies, either acquiring them or developing similar offerings in-house. Their responses to the rise of Snapchat (with Instagram Stories) and TikTok (with Instagram Reels) are testaments to their adaptability and market awareness. However, replicating a competitor's successful feature doesn't automatically guarantee a similar impact in a different organizational context.

In my professional experience, secondary research has been a substantial resource. It can be as insightful as primary research, particularly for initial market pattern recognition that can inform feature development. However, reliance on secondary research can sometimes mislead teams, leading them to believe they have thoroughly understood their users based on generalized findings. Teams using secondary research can better understand their strategic direction and the impact of their features on users. Still, for conclusive insights, primary research is necessary. Absent this, teams are often left to interpret secondary data and rely on their intuition, which underscores the need for further validation of the relationships between User Outcome Connection variables.

Intuition

Product development is an intricate blend of art and science. Although primary and secondary research provide valuable guidance, it is rare for product teams to base decisions solely on data. *Intuition* plays a pivotal role in almost all product development, with the team relying on their collective experience and instincts to make calls on what problems to address for customers and how to approach them. This reliance on intuition spans a spectrum, from complete reliance on gut feeling to leading with data but allowing for instinct to help with how to interpret it. Intuition is a necessary reality in feature creation, as there is almost never enough data to provide a clear direction on what action to take.

The impact of heavily leaning on intuition in product development can be profound, leading to remarkable success or significant misdirection. Apple, particularly under Steve Jobs, is a prime example of intuition-led success. Many of Apple's products, which became household staples, were born from Steve Jobs's vision and the Apple product team's instincts. The iPhone, for instance, broke numerous industry norms and innovated an entire product category, largely based on a gut feeling about user needs.

Similarly, the inception of the Google search algorithm[4] was primarily an intuitive leap by its co-founders. They hypothesized that a page-ranking system would effectively solve users' needs for relevant search results. As they analyzed the entire open web through this lens, this intuition proved to be a game-changer, setting Google apart from other search engines.

Both examples highlight iconic success stories of products that were the output of their founders' intuition, yet these are just that—success stories. Along the

---

4 Quote from https://ayafintech.network/blog/stanford-computer-science-overlords-larry-page-and-sergey-brin-develop-google-as-an-internet-search-company/#:~:text=Brin%2C%20Page%2C%20and%20Schmidt%20trust,fresh%20intuition%20and%20inner%20voice

way, many failed products never rose to the iPhone's or Google Search's prominence because the founders' instincts were wrong. Quibi stands as one of the best examples of a product that failed due to overreliance on assumptions. Their founders believed they understood the trend of media becoming shorter and more quickly digestible and acted upon it. They envisioned themselves starting a new category, even suggesting they were not even competing with Netflix. Instead, consumers had many other options, and Quibi was not offering anything novel to solve a real user problem.

Apple and Google are iconic success stories, demonstrating the power of founders' intuition in creating groundbreaking products. However, it's crucial to remember that these are the exceptions. The landscape is also strewn with failed products, where founders' assumptions did not align with market needs or user preferences. Quibi is a cautionary tale of such failure, born from an overreliance on assumptions. Its founders envisioned a new category of short, digestible media content, positioning themselves as distinct from platforms like Netflix. Unfortunately, they misjudged consumer preferences and needs, leading to Quibi's downfall.

These polarizing examples underscore the dual nature of intuition in product development. Although it can lead to pioneering innovations, it also carries the risk of significant misjudgments, emphasizing the need for a balanced approach that combines intuition with empirical evidence and user-centered research. Product intuition is bound to happen; your role will be to identify its influence and adjust your analysis accordingly.

Adjustments Based on the Main Type of Evidence

After sorting all the gathered data into primary, secondary, and intuition-based categories, the next crucial step is ascertaining which category predominantly influenced the product development process. It's common to find that teams incorporate a mix of data and intuition in their approach. Identifying a reliance on intuition as the main driver is somewhat subjective. A useful guideline is to consider whether the data merely supported a decision or formed its foundation. Teams that primarily rely on product intuition are neither good nor inherently bad, but this approach often indicates a probable absence of solid evidence establishing connections among all facets of the User Outcome Connection.

If your team has minimally employed primary or secondary research in their decision-making, it's important to recognize and adapt to this reality. Such scenarios typically necessitate deeper discussions to effectively identify and define each element of the User Outcome Connection. The path to understanding can be ambiguous, particularly without the guidance of strong product visionaries with deep market and product understanding. In these cases, your role shifts from uncovering absolute truths to striving toward a well-defined framework for each category, laying the groundwork for subsequent validation in the FIA.

On the other hand, teams that have anchored their product development in research are likely to have a firmer grasp on the specific behaviors, user outcomes, and business outcomes they aim to influence. In these instances, research artifacts become the primary tool for dissecting each aspect of the feature. When primary research is involved, it typically offers a more robust and accurate understanding of customer needs, potentially simplifying the process of documenting a feature's purpose. Although helpful, secondary research often requires further interpretation by the team to grasp any assumptions or conclusions fully drawn from it.

With a comprehensive review of the collected documents and a clear understanding of the predominant type of evidence, the stage is set for you to complete the User Outcome Connection. This next step involves synthesizing the information and insights from the categorized evidence, shaping a coherent and validated understanding of the feature's purpose and impact.

Creating the User Outcome Connection

After you've gathered and categorized the relevant data and discerned the primary evidence supporting the feature's intent, the next crucial step is creating the User Outcome Connection. The process varies slightly depending on the nature of the underlying research, but it follows a general flow.

1. Define the feature's intent. For features underpinned by primary research, the User Outcome Connection should be straightforward, as the research directly addresses the feature's intent and impact. When dealing with secondary research, a deeper understanding of the team's interpretation of external sources is necessary to identify each framework component. With

intuition-led features, the responsibility largely falls on you to determine the driving factors behind the feature's purpose. In such cases, consider developing two User Outcome Connections—one based on the team's perspective and another based on your interpretation. The intent should be the long-term change a feature intends to create.

2. Identify the prominent theme. Creating a User Outcome Connection is generally consistent, regardless of the evidence type. It begins with data collection, review, and categorization. From this data, identify the most prominent themes surrounding what led to its design. You are looking for the main reasons that a solution was created to serve the previously identified intent. This step can be straightforward, but you become the arbiter of truth in cases with conflicting perspectives. In these instances, your judgment becomes essential, especially in the absence of clear external guidance. These themes will be the basis on which you select the primary behaviors and outcomes in the next step.

3. Precisely define the outcomes and behaviors. For instance, if your analysis indicates that a feature contributes to user retention, you need to probe deeper: What exactly is the feature doing for users? When the business outcome is retention, the user outcome pertains to the specific benefits the feature provides. Similarly, in a scenario where a feature in a dating app facilitates matches, it's crucial to identify what the feature actually does for the user. Effective implementation might result in increased in-person meetups, making it the user outcome, with retention again being the business outcome.

Usually, the user and business outcomes will become apparent through your data analysis. However, identifying connected behaviors—a key aspect of the Impact Mindset—can pose more of a challenge. Even teams that have meticulously thought through feature development may not have explicitly defined the precise behaviors their feature is meant to influence. In such cases, the onus is on you to creatively outline these behaviors.

A helpful approach is to visualize how users interact with the feature. Consider their actions during use and subsequent behaviors. How do these behaviors relate to the identified user outcome? When still in doubt, consult academic literature, conduct competitive analyses, and perform other forms of quick primary research to understand how others speculate that user outcomes are connected to certain behaviors. Although pinpointing the exact connected behavior on the first attempt may not always be possible, the aim is to establish a plausible link, confident in the potential for a genuine connection. This approach is often iterative, embracing trial and error as a pathway to refining the User Outcome Connection.

4. Once you have an idea of the outcomes and behaviors, draft the User Outcome Connection and share it with a select group for feedback. Ideal reviewers might include members of the product team or the design and engineering teams. Use their feedback for revisions, ensuring a balance between your understanding of the evidence and the insights from those close to the feature. Repeat this process as needed.

Determining whether you have enough data to proceed can be challenging. With no definitive rule for "enough" data, aim to meet two criteria: multiple sources of information and the emergence of one or two dominant themes. Again, understanding the themes here means that you have a few reasons for why the feature design was chosen. Ideally, this would involve at least one discussion with someone involved in the feature's creation and review of a piece of technical or research documentation. Further exploration may be needed if you're still facing conflicting narratives without clear feature definitions. The goal is to feel confident enough to test the User Outcome Connection, not to ascertain its absolute correctness.

Once you have written down the feature's user outcome, business outcome, and specific behaviors, the User Outcome Connection is considered *filled out*. This status does not mean that it is correct or even data supported at this point. It just calls out how each piece of the feature is connected. The next step, detailed in the following chapter, is identifying and attempting to validate the connections between the three variables: business outcomes, user outcomes, and specific behaviors. Going about this may require identifying further materials around the creation of the feature and is likely to determine that a feature lacks some valid connections. A User Outcome Connection in this state is considered *partially validated*. Only once a team has the data to show that a connection exists between each entity can they say it is *complete*.

Generative AI (GenAI) in Practice

Leveraging new powerful tools in the GenAI space can make the process of building out your FIA even easier. The remaining chapters will have a special section for GenAI-based prompts that can be useful for tackling certain aspects of FIA. As I write this, in early 2024, the technology is changing fast, so I don't plan to reference specific technology or approaches beyond standard ChatGPT inputs and outputs. My aim is to show how GenAI tech can be used as an unblocking tool rather than to encourage you to build your entire process around the use of it. As part of the supplemental material for this book, I have included a GPT that is trained on the FIA process.

This first example of leveraging GenAI focuses on a prompt that helps create the User Outcome Connection.

User Prompt

Take the following information describing a feature's intent and break it into three elements: the business impact, the user outcome, and the specific behaviors the feature is changing. Write a single, detailed sentence for each entry.

We are launching a new feature for our dating app that is intended to increase the detail that users provide in their bios. It will do this by prompting them with questions intended to elicit more depth in their responses. We hope doing this will increase the quality of matches that the user has, which will keep them using the app. If it is a success, we may turn it into a premium feature to increase upsells.

ChatGPT

Business Impact: The launch of the new feature aims to enhance user engagement and retention on our dating app, with a potential future goal of increasing revenue through upselling it as a premium feature.

User Outcome: By prompting users with in-depth questions for their bios, this feature is designed to enrich the profiles, leading to higher-quality matches and an improved overall dating experience.

Specific Behaviors Changing: The feature changes user behavior by encouraging them to provide more detailed and thoughtful responses in their bios, moving away from superficial or limited profile information.

Quality Feature Definitions

When constructing the User Outcome Connection, compiling a comprehensive and well-defined list of variables is crucial, ensuring both exhaustiveness and quality in their descriptions. For each feature, consider all the specific behaviors that could influence an outcome and identify all possible business impacts. If a feature influences multiple user outcomes, develop a separate User Outcome Connection for each to maintain clarity. Although it's possible to link numerous behaviors and business outcomes to a single user outcome, avoid including more than one user outcome per framework to prevent confusion. In divergent perspectives, you might create multiple User Outcome Connections for comparative analysis later. However, this approach demands more resources, so when faced with uncertainty, lean toward the interpretation you are most confident about.

Whether you're dealing with one or multiple user outcomes, it's important to articulate every potential behavior and outcome impacted by the feature. Each variable should be described with a high level of detail and precision, as this affects how others perceive the information and establishes the framework as the definitive document for understanding the feature's purpose. The specificity of connected behaviors is particularly important, as detailed descriptions will facilitate the development of metrics in the later stages of the analysis. **TABLE 5.2** includes a few examples of vague versus specific behaviors.

TABLE 5.2 Vague vs. Specific Connected Behaviors

EXAMPLE OUTCOME	VAGUE BEHAVIOR	SPECIFIC BEHAVIOR
Wellness	Our product improves wellness by ensuring the customer adopts a better routine.	Our product improves wellness by ensuring the user achieves eight hours of good sleep and takes stress-relieving breaks throughout the day.
Savings	We help our users save more for retirement by getting them to passively contribute more money.	We help our users to save by rounding up on purchases and auto-depositing that money into their account.
Recruitment SaaS	Our service empowers recruiters with better information so they can make decisions more quickly.	Our service empowers recruiters through the auto-creation of pre-reads before interviews and highlighting of keywords from the interview.

Similarly, business outcomes must be clearly defined, typically linked to essential business goals like increasing revenue or reducing costs. For instance, the broad goal of reducing costs might be more specifically described as lowering the expenses involved in acquiring new customers. Likewise, increasing revenue could be redefined as enhancing customer retention, thereby boosting their lifetime value. Remember, the ultimate objective is to attribute quantifiable metrics to these business outcomes.

For companies operating in the business-to-business (B2B) sector, an additional component, the *business customer outcome*, should be considered. Most user outcomes naturally lend themselves to explaining why a business customer would opt for a particular solution. For example, businesses seek improved productivity to enhance output levels and reduce operational costs or aim for better

A Note on User and Business Outcomes

The nature of user and business outcomes can range from straightforward and measurable to complex and multifaceted. Typically, sectors like health and finance offer clear, quantifiable user outcomes. In the health domain, improvements can be gauged through metrics like weight, vital signs, and well-being assessments. In finance, outcomes are often measured by savings rates, budget compliance, and perceptions of financial security. However, many services present more intricate user outcomes, necessitating a sequence of interconnected results. Consider, for instance, an application designed to boost productivity. While productivity itself is an outcome, its actual implications might include enhanced communication efficiency, reduced rework, and other factors.

Similarly, business outcomes, though ultimately linked to fundamental metrics like revenue and profit, can be more precisely defined. For example, reduced operational costs may stem from lowered customer acquisition costs, attributable to fewer interactions needed to progress a prospect through the marketing funnel. The goal is to progressively identify and define specific outcomes, as this enhances measurability. However, in instances where data is limited or specificity is not yet achievable, broader outcomes can still be associated with distinct behaviors. This approach maintains the focus on tangible impacts, even when dealing with high-level outcomes.

preventative healthcare utilization to lower healthcare expenses. Enhanced communication often leads to more frequent innovation, which can, in turn, increase revenue and reduce costs. These factors feed into the business outcome, as satisfying these needs enables a B2B company to boost sales and enhance customer retention.

Balance Between Feedback and Progress

Creating a User Outcome Connection is not just a systematic task; it involves navigating the dynamics of collaboration and managing the diverse emotions of stakeholders. Particularly in scenarios where the development of a feature was contentious or driven by a few individuals' intuition, officially documenting the perceived purpose and impact of the feature could trigger strong reactions. This sensitivity underscores the importance of discretion in sharing the document for feedback. Your primary objective is to strike a careful balance between soliciting valuable input and steadily advancing the process.

Involving a broad array of contributors in defining a feature's purpose and anticipated impact on business success can lead to dissatisfaction, especially if the evidence contradicts prevailing beliefs. This potential for disagreement doesn't imply that the document should be withheld from everyone but rather that it calls for selecting the right initial reviewers. These individuals should be capable of providing constructive feedback while respecting the integrity of the process and pursuing factual understanding regarding the feature's impact.

This approach is also a safeguard if the initial assumptions about the feature's connections are disproven during the validation phase. For instance, consider a smart lighting app that introduces a "routine" feature to encourage users to experiment with new colors, but preliminary data suggests users predominantly stick to familiar colors. In such cases, discovering that the assumed connections may not hold can alter the narrative and the path forward.

Your main objective is solidifying a User Outcome Connection that is robust enough to undergo testing while facilitating a swift transition to the validation phase. Once the analysis moves beyond theoretical assumptions to actual data-driven insights, the narrative shifts focus, highlighting either the successes or the need for modifications due to shortcomings. The next chapter will delve deeper into this validation process. For now, as you initiate the User Outcome Connection, prioritize building relationships with stakeholders likely to be receptive to the concept of an Impact Mindset. These allies will form your core team as you collect, review, categorize, and analyze all relevant materials. Establishing these collaborative partnerships early on will be instrumental in successfully navigating the FIA process.

Solidifying FIA with a Personal Anecdote

Throughout 2023, I delved deeply into learning about AI-tool development, and in early 2024 I embarked on several projects. Among them was a chatbot named Tasky that was designed to assist users in identifying opportunities to integrate generative AI into their workflows. This project not only achieved widespread usage but also garnered attention from Jakob Nielsen, a luminary in the user experience domain, who referenced my related writings.[5] This story aims to encapsulate the chapter's insights, illustrating the proactive creation of impactful products. Although the principles discussed are applicable to retrospective FIA, this example emphasizes proactive application.

In the define phase of the project, the inspiration to develop a chatbot that was aimed at task identification for AI assistance stemmed from a TEDx Talk I presented. The talk received considerable acclaim, prompting me to expand on the subject through further writing. Encouraged by the positive reception of my articles, I aspired to transform a framework I had developed into an AI assistant. The parts of the framework that I wanted to re-create were the identification of a task to begin automating and the creation of an individual's first ChatGPT prompt.

This proactive approach had its groundwork in the define phase, where I envisioned Tasky as a bot that would nudge users toward leveraging ChatGPT and similar technologies to streamline their daily tasks. The anticipated behavioral shift was in how users tackled routine activities, aiming to enhance their work efficiency and effectiveness. Moreover, empowering users to master these technologies was intended to mitigate their apprehensions. Success with this chatbot could pave the way for developing a product, aligning with the desired business outcome. All this is shown as a User Outcome Connection in **FIGURE 5.2**.

---

5 "AI Habit Formation: Future-Proofing Your UX Career" by Jakob Nielsen

TASKY CHATBOT EXAMPLE

Specific Behaviors	User Outcomes	Business Outcome
The adoption of and experimentation with prompts based on the bot's output.	More confidence using ChatGPT.	Users would purchase this service as a product.

Connection not yet validated

FIGURE 5.2 User Outcome Connection for the Tasky chatbot

CHAPTER RECAP

- **Define phase:** The first part of FIA is focused on understanding why a feature was created and building a solid definition of what it is intended to do, as done through completing the User Outcome Connection.

- **Categorization of evidence:** The evidence for a feature's development is categorized into three main types: primary research (directly conducted by the company), secondary research (external sources), and intuition (instinctive understanding or vision).

- **Role of intuition in product development:** Intuition plays a role in all product development, and in some cases it yields tremendous outcomes. However, you should be aware of the risks of overreliance on intuition without empirical backing.

- **Balancing feedback and progress:** Managing the collaborative process of creating the User Outcome Connection is crucial, especially in balancing stakeholder feedback with the progression of the project. This balance is vital in cases where initial assumptions about the feature are challenged or disproven.

- **Importance of detailed descriptions:** For each aspect of the User Outcome Connection, detailed and quality descriptions are necessary. Specificity in connected behaviors and well-defined business outcomes aid in clarity and later stages of analysis.

CHAPTER 6

Establishing Beliefs About Outcomes with Hypotheses (FIA Step 2)

When outlining user outcomes, you are likely to find that some are straight-forward, like a smart light's on-off functionality or a car app's lock-unlock feature. However, most outcomes are less tangible and more elusive. Take entertainment apps, for instance; do they truly deliver enjoyment, or do they leave you feeling anxious? Apps like Slack and Microsoft Teams aim to stream-line communication, but they often overwhelm users with constant alerts and minor issues, leading to wasted time at the expense of high-value tasks.[1] These complex outcomes pose greater challenges in measurement, and it's com-mon to find insufficient evidence to confirm their effectiveness. In the previ-ous chapter, you explored your feature's dynamics and defined its outcomes. This chapter focuses on validating the assumptions about the ties that exist between each factor in the User Outcome Connection.

---

1 "The Cost of Interrupted Work: More Speed and Stress" by Gloria Mark

Recall the critical features that set your product apart; truly making an impact on your customers demands that these features work as intended. By now you have identified the user outcomes that these features intend to change. How confident are you that your feature is working in the way you planned? Would you confidently wager that it's achieving the desired impact for users? If there's a hint of doubt, you need to bolster your certainty by establishing a method to verify the product's alignment with its intended purpose. Doing so ensures that any improvements will increase the variables most important to your business.

Balancing Rigor and Practicality in Outcome Verification

In the previous chapter, you developed a User Outcome Connection as a foundation for your initial FIA. This chapter concentrates on the validation stage, as shown in **TABLE 6.1**, scrutinizing whether there is adequate data to establish links between each element in the User Outcome Connection. Full validation of these connections is essential before you can confidently assert that your feature influences user outcomes as intended. By the end of this chapter, you'll either have this assurance or recognize the need for more data, prompting further steps in the FIA. With a fully validated User Outcome Connection, you'll be prepared to make that bet with confidence.

TABLE 6.1 Feature Impact Analysis, the Validate Stage

STEP	ACTION	PROCESS	OUTCOME
1	Define	Identify the specific behaviors that a feature alters to impact user and business outcomes.	Completed User Outcome Connection(s) for the feature.
2	Validate	Validate User Outcome Connections assumptions and document evidence gaps.	Validated user outcomes connection and hypotheses to be answered.
3	Collect Data	Scope metrics at each level of the success metric framework and determine how to collect.	Identified metrics and strategy for how each will be collected.
4	Experiment and Analyze	Compare users versus non-users to generate data to support or deny hypotheses.	Determined whether a feature is creating its intended impact.
5	Take Action	Share the results of the analysis and determining the next steps based on findings.	Identified next steps based on the results of an analysis.

Possessing evidence of a feature's efficacy can be immensely empowering. As highlighted earlier, many organizations have lofty mission statements claiming to revolutionize the world. However, the real measure of their impact lies not in these declarations but in their actions. If features are crafted with high-minded goals but executed ineffectively, they fall short of advancing these missions. Companies that purport their product achieves world-changing outcomes without measuring their actual impact are even more problematic, inadvertently distancing themselves from making a meaningful difference. Such a gap between intention and action is ethically questionable and potentially detrimental to users, but it can also lead to disillusionment among employees who perceive this inconsistency.

Although the argument of aligning with mission statements might appeal to the staunch advocates of change, it may appear overly idealistic to many. The drive to increase profits often overshadows other considerations in the practical business world. Fortunately, the rationale for outcome measurement extends beyond merely fulfilling an organization's mission. When products effectively address customer needs, they are more likely to achieve product-market fit, thereby enhancing their profitability. Delving further, effective outcome measurement also aids in crafting impactful marketing strategies and enables teams to identify and address problems early, preventing them from escalating into more significant challenges. This approach is akin to navigating with a full set of instruments, allowing teams to identify and rectify issues proactively rather than reacting to crises after they have already caused significant damage.

Devices that Demand Effectiveness

A product area on one edge of the extreme when it comes to needing to know that something works is medical devices. Companies building solutions in this space undergo significant review to ensure that whatever they build is effective at its intended purpose. Medical devices are assigned one of three categories of risk; we will focus on only the most significant, Level 3. These devices pose a significant threat in the event of a failure and thus require rigorous testing similar to pharmaceuticals. Having confidence that it not only works but that it doesn't create significant adverse effects is a must-have for such devices.

Achieving Level 3 approval for a medical device involves multiple stages. Initially, the device undergoes a review by experts, combining secondary research with product intuition. This is followed by three distinct phases of clinical trials, representing experimental rigor's pinnacle. These trials are meticulously controlled, involving randomly selected individuals from the population divided into treatment and control groups. This design isolates the effect of the treatment, ensuring that any observed outcomes are attributable to the device.

Here is a breakdown of these three clinical trials:

- The first trial is relatively small, focusing intensively on how the device functions and monitoring for any side effects.

- If the device is proven to be safe, the second trial expands to a larger group to explore further effects and start assessing the changes to desired user outcomes—in this case, those that are tied to physical health.

- The final trial significantly increases the sample size, validating the device's functionality on a broader scale.

Completing these scientific trials, which can take months to years, ensures that reliable, quality evidence is generated. This rigorous approach is the gold standard in determining user outcomes and verifying a device's effectiveness. However, companies typically do not adopt such extensive measures in markets that are less regulated than medical devices. Instead, they balance speed, effort, and the desired quality of results, aligning with their culture and specific requirements. At this juncture, forming an informed perspective on your standards for quality evidence is key, enabling you to steer your team toward appropriate actions within the research context you've already established.

The Power of a Randomized Controlled Trial

Randomized controlled trials (RCTs) are the gold standard in research methodology and are highly regarded in the medical field for their precision and validity. The strength of an RCT lies in its ability to minimize external variables, or "noise," allowing researchers to confidently attribute outcomes to the change being studied. This approach ensures that the observed outcome can be directly linked to the intervention being tested when all other factors are constant. In this context, the independent variable is the element being altered (such as a feature in a product), and the dependent variable is the outcome being influenced. Gaining their power from the precise nature of the setup are the three main components spelled out in the name.

Randomization: This involves selecting participants from a broad population without specific conditions, ensuring a diverse and unbiased sample. Researchers often resort to a convenience sample—easily accessible participants like frequent users or responsive individuals. However, this method can introduce biases, as participants may already have a positive disposition toward the product or feature. Randomization avoids this pitfall by including a mix of individuals with varying levels of satisfaction and brand affinity, reducing the likelihood of biased outcomes.

Control: RCTs aim to stabilize external variables that are not being directly tested. For instance, in a trial for a continuous blood glucose monitor, researchers would seek to standardize influencing factors like participants' diets, activity levels, and living environments. Controlling these variables can be challenging and might involve setting specific guidelines for participants or creating a more controlled environment for the study. The goal is to minimize the influence of external elements that could skew the results.

Trial: Every study requires a predefined duration to ensure timely analysis and application of results. While some studies, like the Harvard Happiness study, span decades, most RCTs have a set timeframe to yield actionable insights. The term *trial* underscores a structured approach detailing participant recruitment, control measures, treatment and control group setup, and overall execution. In the medical field, the term signifies a commitment to high-quality research.

Let's walk through a hypothetical example of this entire process using a device manufacturer looking to get Level 3 clearance on a blood sugar tracker, called a constant glucose monitor. When recruiting for this study, they may want to take the path of least resistance and ask people who are currently using their previous device, but this would likely mean over-focusing on those who are early adopters. Instead, they would need to identify a *random* selection of people with diabetes who need to use such a device. With a sample selected, they need to control for as many variables as possible, splitting participants into two groups, one who gets the new device and another who gets a similar but current offering. Pushing this further, they could request that all participants follow the same diet and exercise activities. Lastly, this would be a trial with a defined duration and structure, again controlling as many factors as possible.

Throughout the experimentation community, RCTs are seen as the optimal method for producing valuable evidence. They provide a robust framework for ensuring the reliability and validity of the findings, which is crucial for making informed decisions based on the data gathered. Yet we also recognize that RCTs are uncommon in an applied setting outside this extreme example of medical devices. Research in a corporate setting generally requires constant trade-offs.

The Research Trade-Offs in a Corporate Environment

The detailed exploration of RCTs illustrates the ideal and most comprehensive research methodology rather than setting a benchmark for everyday corporate research. In my decade-long research career, my experience with true RCTs was limited to my academic work. In a corporate setting, while striving toward RCT principles is beneficial, achieving such rigor in every study is often impractical. The task of obtaining a truly random sample can be particularly challenging, especially when investigating the impact of specific product features.

Instead of following the standards of an RCT, research in a corporate context is a balancing act between maintaining methodological rigor and managing practical constraints. The aim is to produce research that provides valuable insights, guiding confident decision-making—the rigor factor. Concurrently, this research must be conducted efficiently, aligning with the team's pace and budgetary limitations—the resources factor.

As you engage in the validation phases of the FIA, it's essential to apply this perspective when evaluating others' research within your organization. Acknowledge that compromises may have been necessary to generate evidence within the constraints of time and stakeholder expectations. In retrospect, it's common for studies to appear lacking, often missing critical elements. Your objective is to discern the acceptable level of rigor and identify when the evidence is insufficient to establish a real connection between the variables in the User Outcome Connection. Remember that in this process, you play a central role in defining feature descriptions and soon will be pivotal in validating feature-related evidence. You become the key decision-maker in determining the existence of genuine connections within the research framework.

Evaluating Assumptions in the User Outcome Connection

Developing the User Outcome Connection is an intensive process that involves meticulous examination of the resources invested in a feature's development and aligning them with the product team's beliefs. However, regardless of the findings and the extent of research involved, the define stage of the FIA charts only the intended function of the feature. The validation phase shifts focus to assessing whether there is sufficient evidence to substantiate a relationship between each variable in this connection. Until this validation occurs, the User Outcome Connection remains a set of hypotheses.

In ideal scenarios, data exists to affirm the connection between all variables: the feature's influence on specific behaviors, how these behaviors enhance user outcomes, and the resulting positive impact on business outcomes. When such comprehensive evidence is available, the FIA can be considered finished, and the User Outcome Connection is complete. With this, you can confidently inform your team that further development and refinement of the feature will likely yield beneficial outcomes.

But often, the validation process reveals either a complete absence of evidence supporting these connections or insufficient data to establish their existence conclusively. In these instances, it becomes necessary to proceed with the remaining steps of the FIA. Your goal will be to generate the necessary evidence to ultimately develop a solid understanding of whether a relationship exists.

In rarer situations, the research might indicate that a feature has no impact or, in adverse cases, a negative effect—for example, showing that interaction with a feature reduces the likelihood of a desired behavior or that certain behaviors are detrimental to achieving user outcomes. These findings require scrutiny to ensure the data's validity. If a negative relationship is convincingly demonstrated, it becomes imperative to communicate these concerns to your team. Chapter 11 will revisit strategies for responding to findings where data either negates a presumed connection or suggests a detrimental impact. Currently, our focus remains on how to methodically validate the assumptions within the User Outcome Connection.

Determining the Three Main Assumptions

Within the User Outcome Connection framework, there are three pivotal assumptions, as shown in **FIGURE 6.1**, that each require validation.

Behavior assumption—The belief that a feature triggers a specific user behavior. For instance, consider Google Tasks, an application known for its simplicity, which includes a feature to star key tasks. This feature presumably encourages users to distinguish and prioritize essential tasks from regular ones, enhancing task organization.

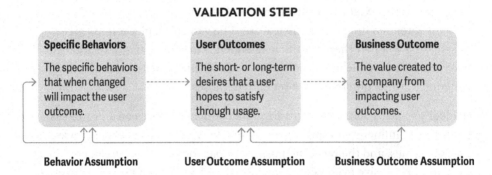

FIGURE 6.1 Behavior, user outcome, and business outcome assumptions

User outcome assumption—The premise that altering a specific behavior positively affects a user outcome. Applying this to Google Tasks, the belief would be that using the important task-flagging feature leads users to complete their significant tasks, instilling a sense of accomplishment and enhancing overall productivity.

Business outcome assumption—The expectation that achieving these user outcomes subsequently leads to favorable business outcomes. In the context of Google Tasks, this could mean that users who find the application effective in managing their tasks are more likely to continue using the platform and perhaps even upgrade to advanced features in Google Workspaces.

Validating these three assumptions is crucial. Only when a team can confirm that enhancing certain behaviors through a feature leads to improved user outcomes, which in turn drives positive business results, can they confidently invest in further developing and refining that feature. In the case of Google Tasks, validation would involve establishing that the starring feature indeed helps users prioritize and complete important tasks, leading to increased retention and potential upselling (**FIGURE 6.2**).

For those operating in a business-to-business context, an additional "business-customer outcome assumption" comes into play. This necessitates validating that achieving user outcomes positively impacts the purchasing business, leading to benefits like continued product usage and increased lifetime value. This process mirrors the validation of business outcomes for your own company but focuses on the customer companies, ensuring that fulfilling user outcomes yields

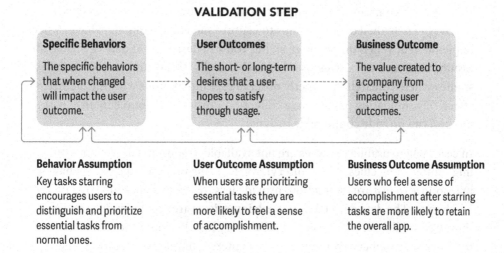

FIGURE 6.2 The three validations as shown through Google Tasks

tangible advantages for them. In the Google Tasks example, if it were being sold as an enterprise suite, then Google would need to validate that it is increasing worker productivity, which is an outcome that business customers would be willing to pay to achieve.

Validating the Behavior Assumption

The behavior assumption, which posits that a feature induces specific user actions leading to significant life impacts, is the most challenging assumption to validate. This concept, central to the Impact Mindset, may be a novel area for many teams. If your team has not previously considered features in terms of their capacity to alter user behavior, then the first FIA step, defining these behaviors, will likely be your most valuable reference for assessing the quality of evidence supporting behavior change.

If the data from the define step is insufficient, expand your search to include behavioral data related to the feature. Passive data collection, often aggregated in dashboards created by products such as Amplitude, through event data collected with tools like Segment, can reveal users' actions. Analyzing user behavior before and after the feature's launch can provide insights into the feature's impact and the extent of its effects. The goal is to discern how the interaction with the feature leads to distinct user actions.

However, it's common to encounter situations where the necessary metrics haven't been defined or the systems to capture such behavioral data haven't been implemented. When this is the case, but you still desire to validate the behavior assumption, turn to existing user research. Ideally, this would involve usability studies where researchers directly observe user interactions with the feature, effectively simulating passive data collection. Although resource intensive, this method can provide comparable insights.

In cases where usability studies are not available, traditional user interviews might offer some clues. These interviews, focusing on predicted user behavior in response to feature interaction, provide less robust evidence of actual behavior change. The data derived from such interviews are often insufficient for thorough validation but can offer preliminary insights into potential behavior modifications induced by the feature. Chapters 7 and 8 cover creating metrics and establishing systems to collect them for all parts of the User Outcome Connection.

Validating the User Outcome Assumption

The next assumption is the user outcome assumption. This assumption explores the link between specific user behaviors and their corresponding outcomes. Many product development teams, often well versed in human-centered design or similar methodologies discussed in Part 1, are likely to have conducted research validating the needs of their users. Ideally, such research would also clarify which behaviors need modification to achieve these desired outcomes, though this is less common.

In some industries, these behaviors are directly tied to the outcomes. Once again, we come back to health and finance, which have some of the most straightforward and measurable outcomes. For companies in these industries, there is likely significant secondary research that points toward the relationship between factors such as exercise minutes and weight loss or the frequency of savings contribution and feelings of financial wellbeing. Additionally, these companies are likely to have market research teams running surveys to better understand what types of actions customers will take to improve their outcomes. An example of this in practice is the financial services SaaS company Brex, which uses market research to test the value proposition of their new features.[2] They found that customers especially resonated with pursuing actions that would satisfy the user outcomes of efficiency, reducing human error, and more accurate data.

Just because your company is not in one of these industries doesn't mean that there will be no research to support a relationship between behaviors and outcomes; it will just likely require more asking around with other teams that conduct research at your company.

In the user outcome assumption, just as with the behavior assumption, the goal is to unearth primary or secondary research underpinning the relationship between behaviors and outcomes. Traditional user research, which generates deep-diving insights into the thoughts and feelings of people, can be particularly valuable here. For instance, Intuit uses diary studies to better understand the process that people follow when doing their personal finances.[3] Through one study, they identified common distractors that people face, which led to them building features to easily resume the tax-filing process across devices, all in an effort to address the user outcomes of ease and accuracy. Large-scale surveys can provide even more robust data, allowing for statistically validating these relationships.

When direct interaction with users is impractical or too expensive, product analytics can serve as an alternative source of insight. However, instead of focusing on behavior changes, the emphasis is on how these behaviors influence outcomes. Taking Apple's three rings fitness feature as an example, Apple could correlate behavioral data (completing the ring activities) with outcome metrics like resting heart rate or weight changes, using passively collected health data to validate the user outcome assumption.

Validating the Business Outcome Assumption

The final assumption, and perhaps the one with the most readily available data, is the business outcome assumption. This assumption is centered on demonstrating that improvements in user outcomes lead to favorable outcomes for the business. Instead of defaulting toward user research or product analytics, it is likely that your validation efforts should focus instead on the work of teams such as marketing insights and business analysts. These teams are instrumental in

---

2 "How Brex uses research to add proof to their value proposition" by SurveyMonkey
3 "Intuit's CFO wants to follow you home and watch you work" by Yahoo News

building the business case for product utility and the potential of new features to open business opportunities.

The contributions from these teams can vary, ranging from secondary research-based reports to insights derived from surveys and interviews. The key is to look for anything that showcases the connection between fulfilling a user's need and creating a positive outcome for the business. Reports featuring intention-to-pay analyses are commonly used to support product requirement documents alongside projections on how specific actions are expected to increase retention or sales.

A prime methodology that effectively validates the business outcome assumption is *conjoint analysis*. This approach asks participants to rank features and indicate their willingness to pay for various feature combinations. Conjoint analysis is a primary method for determining user preferences and their value perception. Although not the sole means of validating the business outcome assumption, it is a powerful example of the depth of analysis that can be achieved. Look for conjoint analyses, Max-Diff analyses, or others that look to identify how successful products impact the business to demonstrate the connection between user satisfaction and business benefits.

In a B2B context, you must also validate the business customer outcome assumption. This process mirrors the approach for the business outcome assumption but focuses on the needs of the businesses purchasing your product or service. This research will likely blend elements of both user outcome and business outcome assumptions, combining user research with business customers and market research to develop a compelling business case.

Navigating the Spectrum of Validation

As you delve into the documents from the define phase and the research undertaken during the validation phase, you'll start to gauge the likelihood of a genuine relationship existing among the variables in the User Outcome Analysis. A common question is how much data is sufficient for validation. The answer isn't straightforward; there's no definitive benchmark. The onus falls on you to decide when the evidence is compelling enough to suggest a direction or to recognize when efforts to uncover more data have reached their limit.

Validation is not a binary process of having enough data or not; it exists on a spectrum. Your threshold on this spectrum will be influenced by various factors, including your industry, the nature of the products you work on, and the ethical standards of yourself and your organization. Some companies might be content with user interviews that suggest connections despite small sample sizes and potential biases. Others may demand rigorous statistical significance from large-scale studies with meticulously designed metrics. Deciding on your validation threshold during this phase is crucial, as it will guide you in determining if you have adequate data. If not, it informs the direction for further steps in the FIA.

When your threshold is set and the data falls short, a final assessment is needed before embarking on new evidence generation. This involves verifying whether the data scarcity is real or if stakeholders obstruct access to existing data. If it's the latter, a renewed push for information may be necessary, potentially involving management or executive intervention. If, after a thorough examination, you conclude that the data simply isn't there—perhaps due to a lack of prior experimentation in your company—you can confidently identify this data gap.

Once all avenues have been explored and a lack of sufficient data for validation is established, the next step is to formally acknowledge this evidence shortfall and conclude the validation stage by formulating hypotheses. These hypotheses aim to guide the generation of new evidence that can eventually validate the connections within the user outcome analysis. This approach underscores the essence of the FIA: It begins by verifying whether existing research has already addressed the necessary questions and only then, if required, initiates new studies to fill the gaps.

Crafting Hypotheses in the Absence of Data

Hypotheses are fundamental to robust research. They articulate the expected outcomes of altering a variable before a study is conducted, establishing a clear benchmark to assess the impact of the change. A well-formulated hypothesis defines a measurable criterion to determine the success or failure of an intervention. This clarity enables the design of experiments to validate the actual influence of the treatment or intervention.

In the context of the FIA, when certain assumptions lack sufficient data for validation, they are transformed into testable hypotheses. Reframing under-supported User Outcome Connection validations into hypotheses facilitates clearer communication regarding the research that needs to be conducted. Hypotheses provide teams with definitive targets, guiding their efforts to validate the existence of relationships between variables. This structured approach helps maintain momentum in the research process, countering any perception that a lack of data signifies a dead end. Instead, it reinforces the understanding that generating hypotheses is a constructive step toward uncovering new insights and confirming connections within the User Outcome Connection framework.

Creating a Robust Hypothesis

Crafting an effective hypothesis doesn't adhere to a singular definition; instead, it's about embodying key characteristics that make it impactful. Applied research has five characteristics that constitute a good hypothesis, as highlighted in **FIGURE 6.3**.

Testable: A hypothesis must be testable, a criterion you're already familiar with from your work in the definition and validation phases. This involves proposing a relationship between two specific variables and designing a method to verify its accuracy.

Falsifiable: Closely linked to testability is the concept of falsifiability. A well-structured hypothesis should be framed such that, following research, it can be conclusively deemed true or false. This apparent dichotomy is crucial for drawing definitive conclusions from your analysis.

FIVE CHARACTERISTICS OF APPLIED RESEARCH HYPOTHESES

1	Testable	Proposed relationship between variables that includes a method for empirically verifying its accuracy.
2	Falsifiable	Structured to allow for conclusive determination as either true or false following research.
3	Specific	Detailed and focused, stemming from an in-depth understanding of the context and variables involved.
4	Contextual	Grounded in existing knowledge and relevant to the specific context of the feature or situation being studied.
5	Measurable	Quantifiable or at least allowing for the assessment of the direction of a feature's impact, even if not to precise statistical standards.

FIGURE 6.3 A good applied-research hypothesis has five characteristics: testable, falsifiable, specific, contextual, and measurable.

Specific: Further hallmarks of a sound hypothesis include specificity and a basis in existing knowledge. Your efforts during the define and validation stages provide a deep understanding of the context in which a feature was developed, offering the necessary details to formulate precise hypotheses. If your hypothesis is not adequately focused on a particular user outcome or a set of behaviors or business outcomes, it suggests a need for a more in-depth exploration of the User Outcome Connection variables. Alternatively, you might consider developing multiple User Outcome Connections, each with its uniquely defined variables.

Contextual: The hypothesis should be built upon the insights of previous research. Doing so requires understanding the situation where the research project will take place and any relevant work that has already been done. With an understanding of the existing knowledge, a hypothesis can be designed to provide evidence that helps create a better understanding of the overall context.

Measurable: The final, often most challenging, aspect is that hypotheses should be measurable. In academic research, this typically involves clearly defined metrics and thresholds, making the hypothesis unequivocally falsifiable based on statistical significance. In the context of the FIA, measurability standards are somewhat more relaxed. You may not yet have a specific metric in mind—that's the goal of the subsequent FIA step. Even if you have a metric, determining the success threshold might still be unclear. Reflect on the validation spectrum discussed earlier; your company's culture and standards will largely dictate the level of measurability required. At a minimum, your hypothesis should enable you to discern the direction of a feature's impact, even if the precise magnitude of that effect isn't yet quantifiable.

Creating the Hypotheses

Creating the hypotheses is a straightforward exercise. Following the best practices outlined you must convert the unvalidated assumptions from statements of fact into testable statements. The following are a few real-world examples of this:

- **Behavioral assumption:** By offering the ability to color code notes in the Google Keep app, users will begin to organize their notes based on a category using colors as the format.

Behavioral hypothesis: Once a user begins using the color-coding feature, they will begin to color code at least 25 percent of their new notes for the following month.

- **User outcome assumption:** When users set realistic calorie goals based on their height and weight in MyFitnessPal, they are at increased likelihood of reducing their caloric intake.

  User outcome hypothesis: If a user engages with the calorie goal feature, they will reduce their caloric intake by at least 10 percent.

- **Business customer assumption:** Businesses that use Square's one-click checkout experience expect to see a decreased cart abandonment rate.

  Business customer hypothesis: Companies that implement one-click checkout will see a decrease of cart abandonment by at least 20 percent compared to before implementation.

- **Business outcome assumption:** Customers who find that they learned a useful skill on Coursera are more likely to purchase another class.

  Business outcome hypothesis: When customers successfully complete a course and report a valuable learning from it, they are 30 percent more likely to purchase another course on the platform.

Generative AI in Practice

Leveraging GenAI for brainstorming is one of its most powerful use cases. In this example, we will use ChatGPT to help turn the assumptions into hypotheses. The prompt is broken down into instructions and further information describing a good hypothesis based on information from this chapter.

User Prompt

I am converting assumptions that my team has made into hypotheses. You will rewrite my assumptions into a hypothesis based on the rules of a robust hypothesis, which are:

Testable - Propose a relationship between variables and include a method for empirically verifying its accuracy.

Falsifiable - Structured to allow for conclusive determination as either true or false following research.

Specific - Detailed and focused, stemming from an in-depth understanding of the context and variables involved.

Contextual - Grounded in existing knowledge and relevant to the specific context of the feature or situation being studied.

Measurable - Quantifiable or at least allowing for the assessment of the direction of a feature's impact, even if not to precise statistical standards.

Now rewrite the following assumptions, and provide only the hypothesis in your response:

Behavioral assumption: By notifying the user of a new simple view to review their billing statement before the upcoming bill, a credit card company increases the likelihood a user reviews their bill for inaccuracies

User outcome assumption: When users catch inaccuracies before paying for them and have to wait for a refund, they feel that their credit card company cares more about them and that they are in control of their finances.

Business outcome assumption: Customers who feel have a higher rating of control and comfort are more likely to retain and secure more lines of credit.

ChatGPT

Behavioral Hypothesis: If a credit card company notifies users about a new, simplified view to review their billing statements before the upcoming bill, then the proportion of users reviewing their bills for inaccuracies will increase, compared to a control group who did not receive such notification, as measured by user engagement metrics within the billing section of the app or website.

User Outcome Hypothesis: Users who identify and report billing inaccuracies before payment and subsequently receive refunds will report higher levels of satisfaction and a sense of control over their finances, as compared to those who do not catch inaccuracies, measurable through user satisfaction surveys focusing on perceived care from the credit card company and personal financial control.

Business Outcome Hypothesis: Customers who express a higher sense of control and comfort with their credit card services, as assessed through customer satisfaction surveys, are more likely to retain their accounts and apply for additional lines of credit, compared to customers who report lower levels of control and comfort.

Incorporating Hypotheses into the User Outcome Connection

When you have completed the validation phase, it's crucial to update your User Outcome Connection to reflect the level of evidence for each aspect of the validation. This scale could range from *No Evidence and Little Support of Relationship* to *Significant Support and Validated Relationship*. It's generally advisable that companies aim for at least Significant Support, with Validated Relationship being the ideal level, indicating a high degree of confidence that specific behavioral improvements will lead to positive business outcomes. When below that threshold, a hypothesis should be added.

After updating the User Outcome Connection with these evidence levels and hypotheses, the next step is disseminating it more widely for additional feedback. Although you might have already involved some key stakeholders, now is the time to extend this circle to anyone with a hand in the feature's development. This broad sharing serves as a comprehensive final review to confirm that no critical information has been overlooked in your definition and validation efforts.

Be prepared for challenges and diverse opinions during this process. Team members may have different perspectives, and some might be concerned about how these findings could affect their personal or team performance metrics. This stage is a natural part of the process and an excellent opportunity to emphasize the benefits of embracing an Impact Mindset. If necessary, consider seeking an executive sponsor to provide support and mitigate any potential negative repercussions. Whatever your approach, your goal should be to gather as much feedback as possible to ensure you haven't missed anything relevant and as it can help with refining the definition and validations.

Sharing the User Outcome Connection requires openness and can be daunting. It's a step that calls for commitment and a deep belief in the value of measuring impact. Reflect on the reasons behind your conviction that impact measurement can enhance both the work environment and the quality of products for customers. Once you're confident in your approach, share the User Outcome Connection. This action will not only reinforce your efforts and gather additional information but also likely increase buy-in from others who see the value in this initiative. By taking this step, you position yourself as a leader in this new methodology, transitioning from mere exploration to leading an innovative experiment focused on metric development and data collection.

Validating the Connections of the Tasky Chatbot Launch

Continuing the narrative from Chapter 5 on the development of Tasky and based on a well-received framework, I rigorously evaluated the User Outcome Connection. My hypothesis was rooted in the belief that integrating generative AI into users' workflows would not only demystify the technology but also foster acceptance over apprehension. This conviction was bolstered by a review of academic literature and secondary research, which collectively suggested that employing these technologies for automating monotonous tasks could significantly boost efficiency and, in many instances, effectiveness. The linkage between specific behaviors and user outcomes appeared robust, indicating a strong case for advancing to a prototype stage.

However, the potential for transforming this idea into a viable product remained uncertain. My literature review and market analysis revealed no existing solutions, leaving a gap in understanding the relationship between user outcomes and potential business success. This gap underscored a critical component of my Feature Impact Analysis, emphasizing the necessity to explore the business dimension without compromising the tool's effectiveness. Given this scenario, I formulated the following hypotheses:

Behavioral hypothesis: After using Tasky, users will be 50 percent more likely to experiment using ChatGPT to speed up one of their tasks.

User outcome hypothesis: By using ChatGPT to automate a task, users will feel more confident about using it going forward.

Business outcome hypothesis: By feeling more confident with ChatGPT after using Tasky, customers will be willing to pay at least $5 a month to continue accessing it.

CHAPTER RECAP

- **Behavior assumption validation:** Examines the influence of features on specific user behaviors using available data and user interaction patterns.

- **User outcome assumption validation:** Focuses on establishing the link between behavior changes and positive user outcomes through existing research.

- **Business outcome assumption validation:** Validates the correlation between improved user outcomes and positive business impacts using marketing and business analysis insights.

- **Spectrum of validation:** Introduces the concept that validation exists on a spectrum, influenced by industry norms and organizational culture, guiding the determination of sufficient evidence.

- **Generating hypotheses in absence of data:** Outlines creating testable hypotheses to explore unvalidated assumptions when existing data is insufficient.

- **Incorporating and sharing findings:** Encourages broad sharing of updated User Outcome Connection findings for feedback, emphasizing stakeholder involvement and the Impact Mindset in organizational change.

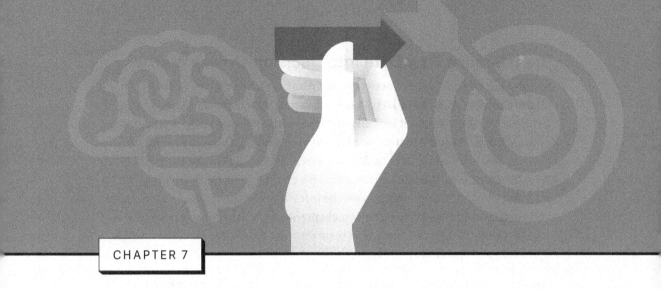

CHAPTER 7

Scoping the Right Measurements (FIA Step 3, Part 1)

Having recognized that you need more data to validate your User Connection Outcome, you are entering the realm of metric creation. What is your current process for creating new data? How do you determine what is possible? What trade-offs you are willing to make when creating new variables? Many product people start their metric exploration by identifying what is already being collected and working from that basis. Although this is a pragmatic approach, it also leads to a limited view of what is possible. Starting with what is already available is a fast path to limiting the scope of research to that which already confirms prior beliefs and an overreliance on vanity metrics, which measure only the surface-level interaction a user has with a product and which are of limited value when measuring true impact, such as usage.

Transforming Raw Data into Decision-Driving Metrics

In this chapter and the next, we cover the data collection phase (**TABLE 7.1**) of Feature Impact Analysis (FIA), which consists of a process that takes the reverse perspective. What would it look like to build on the hypotheses you previously considered and define exactly what is needed to validate them? Then once that vision is set, work from there to determine what is possible and what could be possible given your specific constraints. This chapter focuses on creating metrics, and the next chapter talks about the infrastructure investments required to sustain them. By the end of these two chapters, you will have the knowledge to lead discussions with your technical team on what to build to advance the FIA, spreading an Impact Mindset along the way!

As we delve deeper into the intricacies of the FIA, a critical juncture emerges: the need for comprehensive data to substantiate your User Outcome Connection. This phase beckons a pivotal question: how do we effectively create new data that aligns with our needs? The process of metric creation is not merely about what exists or is easily attainable. Rather, it involves a strategic exploration of what should be measured to validate our hypotheses and how to realistically achieve this within the confines of our resources.

TABLE 7.1 Feature Impact Analysis, the Collect Data Stage

STEP	ACTION	PROCESS	OUTCOME
1	Define	Identify the specific behaviors that a feature alters to impact user and business outcomes.	Completed User Outcome Connection(s) for the feature.
2	Validate	Validate User Outcome Connections assumptions and document evidence gaps.	Validated user outcomes connection and hypotheses to be answered.
3	Collect Data	Scope metrics at each level of the success metric framework and determine how to collect.	Identified metrics and strategy for how each will be collected.
4	Experiment and Analyze	Compare users versus non-users to generate data to support or deny hypotheses.	Determined whether a feature is creating its intended impact.
5	Take Action	Share the results of the analysis and determining the next steps based on findings.	Identified next steps based on the results of an analysis.

This requires a departure from the conventional approach. Often, the quest for metrics begins by sifting through existing data, a method that, while practical, can inadvertently constrain our perspective to what is readily available. Although this path is commonly taken for its fast results, it risks a myopic focus on surface-level metrics like usage, potentially overlooking deeper, more impactful insights. In the next chapters, I propose an alternative strategy. Imagine reversing the process: beginning with the hypotheses crafted earlier and defining the precise data needed for validation. This approach fosters a vision-first mindset, prioritizing the ideal metrics that would provide the most meaningful insights. Once this vision is established, the next step is to assess feasibility—discerning what currently exists, what can be feasibly developed, and what requires more significant investment or innovation.

The adage "data is the new oil" encapsulates the burgeoning value of data in our digital era, yet it barely scratches the surface of its complexity. Data is like crude oil mined straight from the earth; in many cases it can be extraordinarily valuable, but in its raw state, it is not that effective. Instead, it must be refined and piped to the right sources—known as the technical infrastructure requirement—before it can be useful. It must also be handled by people who understand how to "chemically" transfer it into "refined oil" usable by consumers across domains—known as the functional requirement.

The true utility of data, akin to oil, emerges only after it undergoes a meticulous process of refinement and is channeled appropriately. This transformation is twofold, encompassing both the technical infrastructure to process and channel data and the functional expertise to convert it into refined, user-friendly metrics. In the realm of product management, the potential of data to unlock insights and drive decisions has not gone unnoticed. Product managers increasingly aspire to harness data for informed decision-making and acknowledge its potential as a key area for development.[1] Yet many find themselves trailing behind their competitors, hindered by a shortfall in effective data management. This gap is highlighted in a 2020 Mixpanel survey,[2] revealing that only 10 percent of teams felt fully equipped to leverage data for all pivotal product decisions.

---

1 "The State of Product Analytics" by Mixpanel "2020-2021 Pragmatic Institute Annual Product Management and Marketing Survey" by Pragmatic Institute
2 "The State of Product Analytics" by Mixpanel

As we navigate through data transformation, we must understand that the path to actionable metrics is not linear. It demands a harmonious blend of technical acumen and functional insight. This understanding is the cornerstone upon which we build systems capable of not just collecting data but transforming it into strategic metrics that guide and enhance our decision-making processes.

The Technical Challenge

In 2023, the sheer volume of data generated by businesses reached astounding levels. This abundance presents a formidable challenge for data leaders: determining what data to capture and retain.[3] Opting to store everything is a simplistic approach but brings with it hefty costs and heightened risk of data breaches. Conversely, limiting storage to currently utilized data risks a lack of historical context for future metric development. Striking the right balance is a complex endeavor, often leading to significant gaps in metric creation.

Capturing data is only the beginning of the data's journey to becoming valuable insight. Several obstacles[4] stand in the way, including unrefined, siloed data; a dearth of knowledge around what metrics are available; and more. The process of refining raw data typically involves cleaning to align with established data structures, followed by organizing it for scalable querying. This data then must be integrated with other datasets, enabling more comprehensive analyses. Throughout this process, sensitive personal and proprietary data, which commonly come with regulatory requirements, must be meticulously flagged and secured. An ongoing requirement is the frequent monitoring and visualization of this data, ensuring it remains comprehensible and accessible to non-technical stakeholders.

As an example of this full process, consider a mobile banking application looking to evaluate the impact of a new budgeting feature. You would start by building out the systems to collect the raw event data created by a user as they navigate through the interface. Event data is insightful, but it is a lot; imagine the granularity of an every-click-on-a-screen level of data. Transforming this voluminous raw data into a functional format is a task for skilled data engineers, using an array of specialized tools. For the banking app this would look like managing all the clicks on the feature into user flows, showing the path from start to finish for each visit. Additional variables, such as time on page and clicks

---

3 "Data: A double-edged sword" by Deloitte Insights
4 "Top 6 Data Challenges and Solutions in 2024" by Atlan

within a page, might be created to add more detail to what a person did each step along the way.

Once the data is organized into accessible tables, it offers insights into user behaviors within the app. However, this alone doesn't provide a complete picture of the feature's efficacy. The next step involves linking this behavioral data with customer profiles and account details. This integration phase is delicate because it involves sensitive customer information, necessitating rigorous data privacy measures. Finally, the consolidated data must be presented in a format that is easily interpretable by the product team, paving the way for the subsequent challenge: the functional definition of meaningful metrics. The same process must be instituted for attitudinal metrics but with the additional complexity of capturing and evaluating user input.

System Performance and Health Metrics

Another common category of metrics referenced by data engineers and software developers is system performance and health metrics. This includes metrics such as the amount of time that a service is available for customers, known as *uptime*, and the average load time for a webpage. These metrics are essential to building a good product experience and one that will have a high usability score, but this chapter does not reference them, because they are generally handled by the technical team. I recommend asking your team what system health metrics they collect and seeing if you can leverage any of them to paint a better picture of your product's overall usability and impact.

The Functional Challenge

The journey of transforming data into actionable insights isn't just about data collection and refinement. The crux of this process lies in the functional aspect: the precise definition of metrics. This stage demands a clear vision for data utilization, spearheaded by individuals who possess a deep understanding of the business context and can adeptly translate raw data into company-relevant metrics. Often, the pivotal limitation at this stage is the maturity and capability of the team handling the data. A notable rise in teams specializing in product analytics has occurred with the growth of the team in this respect, manifesting under titles such as UX Metrics, Data Science, and others. Despite variations in their approach, these teams share a common goal: to enhance understanding of product performance.

Initial efforts typically focus on fundamental metrics like usage and retention, readily provided by tools like Amplitude and Mixpanel. Although these metrics are useful due to their simplicity, they are limited in scope and cannot be the sole focus. As teams evolve, they venture beyond these basic metrics, refining and expanding their approach to include advanced, specific metrics that delve deeper into user behavior, outcomes, and other proprietary measures directly tied to their business. Advanced metrics might include activation funnels, churn rates, and net revenue retention, among others.

Defining these metrics requires human expertise or the use of software that has metrics predefined and ready to be instrumented. To address this need, there has been a surge in educational resources aimed at aiding teams in metric development. Analytics-focused software-as-a-service (SaaS) products frequently offer guidance on metric creation, and webinars on this topic are becoming increasingly common. Moreover, the emergence of startups developing advanced analytic tools has introduced the idea of productized expertise of metric creation.

In the realm of education and products, there's ample inspiration for identifying potential metrics. Two popular frameworks are Google's HEART (**TABLE 7.2**), which emphasizes metrics centered on user experience, and the Startup Pirate's AARRR (**TABLE 7.3**), focusing on user engagement throughout the product. Both frameworks exemplify the extensive possibilities in developing an array of metrics, from easy-to-collect vanity metrics such as Net Promoter Scores (NPS) and page views through well-defined variables that cater to different aspects of product interaction and user engagement.

Although these frameworks and numerous other solutions are helpful in brainstorming new ideas, it takes knowledgeable team members to convert this raw knowledge into metrics. By embracing an Impact Mindset and creating User Outcome Connections for your feature, you have already begun the journey of learning what is needed to functionally define variables that are useful to truly understand if features are working. While working through the data collection chapters (Chapters 7 and 8), remember that although the technical part is a science, building the best metric is more of an art. You are entering the realm of experimentation; trial and error are your friend and the path toward the best outcome.

TABLE 7.2 Google's HEART

	DESCRIPTION	METRIC
Happiness	Users find the overall experience pleasant and helpful to use.	Net Promoter Score
		CSAT score
		Thumbs up/down
Engagement	Users enjoy using the feature and continue to expand their usage.	Conversion rate
		Average session length
		Page views
Adoption	Users find the feature interesting and actively choose to use it.	Growth rate
		Download rate
		Upgrades to new versions
Retention	Users continue to return to the application to satisfy a need.	Churn rate
		Daily and monthly active users
		Repeat purchases
Task Success	Users are able to complete their goals quickly and easily.	Flow stage rates
		Error out rate
		Level of completion

TABLE 7.3 The Startup Pirate's AARRR

	DESCRIPTION	METRIC
Acquisition	How easily do new users find the product?	Signup page visits
		Account creation
Activation	How quickly can customers get to a significant moment that matters?	Complete onboarding
		Ingestion of data
Retention	How many customers are you retaining and why are you losing them?	Churn rate
		Survey feedback
Revenue	How can customers be turned into lifetime users?	Expansion rate
		Arr growth
Referral	How many customers are turning into product advocates?	Referral shared
		Reviews created

Approach to Generating Metrics at All Five Levels

The prevalent gaps of technical infrastructure and functional expertise in metric creation, coupled with an escalating need for robust data systems, are inadvertently steering teams toward an overreliance on vanity metrics. In scenarios where teams are constrained by inadequate systems or lack the necessary know-how, there's a tendency to hastily assemble makeshift solutions. These often result in defaulting to generic metrics provided by analytic tools and superficial measures like NPS. Such measures, though providing immediate data influx, often fail to paint a complete picture of the product's impact.

Fallout from this approach becomes evident when these lagging, loosely connected indicators start reflecting negative trends, directly affecting the bottom line. It's usually in these moments of crisis that teams realize the superficial nature of their metrics and how little they truly reveal about their product's performance and user engagement.

Metric Development That Spans the Five Success Levels

Adopting an Impact Mindset necessitates a more holistic approach to metric development, one that spans five layers of success metrics: usage, usability, behavioral outcomes, and user outcomes, as shown in **TABLE 7.4**. This extends beyond mere usage metrics, encompassing satisfaction, behavior, and outcomes—each offering a vital piece of the broader puzzle. It's crucial to recognize that each metric category serves a specific purpose, and over-reliance on any single category can lead to skewed perceptions of product success.

In the following discussion, we delve into each of these metric categories in depth. The aim is to provide a clear understanding of the unique value each brings and to underscore the importance of a balanced metrics strategy that captures the full spectrum of user and business impact.

Usage: Usage metrics form the most fundamental layer of data analysis, often already in place within organizations. Tools like Amplitude or Looker facilitate the passive collection of this data, particularly for digital products. In non-digital contexts, proxies like sales figures may be a substitute, assuming a correlation between purchase and use.

TABLE 7.4 Five Levels of Success Metrics

	BENEFIT	DRAWBACK
Usage	Easy to capture Product teams are familiar with it	Does not explain anything about the outcome the feature is creating
Usability	Lots of resources to help capture and understand Product teams are familiar with it	Biased by users responding at the moment and not about long-term outcomes
Behavioral Outcomes	Can be built from understanding actions taken within a feature	Does not explain the benefit a user experienced
User Outcomes	Captures outcomes from usage	Difficult to measure Can require soliciting user feedback
Business Outcomes	Connected directly to the success of the business	Doesn't articulate anything about why a product is selling

This usage metric will be a binary yes or no at its simplest. As it gets more complex (**TABLE 7.5**), usage data can look over a longitudinal period (that is, retention) or be displayed as a funnel analysis showing where someone stopped using the product. As usage metrics mature, they can also begin to look at the degree of interaction between users. For example, a social media company can track how frequently someone logs on and the number of likes a user gives on their own content, their friend's content, or the content of those further removed from their immediate network.

TABLE 7.5 Usage Examples

EXAMPLE	METRIC
Whether an individual used a delay delivery feature within Gmail	Binary usage
How many meditation videos did a user fully watch in the previous week?	Count of finished content by week
Where are we losing the most users during the Fivetran data pipeline setup?	Dropoff per step in the setup process
How many Grammarly customers still use the platform six months after signing up for a premium account?	Six-month retention per user

Usability: Usability metrics (**TABLE 7.6**), the attitudinal counterpart to usage data, aim to capture user enjoyment and other sentiments related to their experience using the product. They are the first step toward understanding user perceptions and feelings about the product or service. At their simplest, these are basic variables that cover the holistic experience, such as "Rate your satisfaction with the experience." As they get more focused, their value continues to grow by targeting specific aspects of the feature and the interaction a user had with it, such as asking about a button or how confident someone felt after completing setup.

TABLE 7.6 Usability Examples

EXAMPLE	METRIC
Prompting a user with a "how satisfied were you during this experience" question after finishing the onboarding flow	CSAT score
Asking an in-product survey question focused on the level of discoverability of a new feature	Perceived discoverability metric
Conducting a sentiment analysis on the comments left on the app store page	App ratings

Direct surveys, whether through established frameworks like the System Usability Scale (a battery of tailored questions) or through custom questions, are key to gathering this data. Ideally, surveys should be integrated within the app at relevant interaction points to minimize response bias, using tools like Chameleon or Appcues. In cases where digital integration isn't feasible, traditional methods like Qualtrics or paper surveys can be effective.

Although this user feedback is valuable in extending what is learned from usage metrics, it still needs to answer whether the product or service *satisfies* the user's purpose for purchasing it. It is not uncommon for an individual to like something but not find it helpful; how often do you hear people say that they enjoy Netflix but are ashamed of how much time they spend binge-watching? A single view of how an individual feels at a single point in time also incorporates bias. How and when the surveys are disseminated may capture only those with strong negative or positive feelings. Being thoughtful about collecting this data can overcome some of its drawbacks.

Behavioral outcome: Behavioral outcome metrics offer insights into user actions within the product or service environment. They are more challenging to collect than usage data and require more advanced technical setups when companies desire to have these user actions passively collected. Metrics here begin to describe the behaviors users exhibit; in a digital environment this can be down to the specific click, text typed, and so on. In a physical environment, exact data collection is nearly impossible and requires developing proxies using whatever systems are available, from user-reported tracking through artificial intelligence systems scanning video footage.

Behavioral metrics (**TABLE 7.7**) can be leading or lagging. Leading behavioral metrics track individual actions when interacting with the solution. Lagging metrics, on the other hand, follow actions that individuals take after an interaction. In an ideal situation, you can create behavioral metrics that track the direct behaviors, so proxy metrics are the desirable alternative when that is not possible.

The most straightforward approach to measuring behavioral metrics is to collect specific user actions within the digital platform. An example of this is tracking every click that a user performs on a website as they set up their banking account. This can be distilled into two primary metrics: a drop-off metric that shows the last page they visited (with an option for completed setup) and a metric for which page the user spent the most time dwelling on. This metric level is also where the development of proxies becomes much more necessary, as the particular behaviors may not be measurable.

TABLE 7.7 Behavioral Outcome Examples

EXAMPLE	METRIC
Amount of time that an individual reads on their device	Time on platform
	Pages read
	Average reading speed
Disconnecting from work after using the Microsoft Office Plan Your Time Away feature	Emails sent and read during away time
	Meetings attended during away time
	IMs sent and read during away time
Ease of setting up a data pipeline	Clicks on page versus expectation
	Count of triggered errors
	Time per setup page

User outcome: User outcome metrics are pivotal for validating the primary hypothesis about a new feature. Outcome metrics (**TABLE 7.8**) indicate whether an individual experienced a change to their lived experience through the product or service usage. This metric level can be by far the most difficult metric to track. In some cases, metrics exist to measure the change that occurs, such as digital weight loss products that can count the number of calories the individual consumes compared to those they burn, or financial services that measure savings. Although these types of metrics are not the norm, in most cases the product team will measure an individual's attitudinal feedback to determine if there is a change to their sentiment or progress toward goals or find a behavior that can serve as a proxy for the outcome.

TABLE 7.8 User Outcome Examples

EXAMPLE	METRIC
Marketers' effectiveness with marketing campaigns after using personalized email attributes	Customer conversion rates
	Unsubscribe rates
Employees' stress levels after engaging with Modern Health's app and complementary therapy services	Self-reported stress levels
	Usage of emergency stress-relief content
Customers' savings after using Acorn's auto savings feature	Savings amount
	Self-reported sentiment regarding savings confidence

Ultimately, creating this metric requires the product team to start at the outcome they agreed the feature intends to change. From there, they can either measure that specific change or begin to abstract until they reach a reasonable substitute. For example, a new mobile app plans to increase an individual's confidence. To measure this, you would have to see how that person interacts with others throughout their days and in varying contexts. This process is only practical if done through an ethnographic methodology with limited sample size and, thus, potentially inherent bias.

The team would need to break down this idea of confidence into more measurable components such as positive interactions, positive sentiment after conversations, and positive self-image, among other subcomponents. These refined constructs are easier to measure—some of them you can directly ask the individual, such as their perceived self-image. Others are measurable through a proxy behavioral metric, for example, increased length of conversations, repeated eye contact, sentiment analysis of transcript, and so on. The infrastructure your team has developed will constrain how easy it is to get these measurements; attitudinal feedback received from the user should be possible at a minimum, with the others as ideal add-ons.

Business Outcomes: Products exist to satisfy user outcomes such that the end-user chooses to continue purchasing the solution. All the financial metrics associated with the cost to develop products and the actual sales of them can be encapsulated into business metrics (**TABLE 7.9**). At its core, this entails tracking revenue (the income generated), costs (the expenses incurred), and profit (the financial gain after expenses). Beyond these fundamental metrics, companies explore various avenues to assess success, including analyzing the number of distinct clients, the revenue contribution of each client, and the lifetime value (LTV) representing the total revenue a customer is expected to generate over their tenure with the company.

TABLE 7.9 Business Outcome Examples

EXAMPLE	METRIC
Determining if a ticket marketplace that assists users chose the ideal ticket based on their budget will create loyal users	Return Customer Rate Life Time Value (LTV)
The level of success that users feel after using a engaging with a fitness tracking application leading to increased word-of-mouth marketing	Customer acquisition costs Subscription Retention
Identifying whether a research tool is assisting design teams become more effective at their job and if that leads to continued purchase	Annual Recurring Revenue by Account Upgrades Purchased

Revenue can be calculated in many ways but can be categorized as simple as what money is being brought into the company. Delving into costs reveals a more intricate picture, as modern products often involve numerous contributing factors. Human capital, typically the most substantial expense, are scrutinized in terms of the time invested in product development and maintenance. Marketing expenses, another significant outlay, lead to the creation of metrics such as the customer acquisition cost (CAC), which calculates the expense of acquiring a new customer. For physical products, the costs of raw materials are pivotal, while digital products focus on expenses related to digital services, such as server use and software integrations.

Although these financial measurements are crucial for fleshing out the User Outcome Connection, there is less instruction on finding the correct ones for two reasons. First, these metrics are often determined by broader organizational teams beyond the product team, with numerous variables influencing their selection. Second, a wealth of resources already exists to guide product teams in measuring the financial impact of their features. In the context of FIA, your primary responsibility is to grasp the business's key performance indicators (KPIs) and ensure your features align with them. This approach acknowledges the complexity of financial metrics while emphasizing the FIA lead's role in linking feature performance to overarching business objectives, respecting the nuanced interplay between product development and financial health within the firm's culture.

Blueprint for Developing Impactful Metrics

Embarking on the journey to develop metrics across different stages of the User Outcome Connection might appear overwhelming at first. It demands not only technical resources but also the functional acumen to define and implement new measurements. Fortunately, if you've been diligently following the methodologies outlined in this book, you've already navigated the most challenging part. By meticulously defining each element of the User Outcome Connection, you've essentially sketched the framework required to validate these connections, setting the stage for metric creation. This marks the commencement of a six-step process (**FIGURE 7.1**) that transforms a conceptual plan into actionable metrics.

The six-step metric creation process spans from conceptualization to collection and refinement. Three functional steps at the beginning focus on understanding

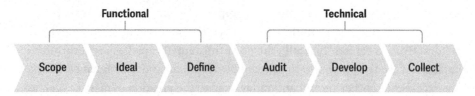

FIGURE 7.1 The six-step process for developing impactful metrics; the first half is functional and the second is technical

what is needed, followed by three technical steps that develop the actual metric. The initial step involves defining the scope of the metrics, which can be a perplexing stage due to the plethora of potential directions available. However, by focusing on the User Outcome Connection within the FIA framework, you've already completed the scope step by homing in context to concentrate on measuring impact. With this defined scope, the subsequent step is to envision the ideal dataset required to fulfill the needs of this setup. This is a visionary exercise, where you imagine the most ideal scenario, setting the foundation for subsequent steps that tailor these ideals to practical realities.

Once you have a narrative of the ideal data needed to validate the User Outcome Connection, the next phase is to translate this into concrete, functional metrics. This stage involves defining specific variables for data collection, still devoid of any practical constraints. With a preliminary list of metrics in hand, the process then shifts to aligning these metrics with the unique context of your operation. The audit step involves evaluating the discrepancies between your ideal metrics and the actual capabilities of your company's technical infrastructure. Following this is the develop step, where metrics are reshaped to fit the realities of your organization's resources and willingness to invest in data infrastructure. The culmination of this process is the actual collection and refinement of these defined metrics.

By adhering to this methodical process, you transition from a conceptual desire to develop multifaceted metrics to being primed for implementation. Throughout this journey, you are not only enhancing your proficiency in functional metric development but also bridging the gap between your current state and a future rich in meaningful metrics, shifting the focus to the technical necessities of your company. We will now delve deeper into the five steps following the scope step, addressing the two additional functional steps in this chapter and the three technical steps in Chapter 8.

Ideal: Starting with a Vision

Envision yourself sitting on a bench in a bustling major city, immersed in a tapestry of life where people, animals, and vehicles interweave in a vibrant urban dance. This scene, a microcosm of human societies and cultures, is a living canvas for anthropologists who study the development of civilizations. Here, the observer has the choice to either embrace the grandeur of societal complexity or zoom into the nuances of individual experiences, akin to ethnography, which focuses on understanding people, and their unguided actions, in their natural environment.

This concept of observation is pivotal to our understanding of measurable behavior. Earlier in this book, I posited that all behavior is measurable, drawing upon ethnographic research as my rationale. This field of study exemplifies that at its core, observation is a fundamental form of measurement. Although direct observation might not be scalable in reality, it reminds us that the actions of individuals in the physical world are indeed quantifiable; the challenge lies in determining how to measure them effectively for metric development.

When it comes to measuring internal processes such as thoughts and feelings, the approach is less direct, but not impossible. Psychology, with its myriad subfields, offers a wealth of methodologies for quantifying mental processes. For instance, affective psychology helps in understanding emotions relevant to apps focused on health and wellness, while social psychology can be instrumental in measuring social sentiments crucial for social media platforms. Similarly, industrial and organizational psychology offers insights into measuring knowledge, skills, and abilities that are invaluable for applications aimed at enhancing customer learning.

The reference to anthropology and psychology here is not to advocate for expertise in these fields but to illustrate that metrics can be developed for nearly every aspect of human experience. The shift in focus should be from "if" to "how" you can develop these metrics. Adopting this perspective broadens the horizons of functional metric definition, encouraging a thought process that considers real-life observations and hypothetical, ideal questions to gather truthful insights.

Crafting the Ideal Narrative

Building upon the hypotheses you've formulated, the subsequent phase in metric development is envisioning the ideal data collection scenario. Picture a world where you have the means to monitor every interaction of your users with your product, capturing every click and subsequent action. Reflect on the hypotheses at hand—what specific user actions would you need to observe to validate these hypotheses? And in cases where the change you're anticipating occurs internally within the user, what questions would you ask to gauge the impact of your feature? These contemplations form the foundation of your ideal data collection narrative.

The objective here is to construct a visionary blueprint of the data you aspire to gather. This step transcends the limitations of your current technical and operational environment, allowing you to define your data collection goals without constraints. It's an imaginative exercise that paves the way for actionable steps in the subsequent phases. By the end of this exercise, you should have a concise narrative delineating precisely what you would observe in your users or the questions you would pose to them. Ensure that this imaginative process encompasses each level of success metrics, crafting a comprehensive vision of data collection in an ideal setting. The richer the detail in these envisioned scenarios, the more effective they will be.

Example Vignettes

Sharing these envisioned narratives as succinct vignettes with other teams can be instrumental in refining and enhancing their feasibility. Here are two illustrative vignettes to demonstrate this approach:

- **B2C vignette—muscle growth connected fitness device:** A user engages daily with our fitness app, which offers tailored workouts for their goals. We observe their interactions with the app, discerning their comprehension of the exercises. Additionally, you inquire about their sentiments toward the workouts and their belief in achieving the recommended fitness levels. As they commence their workout, you monitor their performance, noting any adjustments in weights or difficulties encountered. Post-workout, you gather their feedback on physical and mental well-being. Tracking these metrics over time allows you to correlate the effectiveness of the workouts with the users' physical and psychological outcomes.

- **B2B vignette—sales conversation improvement platform:** A customer employs the platform to enhance their salesforce's conversational skills via analysis of call recordings. The primary focus is to ascertain whether the end users engage with the platform and the duration spent reviewing the recommendations. You seek feedback from these users on the utility of the suggestions and potential enhancements. Subsequently, you listen to their calls to determine if they implement your advice. The aim is to measure the improvement in the salesperson's effectiveness and whether the company observes overall enhancements in their salesforce performance.

Generative AI in Practice

Content creation is another powerful aspect of GenAI, especially for its ability to turn thoughts into cohesive paragraphs. We can see this illustrated by its use in the development of vignettes. To make it more effective, in this prompt we offer ChatGPT a persona that it should adopt.

User Prompt

You are an experienced vignette writer who will be assisting me in creating a single paragraph that describes, in the third person, a person's behavior when interacting with a product in great detail. I will offer you a collection of notes, and you will write the narrative.

- The product is intended to help users create simple invitations for events.

- The specific feature is the seasonal and timely templates that are intended to inspire the user to create something they are confident in sharing.

- I want to ultimately measure how much they use the template and how that changes their experience creating the invitation.

- If the feature works it means the user is willing to share the invitation and even send it to be printed by one of our partner organizations.

ChatGPT

Jessica had always struggled with designing invitations for her events, often spending hours tweaking every little detail. But today, she discovered something new - a feature within her go-to invitation creation app that offered seasonal and timely templates. With a sense of curiosity, she scrolled through the autumn-themed designs, her eyes lighting up at the sight of a template adorned with golden leaves and elegant typography. It seemed to capture the essence of her upcoming fall harvest dinner perfectly. Selecting it, she noticed how the template guided her effortlessly through the process, from inserting the event details to choosing the right font. The design process, which usually felt like a chore, was surprisingly enjoyable and took significantly less time than her usual attempts. She found herself smiling, confidently adding personal touches here and there, making the invitation uniquely hers. Once satisfied, she didn't hesitate to share the finished invitation with her friends. Feeling proud of her creation, she even decided to have it professionally printed, opting for one of the app's partner organizations. For Jessica, the feature had transformed invitation designing from a tedious task into an enjoyable and fulfilling experience.

Define: Turning the Idea into Measurable Variables

When talking about metrics, there are a lot of different manifestations that might be described. Metrics at their core are any measurement of something. Thus, they can come in many forms. Three primary qualities are especially important for this book: qualitative and quantitative; attitudinal versus behavioral; and active versus passive collection.

- **Qualitative and quantitative:** Qualitative data encompasses non-numerical insights that capture the subjective experiences, opinions, and feelings of users. This type of data is gathered through methods like interviews, focus groups, or open-ended survey questions. It provides depth and context to the user experience, uncovering the why behind user behaviors. For example, a company might conduct user interviews to understand the reasons behind a product's appeal or the challenges users face while using it. Qualitative data is crucial for gaining a deeper understanding of user motivations, preferences, and perceptions, which cannot be obtained from numerical data alone and are the primary data sources that will assist you in defining the User Outcome Connection.

  Quantitative data, on the other hand, in product impact analysis refers to numerical, measurable data that quantifies user behavior and interaction with a product. This type of data is objective, providing hard facts and figures that can be statistically analyzed. It typically includes metrics like usage frequency, sales numbers, or user demographics. For instance, an app might track the number of downloads, session lengths, or the frequency of feature usage, offering precise, numerical insights into how a product is being used. Quantitative data is invaluable for making data-driven decisions and identifying trends or patterns in user behavior. *The metrics that are developed as part of FIA will be quantitative.*

- **Attitudinal versus behavioral:** Attitudinal measurement in product impact assessment focuses on the attitudes, beliefs, and opinions of users toward a product. It captures subjective elements like user satisfaction, preferences, and perceptions, providing insights into how users feel and think about a product. Attitudinal data is typically gathered through surveys, questionnaires, or interviews, where users express their opinions or rate their experiences. For instance, measuring user attitudes toward a new software feature might involve asking them to rate their satisfaction or likelihood to recommend the feature to others.

  Behavioral measurement, in contrast, tracks the actual actions and behaviors of users when interacting with a product. This objective approach provides concrete data on how users engage with a product, such as usage frequency, duration of engagement, or specific actions taken within an app or software. Behavioral data is best captured through analytics tools that track and record user interactions, offering a factual record of user behavior without the influence of personal opinions or biases. For example, assessing the impact of a website redesign might involve analyzing metrics like click-through rates, time spent on the page, or the number of completed transactions.

- **Active versus passive collection:** Active data collection in product impact involves directly engaging with users to gather data. This method requires user participation, often through surveys, interviews, or focus groups. Users actively provide feedback, opinions, or information about their experiences with a product. For example, a company might conduct a survey to understand user satisfaction with a new app feature. Active data collection is ideal for obtaining detailed, subjective insights, particularly attitudes, preferences, or feelings that aren't observable through user behavior alone.

  In contrast, passive data collection involves gathering data without user interaction, typically through automated means. This method relies on tracking tools and analytics to observe and record user behavior as it naturally occurs. For instance, an app might use embedded analytics to track user engagement levels, time spent on different features, or navigation patterns. Passive collection is unobtrusive and offers objective, behavior-based insights into how users interact with a product in real time, providing a factual basis for understanding user behavior patterns and product usage. *Almost all attitudinal data collected is active*, except for cases where sentiment can be assessed using text analysis or other advanced techniques. That said, it can be done in a nearly passive way, such as in-product, where a user must do only an additional click.

As you convert the description of your idea measurement from the ideal narrative into a specific description, you will want to think through these three types. If your description details observing the types of products a user shops for after engaging with your coupon collecting application, you would want to start by identifying that it is an objective metric you are looking for, since it is something happening in the real world and can have a right answer. Next, it is likely that you would want to classify it as behavioral, since you are looking for someone's actions, not their perceptions, on what they want to purchase. Lastly, this data could be collected by actively watching someone but is done at scale by passively collecting it through digital systems. Starting here, you begin with a solid understanding of what you will need from the metric.

Precision in Metric Development

With a preliminary outline of your desired metrics in hand, the next step is to refine and fully define these metrics. The depth of your initial narrative will significantly influence this stage; a detailed narrative can serve as a robust foundation. The goal here is to craft a metric description so comprehensive that even a technical counterpart, who may not share your intimate understanding of the product, can accurately construct the metric as envisioned.

Detail is paramount in this phase. Technical development thrives on specificity, necessitating well-defined parameters. As you document your desired metrics, continually assess the level of nuance required to effectively capture the outcomes you seek. For instance, if your goal is to gauge customer satisfaction with a new feature, consider how you will define and measure satisfaction. What specific questions will you ask, and what range of responses will you allow? Similarly, if assessing the impact of a feature on email behaviors, pinpoint the exact behaviors of interest. Is it the volume of emails sent or received, the timing of these emails, or patterns in email activity?

Leverage the User Outcome Connection definitions and your ideal narrative to help identify the necessary elements of each metric. Once you have a clear idea of what is required, write it down and start infusing it with specificity. For behavioral metrics, this might include the context of the behavior, the precise actions taken, and the extent to which these actions represent the behavior in question. For metrics focused on sentiment, define the exact feelings you aim to capture. The objective is to provide such clarity in your description that anyone reading it can grasp exactly what is being measured.

To illustrate the difference between low-quality and detailed descriptions, **TABLE 7.10** provides examples of both. These comparisons will highlight the importance of precision in metric development, ensuring that your metrics are not only accurate but also meaningful and aligned with your product's goals.

TABLE 7.10 A Comparison of Low-Quality and Detailed Descriptions

LOW-QUALITY DESCRIPTION	DETAILED DESCRIPTION
Someone used the feature.	A user clicked the page at least once or dwelled for more than three seconds.
How much a user liked the feature.	The rating, on a scale of 1 to 10, that a user provided to the question "What level of satisfaction did you have with the overall product experience?"
The degree that a user exercised after using a feature.	The total level of exercise minutes that a user completed in the 24 hours after interacting with a feature.
The change in confidence a user experienced.	The rating, on a scale of 1 to 5, that a user provided to the question "What degree of change in confidence did you have after your interaction?"

Metrics Connected Back to the FIA

For teams with advanced data infrastructures, the luxury of already capturing essential data for their FIA might be a reality. Many teams will discover that they have already implemented several pertinent metrics. In such scenarios, the focus shifts to updating your FIA worksheet to incorporate these metrics, thereby consolidating all necessary elements in one accessible location. To ensure comprehensive and effective integration, I advise including at least the following five key elements for each metric: title, description, collection method, the nature of collection (passive or active), and the associated User Outcome Connection assumption.

Generative AI in Practice

Enhancing while brainstorming new ideas is another powerful application of GenAI. In what is being called a "punch-up," these systems can enhance the quality of information. In this prompt we will do exactly that with a low-quality metric description, creating three versions of the more detailed description. The person running the FIA could take these descriptions and create a final one that works best for their use case.

User Prompt

You are an experienced product developer who is assisting in the creation of definitions describing metrics. A short description of a feature and a brief explanation metrics will be provided and you will write three versions of a detailed single sentence explaining the metric.

Feature: A tool to assist in finding lost devices

Metric explanation: How quickly a person can find their lost device

ChatGPT

Version 1: The metric measures the average duration, from the moment a user initiates the lost device finding feature until the device is successfully located, quantifying the efficiency and speed of the tool in facilitating device recovery.

Version 2: This metric quantifies the time efficiency of the lost device assistance tool by tracking the elapsed time between a user activating the search feature and the moment the lost device is reported as found, providing insight into the tool's effectiveness in real-world scenarios.

Version 3: The metric evaluates the tool's performance in assisting users to recover lost devices by calculating the average time taken from initiating the search process to the successful location of the device, offering a direct measure of the tool's utility in reducing recovery time.

The title of each metric is crucial for easy reference, while the description provides the necessary details for its construction and understanding. The collection method outlines the specific approach to gathering the data. Distinguishing between passive and active data collection is equally important, because it influences resource allocation and feasibility; generally, passive collection systems are more straightforward to implement. Finally, linking each metric to a specific assumption in the User Outcome Connection enhances clarity in tracking and testing its relevance and impact.

TABLE 7.11 exemplifies how these elements come together. They are taken from a real application of the FIA conducted with an education technology. Jochi is a platform that empowers academic support teams to be more effective at helping students do their best work. Their platform is a collection of features curated to encourage students to act in a way that will increase their academic performance. On the flip side, they surface this data to those who work with these students, so they are always up to date with students' actions.

TABLE 7.11 Fully Defined Metrics for Jochi

Metric 1

METRIC	FEATURE USAGE FREQUENCY
Description of metric	Number of times students interact with task management and communication features
System collecting metric	In-app analytics
Actively or passively collected	Passively collected through app usage and actively collected through feedback at the end of every study session
Associated user outcome assumption	Specific behavior

Metric 2

METRIC	INCREASED TASKS COMPLETION
Description of metric	The percentage of tasks that a student marks as completed
System collecting metric	Product analytics
Actively or passively collected	Passively
Associated user outcome assumption	Specific behaviors

Metric 3	
METRIC	INCREASED GRADES
Description of metric	The average grade received on a student's assignments broken down by month during period of usage
System collecting metric	Integration from Learning Management System.
Actively or passively collected	Passively.
Associated user outcome assumption	User outcome.

Metric 4	
METRIC	FEELING OF ACCOMPLISHMENT
Description of metric	The response that a student gives to the prompt "Please rate your level of feeling accomplished at the end of this quarter."
System collecting metric	In-product survey.
Actively or passively collected	Actively.
Associated user outcome assumption	User outcome.

Metric 5	
METRIC	DECREASED LIKELIHOOD OF USER CHURN
Description of metric	Student discontinues usage of any features on the platform for at least one month.
System collecting metric	Product analytics.
Actively or passively collected	Passively.
Associated user outcome assumption	Business outcome.

One of the core features that Jochi offers students is the ability to track their tasks, like a professional would do, in a tool such as Asana or Trello. When Jochi set up a FIA on this feature to determine if it was effective at increasing students' ability to get work done, they first needed to define the intent of the feature. This yielded the User Outcome Connection shown in **FIGURE 7.2**, which suggested feature use would create more organization behaviors that increased academic performance and decreased student churn.

JOCHI CHATBOT EXAMPLE

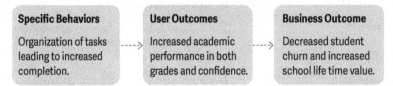

Specific Behaviors	User Outcomes	Business Outcome
Organization of tasks leading to increased completion.	Increased academic performance in both grades and confidence.	Decreased student churn and increased school life time value.

FIGURE 7.2 Jochi User Outcome Connection

With a *filled-out* User Outcome Connection that required validation, metrics were created and detailed as shown in Table 7.11. These illustrations demonstrate how each variable can be seamlessly integrated into the FIA framework, offering a clear roadmap for the creation and application of these metrics. This integration is a vital step in ensuring that the metrics you develop are not only technically feasible but also functionally aligned with your FIA goals, thus contributing effectively to the overall success of your product analysis.

CHAPTER RECAP

- **Functional versus technical metric definition:** Functional metric definition involves conceptualizing what needs to be measured and how it aligns with business goals, while technical metric definition focuses on the actual data collection, processing, and analysis techniques.

- **Process of creating new metrics:** A comprehensive six-step process for creating new metrics was introduced which includes scoping what is needed, creating an ideal narrative, documenting the metric, auditing current technical systems, developing needed systems, and refining the metric until validated.

- **Ideal narrative:** Envisioning an ideal scenario is an important first step to data metric development as it breaks the team free from perceived constraints.

- **Proxy metrics:** The use of proxy metrics is the best alternative when ideal metrics are unfeasible, emphasizing their role in balancing metric quality with practicality and resource constraints.

- **Integrating metrics with the FIA framework:** When integrating metrics into the FIA, it is important to provide a solid definition, outlining necessary elements like title, description, collection method, nature of collection, and User Outcome Connection assumption.

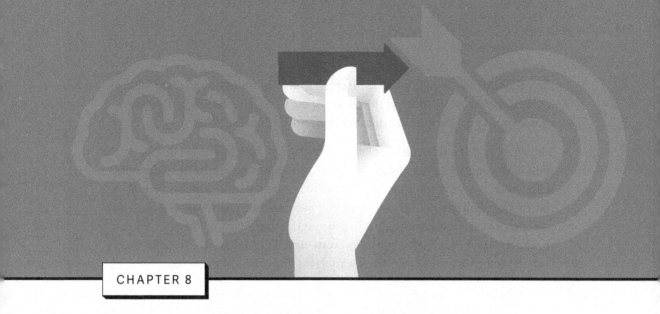

CHAPTER 8

Building Data Collection Systems (FIA Step 3, Part 2)

Before delving into this book, you might have questioned whether it is possible to construct metrics for any given behavior or sentiment. However, the previous chapter illuminated the immense potential of starting with a functional definition of metrics, encouraging you to look beyond the perceived limitations of current infrastructure and expertise. The process of crafting an ideal metric narrative demonstrated that, in theory, anything is measurable. By now, you should have a list of ideal metrics to capture as part of your FIA. It's time to confront the practical realities and acknowledge that not all metrics can be captured within the constraints of available resources.

While numerous resources are available to guide the engineering of metrics, this chapter will provide an overview of the process of capturing new data without delving into the specifics of coding or technical implementation. For those seeking a more in-depth technical understanding, consult resources such as *Fundamentals of Data Engineering: Plan and Build Robust Data Systems*, by Joe Reis and Matt Housley; the *IBM: Data Engineering Basics for Everyone* course on edX; or various instructional video series on YouTube.

This chapter will guide you on what to consider and how to initiate discussions with your product and engineering teams regarding metric development. Remember, there are multiple approaches to metric creation, and by the end of this chapter, you should feel confident that you can find a pathway to either your ideal metrics or a close approximation through proxy metrics. This journey into the practical aspects of data collection systems is a critical step in transforming your theoretical metrics into tangible tools for impact analysis.

Technical Stages of Metrics Development

As we shift to a technical focus, we will look at an overview of the technical process of creating new metrics, as shown in **FIGURE 8.1**. The transformation of raw data, whether attitudinal or behavioral, into meaningful metrics is a nuanced journey that starts with its raw collection and ends with refined metric formation. Initially, raw data is a simple collection of information in a recallable format. To unlock its potential, it must undergo a series of structured transformations. This overview is not meant to delve into the complexities of data engineering but rather to provide a foundational understanding for discussions with technical partners. For those leading the functional aspect of metric creation, a basic grasp of the technical process is invaluable.

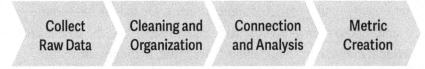

FIGURE 8.1 Four steps to the technical creation of a metric

1. **Collect raw data:** The journey begins with data captured in its raw form. For many digital companies, this often involves passively collected behavioral data from user interactions with a product. Other methods include direct user observation or gathering attitudinal data through user feedback. This stage lays the groundwork for the technical creation of metrics.

2. **Cleaning and organization:** Following collection, the data needs to be stored for future access and cleaned for uniformity. Common storage solutions include relational databases and data warehouses. The transformation of raw data to fit these structured formats allows for integration of additional data sources, paving the way for a unified database.

3. **Connection and analysis:** Single databases are not enough for data at the scale of most modern organizations. Thus, the third stage involves linking various data sets to create a cohesive understanding. You can visualize this as merging multiple spreadsheets based on common data points. Establishing a central repository for all data enables pattern recognition and the identification of new metric opportunities through tools like dashboards.

4. **Metric creation:** The final stage circles back to the functional requirements outlined in the previous chapter. Here, the insights gleaned from the connected and analyzed data are used to formulate precise metrics, completing the transition from raw data to actionable insights.

Collect Raw Data in the Digital Realm

The method you choose for raw data collection in a digital environment hinges on your team's technical prowess and the objectives you aim to achieve. Raw data comes from either direct user interaction with a product, asking them for their feedback, or by collecting data from integrations with other sources. When collecting data from product interactions, it can come in a highly detailed flow with *event data* or more aggregate patterns in *user activity data*. Asking users about their perceptions is considered *attitudinal data* and requires active participation. Integrations with other platforms means any time that data is being pulled in from another platform.

One of the most common approaches for gathering raw behavioral data at scale involves developing trackers that log every user-generated action, known as event data. These streams of data provide a comprehensive understanding of user interactions within a product, capturing details like clicks, page changes, and other actions, along with contextual user information.

As of this writing, there are notable players in the *event data* collection field. Segment, which is recognized as a market leader, offers a user-friendly solution to implement event trackers across various digital platforms of a company.

Operating as a customer data platform, Segment specializes in capturing and storing extensive user data for subsequent processing. Another notable company, mParticle, follows a similar path but with a strong emphasis on mobile platforms. Although numerous other solutions are available for exploration, directly embedding such systems into your product is an alternative, although generally less cost-effective, option.

Event data provides a detailed, microscopic view of user actions but can be voluminous. An alternative is using user-monitoring services that offer a more aggregated perspective. Notable examples include Hotjar and Fullstory, which provide detailed tracking and reports on *user activities*. Hotjar, for instance, is popular among designers for its heatmaps that show cursor movements. It's important to note that such monitoring can raise privacy concerns, so it's essential to establish ethical boundaries. For a more limited scope, classic eye-tracking studies can offer insights into user behavior, though they are not scalable for large user bases.

Capturing *attitudinal data,* which involves understanding user thoughts and feelings, is inherently more challenging, as it requires active user participation. Commonly, this is achieved through in-product surveys using tools like Chameleon and Pendo, which facilitate easy integration and rapid data collection. Product teams can build their own surveys into the interface with limited resource involvement. Plenty of examples of thumbs-up/down feedback buttons and similar elements are embedded throughout services across the web. However, this method is limited to users interacting with specific features and can encompass only a certain range and depth of questions.

For broader surveys, platforms like Qualtrics and SurveyMonkey can be used to disseminate surveys via email or text. Although less immediate than in-product surveys, this approach allows for more comprehensive data collection. Thoughtfully conducted, attitudinal data collection can yield valuable insights on a recurring basis, complementing the behavioral data gathered through other methods. When all these options cannot be deployed, the final option is to ask users through interviews done either live, in a moderated sense, or through asynchronous mechanisms provided by tools like UserInterviews, in an unmoderated way.

When data is needed but cannot be collected from the user—either through interaction or active participation—the team can seek it out from an additional system. Piping data in from additional sources is considered an integration and is a common practice on most data teams. The options for other data systems are endless but are commonly from systems such as customer relationship management systems like HubSpot and Salesforce and Enterprise Resource Planning systems like SAP and Oracle. Connecting these systems can offer other relevant raw data on users' actions.

Cleaning and Organization

Once raw data has been collected, the next step is preparing it for easy access and analysis. This involves determining the appropriate storage location and schema for the data. The landscape of data storage is varied, each option coming with its unique specifications for transforming raw data into a compatible format. In the contemporary digital environment, cloud-based databases have emerged as a prevalent solution, offering powerful and accessible data storage capabilities. Leading cloud service providers like Amazon Web Services, Microsoft Azure, and Google Cloud provide robust platforms for data storage and management.

As the volume of data grows, companies are increasingly seeking larger, yet cost-effective storage solutions. Although immediate accessibility is crucial, managing storage costs has also become a priority for many data teams. This balance has led to the rising use of data warehouses, both physical and cloud hosted. Snowflake, for example, has gained prominence for its user-friendly setup and a broad array of tools tailored for data warehousing.

The schema, the framework that dictates data organization and interconnectivity, plays a pivotal role in a data warehouse's functionality. However, as the diversity of data types expands (such as audio clips in note-taking apps or images in photo-editing apps), traditional data warehouses may encounter limitations. This challenge has given rise to the popularity of data lakes in recent years. *Data lakes* offer semi-structured repositories capable of housing mixed media. Databricks stands out in this domain, offering not just data lake solutions but also the foundation for developing AI applications using this data.

Databases, data warehouses, and data lakes each present trade-offs between accessibility, cost, and complexity. Databases, while structured, allow quick access; data warehouses offer a cost-effective solution with some trade-off in speed; data lakes provide versatility for complex data setups but may be less accessible. The key is to collaborate with your technical team to determine the best method for cleaning and integrating data into these storage systems. The ultimate objective is to transform raw data into a format that facilitates easy storage, retrieval, and connection with other pertinent data for comprehensive analysis.

Connection and Analysis

After securing a storage solution for your raw data and choosing an appropriate organizational framework, known as a *schema*, the next crucial step is to enrich this primary data by adding related information from other sources. Think of this as linking pieces of a puzzle where each piece is data from a different source, and when connected, they form a complete picture. If the schemas of different data sets are compatible, they can be connected, much like linking two data tables that have a common element. This linkage enhances how easily you can access and use the data, although it might not always be as simple as it sounds.

A modern technique used in this process is called *extract, load, transform* (ELT). A breakdown of what this means is as follows:

1. **Extract:** This is where data is gathered or pulled from various sources, like customer databases or employee records.

2. **Load:** The extracted data is then transferred into your main data storage area.

3. **Transform:** The data is reorganized, or *transformed*, to fit the structure of your main storage area.

By connecting more consistent types of data (such as customer demographics or preferences) with the dynamic behavioral and feedback data from users, you can begin to see valuable patterns. These patterns can help in creating meaningful metrics. Although understanding ELT is beneficial, the detailed execution is usually handled by specialists known as data engineers.

Once you have a mix of clean, well-organized, and interconnected data, it's time to start digging into it to see what stories it tells. Platforms like Looker, a leader in this space, provide a central point for examining all your data. Though setting up Looker requires some technical know-how, once it's up and running it becomes a user-friendly tool for exploring your data. In Looker, *views* are basically different ways to look at your data. They allow you to play around with the data, rearrange it, and look at it from various perspectives. This is where you, even without deep technical expertise, can start identifying what new metrics can be created from the data you have.

Metric Creation

The culmination of the metric creation journey is the actual development of new metrics, which transforms your conceptual work into tangible, actionable data. Some metrics might already have taken shape during the transition from raw to organized and cleaned data, particularly basic metrics like usage, retention, and page clicks. However, your unique contribution becomes crucial when adapting these simpler metrics to meet the specific needs of the FIA.

Consider an example where you aim to analyze user conversion through a feature's setup flow. Suppose the cleaned event data in your warehouse already tracks each page click-through and screen interaction. Your task would be to meticulously define what you need technically to align this data with the functional description you provided earlier. This precise detailing enables the data team to construct the specific metric you require. Another example could be to observe how users adjust their savings goals in a finance app. If you need to quantify the frequency of these adjustments, a new metric must be crafted atop the existing event data.

This end-to-end walkthrough exemplifies a common methodology for developing new metrics. However, it's important to recognize that this is not a one-size-fits-all process. Each organization will have its own set of methods, needs, and limitations. Although you don't need to be a technical expert in data processing, a deeper understanding of how raw data is transformed into meaningful metrics will make you a more effective collaborator. By bridging the gap between functional objectives and technical execution, you not only enhance your role but also drive the adoption of an impact mindset within your team. Engaging actively in metric and key product indicator discussions reinforces your position as a crucial player in the data-driven decision-making process.

Audit: Assess What Systems You Have Available

As you progress from the conceptualization of new metrics (referred to as functional creation) outlined in the previous chapter, you now shift to the technical creation of metrics. The audit step focuses on first identifying what systems are currently in place and your team's readiness for each metric's collection. Conducting a thorough audit is essential as a fit-gap to see what is missing, ensuring that redundant systems are not created and reducing the overall effort needed to create new metrics. This stage marks a transition from the functional aspect of metric definition to the technical realm of metric creation (**FIGURE 8.2**).

FIGURE 8.2 The second half of the six-step process for developing impactful metrics is technical in nature.

If you haven't already partnered with technical experts, commonly in engineering, for your FIA, now is the time to engage them. Request a comprehensive list of systems currently in use for data collection, management, and access. This should include not only data collected through product interactions but also customer feedback from various channels. Engaging with user research and market research teams may also be necessary to gain a complete picture. With an understanding of existing systems and data sources, collaborate with your technical partners to categorize each proposed metric according to its readiness for collection. I recommend a four-tier classification system:

- **Already collected:** Metrics that are currently being gathered and are readily accessible.

- **Needs transformation:** Metrics that require new formulations, albeit with existing raw data.

- **Needs new systems:** Metrics necessitating the development of new data collection systems.

- **Unlikely to occur:** Metrics that are currently infeasible given the team's constraints.

The distinction between *needs new systems* and *unlikely to occur* is nuanced, influenced by your company's technical capabilities, financial resources, and the level of commitment from your technical partners. This is particularly relevant for metrics that require significant infrastructural changes, such as attitudinal metrics necessitating in-product surveys. Determining the feasibility and classification of each metric will require thoughtful dialogue and reflection with your technical team.

For metrics classified as *needs transformation* or *needs new systems,* you face a subjective decision based on the required development effort and your FIA timeline. Although it's ideal to implement all envisioned metrics, practical considerations may necessitate prioritization or delays. If extensive development time is required, consider the potential loss of momentum and gauge this against your project's timeline and your organization's culture.

For metrics that are either time intensive to develop or deemed *unlikely to occur,* consider the creation of proxy metrics as an alternative. These are metrics that approximate your ideal metric but are more readily obtainable. For instance, to measure "the ability to send emails more effectively," you might use related but indirect metrics like average email composition time or email thread length. The trade-off here is between the quality of the metric and the feasibility of measurement. The guiding principle should be to create data that, although not perfect, is more valuable than having no data at all.

With a thoroughly audited list of metrics, you gain a realistic perspective on which hypotheses you can validate immediately and which ones require further development. For each metric that is not immediately actionable, you'll need to decide whether to invest in developing it or opt for a more accessible proxy.

Develop: Data Collection Systems

With an understanding of what systems are needed to create the metrics that have been outlined, you now enter the develop phase. This phase ensures all the systems are in place to capture and properly store the data needed for each metric. For metrics lacking existing raw data collection mechanisms, this phase marks the initiation of building systems to capture such data. Following a similar four-step process as discussed earlier—collecting raw data, organizing it, connecting it to relevant information, and refining it post-collection—is crucial. Collaborating closely with your technical team is key to balance your requirements with their insights to identify the most efficient path forward.

The first step in developing new metrics involves pinpointing which of the four stages each variable falls into, based on the previous assessment of raw data availability. Those that are *already collected* require minimal effort, and your goal is just to ensure the metrics are being directed to the right location for future experimentation. For metrics classified as *needing new systems*, your focus will be on collaborating with the technical team to devise methods for gathering raw data relevant to your topics of interest.

Consider a meditation app seeking to evaluate the effectiveness of a new feature designed to expedite sleep onset through white noise. The metrics defined include feature usage, interactions within the app and phone post-white-noise initiation, and reported restfulness the following day. Although usage is already tracked through product analytics, capturing interaction data necessitates new systems. This could involve implementing an event data capturing system to record all in-app activities and subsequently using this organized data to construct the metric of *app interaction post-feature initiation*. More complex yet, to track the metric of *phone interaction post-feature initiation*, exploring methods to access phone usage data may be required. Additionally, gathering attitudinal feedback on restfulness would involve creating an in-product survey.

For metrics classified as *needing transformation*, understanding the current state of the data and how it can be manipulated into a usable metric is essential. Taking an example of an SaaS product designed to expedite mockup creation, if event data capturing is already in place, the focus would be on proper data storage and accessibility. It falls upon the FIA team to determine the data's current state and devise a strategy for its utilization.

Similarly, for outcome metrics like task completion speed, mockup utilization, and confidence in the mockups, the approach mirrors that of the behavioral metrics. If, for instance, confidence in mockups is already queried in a monthly survey, the task would be to integrate this data regularly into the main database for comprehensive analysis alongside other metrics.

Creating effective data collection systems is an intricate task that involves aligning functional requirements with technical feasibility. When achieving the ideal metric is not possible, identifying proxy metrics becomes a strategic alternative. For example, in a dating app scenario where dwell time on profiles is unattainable, the number of profiles viewed per session could serve as a proxy. Though not identical, this proxy metric might reveal insights into user engagement patterns post-feature implementation.

Throughout this process, maintaining a synergistic relationship with your technical team is invaluable. Their broader understanding of current data capabilities and possibilities complements your in-depth knowledge of what is required and why. This collaborative dynamic enhances the likelihood of developing robust systems and, when necessary, proxy metrics that closely align with your objectives, given the realistic constraints of data availability.

Collect: Collection and Validation

Transitioning to the collect phase, you reach the pivotal moment of commencing data collection for your newly scoped metrics. Until now, your endeavors have been preparatory, laying the groundwork for this crucial stage. The process may vary based on the nature of the data: passive behavioral data collection typically involves activating existing mechanisms, while attitudinal data collection might require deploying surveys or other tools to garner real user feedback. For metrics created from data collected manually, the collect phase commences with the beginning of that collection.

As data starts to flow, the emphasis shifts to validating the metrics to ensure they accurately capture the intended information. The approach varies depending on the type of data and the specific context, as shown in **TABLE 8.1**. For passively collected behavioral data, simple scenario testing can be effective. This involves having mock users or team members simulate specific interactions that the metric is supposed to track, then verifying that the metric changes as expected. For instance, in a smart-light app measuring the frequency of default color changes, testers could perform various schedule adjustments to see if the metric accurately reflects these nuances. Similarly, passively collected attitudinal data, like social media sentiment analysis, would follow a comparable validation method.

TABLE 8.1 Matrix of Ways to Validate Data Based on Its Type

	PASSIVE	ACTIVE
Behavioral	• Scenario testing • Statistical analysis	Inter-rater bias reduction
Attitudinal	• Scenario testing • Statistical analysis	Measuring content, criterion, and face validity

In cases where behavioral data is actively collected, detailed validation is essential, especially when multiple observers are documenting the same behaviors.

This is to ensure consistency in how behaviors are recorded, minimizing the inherent differences between individual raters, commonly referred to as *inter-rater bias*. Consider a scenario where a team is reviewing edits made in journal entries using a feature designed to encourage depth. Standardizing the definition of an *edit* across observers is crucial to reduce subjective interpretation and ensure reliable data collection. By ensuring that each rater uses a similar scale and that their judgments are aligned, it reduces the noise created by individual perceptions. Further reducing bias by the active collecting device, commonly people, the use of established methods from academic sources is ideal, or the creation of new ones from experts in the field that you are operating within. Here, the aim is to ensure the data is being collected as uniformly as possible and then to move on to making sure the metrics are accurately reflecting reality.

Validating attitudinal data, which is captured by surveys, interviews, or other forms of asking a person, takes a different approach. Since there is not an objective truth to test against, the goal is instead to ensure the specific phrasing for the question results in a response that is in line with what you are aiming to achieve. I will briefly introduce a few concepts to help you think through how to build the best survey. (If you desire to chase these down further, I suggest consulting industrial/organizational psychology resources.)

The first is face validity, which asks if the survey questions *look* as though they are phrased correctly. For example, take a question that is attempting to determine a respondent's sense of financial security: "On a scale of no confidence to fully confident, how prepared are you to handle an unexpected expense of $500?" Assessing its face validity would be asking external individuals how likely it is that the wording is yielding the right data. It is using the opinions of others to assess the quality of a question.

Another measurement of validity of actively collected attitudinal data is content validity, which asks if the question is capturing all components of what you are trying to measure. Take the question "How much did the e-learning content contribute toward your educational growth?" Although this question does directly ask how the content helped with growth, that is a vague variable. The team would be better suited to select one specific element of growth, such as understanding, applicability, or something else. By getting specific, the question is sure to holistically capture the area of interest rather than vaguely cover a breadth of topics.

The final assessment relevant to these types of questions is *criterion validity*. Measuring the effectiveness of a question is measuring the subject domain that it was intended to focus upon. This type of validity is the most relevant for good research but also the most challenging. An example for a fitness application would start with the question "How accurate do you find the fitness tracking app in measuring your daily physical activities?" and assess its validity by comparing responses to actual behaviors captured by the device and other comparable services (iPhone native activity capturing versus a Garmin watch).

For all these metrics, in addition to the unique attributes that each carry when actually collecting the data, an essential aspect to consider is the distribution of the data you gather. Ensuring that your data adheres to a normal or somewhat normal distribution is crucial for the validity and reliability of your metrics. This concept of normal distribution implies that most data points will cluster around a central peak, which typically represents the average value. This peak is flanked by a symmetrical spread of data points, diminishing as they move farther from the center. In some instances, you might encounter a multi-modal distribution, characterized by multiple peaks or *humps*. Each peak in such a distribution should exhibit a relatively equal spread of data points above and below it. This pattern ensures that the distribution remains balanced and reflective of the underlying metric's nature.

Collaborating with your data science team is pivotal. Their expertise in validating the descriptive statistics of a metric is invaluable in identifying and addressing any significant biases that might be present in the data. Additionally, analyses conducted by these teams will provide reassurance that the metrics are not only collected accurately but also that the values derived from this data are trustworthy and representative.

It is recommended to consult with these subject matter experts or explore additional resources to deepen your understanding of data distributions. As the FIA leader, your main goal in this phase is to confidently ascertain that the metrics are not just accurately collected but also that their foundational values exhibit validity. This scrutiny ensures the integrity of the data, paving the way for impactful insights and informed decision-making based on the FIA.

Once metrics are validated—and ideally before commencing your experiment—it's time to refine them to align closely with your data goals. Depending on the gap between the current metric and the desired outcome, you may need to consult experts for substantial reworking or employ a trial-and-error approach for minor adjustments. These steps ensure that your metrics are as accurate and relevant as possible.

Finally, establishing a system to monitor the incoming data is crucial. Using tools like Data Dog, you can set alerts for significant metric deviations, signaling potential issues or interesting trends. For example, if a smart-light app typically records two color switches per user but suddenly observes a spike to ten or more, it would trigger an alert for further investigation. Consistent monitoring not only prepares you for the experimental phase but also reinforces the reliability of your data, ensuring that your metrics truly reflect reality.

Generative AI (GenAI) in Practice

Showcasing the brainstorming potential of GenAI again, we will use it in this case to help think through ways to validate that a metric is being adequately collected. In this prompt, instructions are given followed by a description of an attitudinal metric. Then a second behavioral metric is shared. The researcher could take these results and dig further into them by having a conversation with ChatGPT, beginning the process when they are ready.

User Prompt

You are an experienced researcher and data engineer who has years of experience consulting with companies to determine the best way to validate whether their metrics are being collected properly. Share three ways, in no more than two sentences each, describing how I can go about validating that the following metric is being adequately collected in a way that reduces noise as much as possible:

The response to a survey question focused on understanding how use of a new music discovery feature led to users feeling a sense of novelty with their song selection.

ChatGPT

Implement Response Validation Rules: Use validation rules on survey responses to filter out inconsistent or illogical answers, such as responses that contradict each other or are outside the expected range, ensuring that the data collected reflects genuine user experiences with minimal noise.

Statistical Analysis for Outliers: Apply statistical techniques to identify and analyze outliers within the survey data, allowing for the removal or further investigation of responses that significantly deviate from the norm, which may indicate misunderstanding of the question or random response selection.

Cross-Validation with Usage Data: Cross-validate survey responses with actual usage data of the music discovery feature, checking for correlations between reported feelings of novelty and patterns in music exploration behavior (e.g., frequency of feature use, variety of songs listened to) to ensure responses accurately reflect user engagement and experience.

User Prompt

Now do the same for a metric that is built around behavioral data detailing how the user's interaction with the feature changed their song searching actions.

ChatGPT

Event Tracking Verification: Ensure accurate event tracking implementation by performing regular audits of the tracking codes or pixels associated with the music discovery feature's interactions, verifying that every action (clicks, searches, plays) is correctly captured and attributed to the feature to accurately reflect user behavior changes.

A/B Testing Analysis: Conduct A/B testing where one group of users has access to the new music discovery feature while another does not, and compare the song searching actions between these groups. This method isolates the impact of the feature on user behavior, helping to validate that observed changes in actions are directly attributable to the feature's use.

Segmentation and Trend Analysis: Analyze the behavioral data across different user segments (e.g., by demographic, device type, music genre preference) and time periods to identify consistent patterns or trends in song searching actions that can be attributed to the introduction of the music discovery feature, helping to reduce noise by accounting for external factors that might affect user behavior.

Updating the User Outcome Connection

Maintaining a central record of metrics throughout their development and data collection stages is crucial. This centralization ensures alignment among all stakeholders, from those casually observing the experiment to those intimately involved in metric development. Recall that in the last chapter, you incorporated these metrics into your FIA document, though some details might have been preliminary at that stage. Now, following the completion of the collect phase, it's time to revisit this document to update it with the most current information.

Once your document reflects the latest metrics data, you're positioned to start disseminating this information more broadly. Soliciting feedback from others, particularly on the behavioral and outcome metrics, is invaluable. This collaborative approach aids in refining metrics that are aligned with your team's needs and is crucial for validating the hypotheses underlying the User Outcome Connection. It's also a time to identify and agree on the key metrics that will be pivotal in assessing the impact of your feature. Pinpointing one or two high-value metrics is especially important as you gear up for the experimentation phase.

By broadly sharing the metrics, you are also laying the groundwork for extended use of these new metrics. Your stakeholders may appreciate the perspective the variables offer and want to incorporate them into other dashboards or reviews. As Chapter 11 will discuss, the metrics you create as part of the FIA are deliverables themselves and can be just as valuable for your team as the output of the experiment.

Navigating the data collection phase might be a new experience for you and your team, particularly regarding the creation of behavioral and outcome metrics. The guidance provided in the previous two chapters aims to equip you with a comprehensive understanding of how to functionally define metrics across all five levels of success. This newfound knowledge prepares you to engage with your technical team effectively, armed with actionable ideas for capturing these metrics.

As you edge closer to the experimentation stage, highlighted in the next chapter, it's crucial to ensure you are thoroughly satisfied with the metrics you've developed. Remember, the quality of data you input significantly influences the reliability of your experiment's outcomes. The adage "garbage in, garbage out" holds particularly true in data analysis. Ensuring that your metrics are well conceived and accurately captured is essential to avoid presenting findings that might be perceived as "garbage" by those who will ultimately review the final analysis.

Building Metrics for the Chatbot Launch

With the need to validate hypotheses for Tasky firmly in place, it became evident that the next step involved establishing metrics for a forthcoming experiment. Given the proactive nature of this project, no pre-existing metrics were available for evaluation. In a scenario where the chatbot was already operational, my first action would have been to consult the product analytics platform and any existing qualitative feedback mechanisms, such as an in-product survey or feedback button.

Starting from the ground up, it was essential to track user interactions with the chatbot. The hosting website came equipped with a product analytics tool, providing basic usage data. For a more sophisticated tech setup, I might have considered embedding a simple thumbs-up/thumbs-down feedback system for quick satisfaction metrics. However, given the limitations, I opted to include a feedback form at the page's bottom, featuring satisfaction and outcome-related questions.

The chatbot's primary goal is to help users discover new ways to integrate these advanced systems into their workflows. Direct measurement of this behavioral change would ideally involve complex integrations with productivity suites, task trackers, and other work-monitoring systems or tapping into the generative AI systems to track customer usage. Such extensive integrations were beyond the scope of my prototype, prompting reliance on the feedback survey complemented by a series of interviews.

The chatbot aims to enhance task completion efficiency and reduce automation apprehension. While the former could theoretically be measured using behavioral data from the integrations, the latter—an attitudinal measure—would require direct participant inquiries or possibly text analysis of social media responses. For this experiment, only the inclusion of automation fear sentiment in the feedback form was feasible.

This walkthrough highlights the pragmatic limitations and possibilities within this project's scope. As it was a prototype test, I was prepared to work with lower-fidelity data and an incomplete picture to assess whether further investment in the idea was justified. A final pre-launch test for a major marketing initiative would necessitate far more rigorous metric quality.

CHAPTER RECAP

- **Four-step process for metrics development:** A four-step process for developing new metrics includes collecting raw data, organizing it, connecting it to other relevant information, and refining it post-collection.

- **Metric audit process:** This process introduces a four-tier classification system for evaluating metrics based on readiness for collection, including already collected, needs transformation, needs new systems, and unlikely to occur.

- **Developing collection systems:** Whenever there are metrics that require new systems to be created, the team must identify how to best capture that data and transform it in the right format.

- **Collection and validation:** The final step in the overall development of new metrics is the collection and validation of metrics. There are many ways to approach validation, depending on the type of data being collected.

- **Importance of proxies when ideal metrics are infeasible:** Identifying proxy metrics is necessary when perfect metrics are infeasible due to technical or resource constraints.

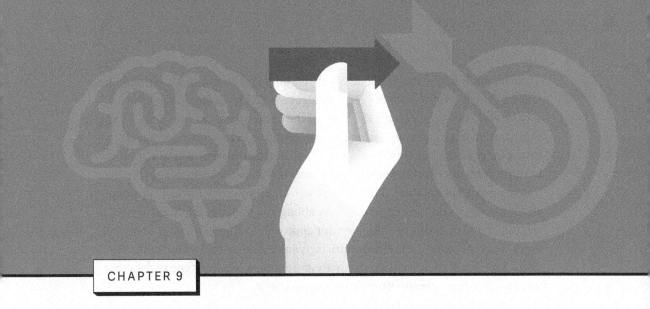

CHAPTER 9

Conducting the Experiment (FIA Step 4, Part 1)

Performing a Feature Impact Analysis (FIA) is more than just a methodical process; it's an avenue to foster an Impact Mindset within your team. By meticulously following the designated steps, you're advocating a philosophy that values scrutiny of product components, assessing each element's efficacy. The approach is a testament to the belief that incremental enhancements can collectively forge a solution profoundly impactful for your customers. As a torchbearer of this initiative, you are pivotal in steering your team, the entire company, and, ultimately, the customer experience toward a brighter horizon.

Armed with a suite of newly minted metrics, you are ready to commence the Experiment and Analyze phase of the user outcome connection. The term *experimentation* may conjure a spectrum of reactions—from exhilarating anticipation of discovering new insights to daunting memories of rigorous academic endeavors.

This chapter is dedicated to the detailed planning and execution of experiments, aiming to yield robust evidence. This evidence is crucial in elucidating the relationships between various elements of the user outcome connection. Every organization has its unique testing culture, resource limitations, and benchmarks for evidential quality. In almost all cases, these prevent you from performing academic-quality research, but that should not be used as a reason not to pursue experimentation. This chapter will equip you with critical considerations for setting up your experiment, enabling you to make informed decisions and judicious trade-offs to calibrate your approach to align with your organization's specific context, thereby optimizing your experimental framework. The next chapter will then focus on the analysis possible given the type of data that you and your team create through your experiment.

Developing a Culture of Experimentation

In our modern corporate arena where companies vie for supremacy with groundbreaking products and compelling marketing strategies, the need for product testing has never been greater. This competitive urgency has catalyzed a surge in the development of corporate experimentation capabilities. This growth is not only in assembling specialized teams but also in enhancing technical prowess for swift and effective testing. A striking indicator of this rapid escalation is the remarkable 227 percent increase in tests conducted from 2018 to 2023 by organizations fusing the leading experimentation platform, Optimizely.[1]

However, effective experimentation transcends the mere presence of dedicated teams or the availability of sophisticated testing tools. It's fundamentally about fostering a culture that prioritizes evidence-based decision-making and perceives failure not as a setback but as an opportunity for innovation and learning. The true value of experiments lies not just in the insights they generate but in how these insights are disseminated, embraced, and integrated to sculpt impactful outcomes. The full potential of these experimental endeavors can be harnessed only when an organization wholeheartedly adopts a culture of experimentation.

---

1 "Evolution of Experimentation" by Optimizely (https://www.optimizely.com/the-evolution-of-experimentation/)

Each experiment has the potential to overturn preconceived notions or expectations. In environments where evidence-based decision-making is not yet deeply ingrained, there's often a tendency to dismiss or rationalize insights that contradict existing beliefs or hypotheses. The real transformative power of experimentation is unlocked when a team is ready to pivot from long-held assumptions considering new, compelling evidence. This paradigm shift is the cornerstone of fostering a team that not only experiments but also ensures that these experiments substantially influence outcomes.

Even with a strong commitment to an evidence-based philosophy, numerous cultural and organizational obstacles (**TABLE 9.1**) can impede the initiation of tests or the acceptance of their outcomes. Navigating these challenges requires a nuanced understanding of the organization's dynamics and a strategic approach to embedding experimentation into the company's ethos. This chapter delves into the strategies and best practices for cultivating a robust culture of experimentation, ensuring that the insightful revelations of each test are acknowledged and harnessed to drive meaningful change.

TABLE 9.1 Potential Hurdles Preventing an Experimentation Culture	
CULTURAL HURDLES	**ORGANIZATIONAL HURDLES**
• Aversion to risk	• Perceived complexity and effort
• Fixed mindset	• Restrictive rules and regulations
• Democratizing evidence creation	• Lack of collaboration

Cultural Hurdles

Aversion to risk is one of the most pervasive challenges faced by many companies.[2] This apprehension often manifests in a propensity to cling to established methods and patterns, even when evidence suggests their ineffectiveness. Risk in this context is twofold: the potential of alienating customers or stakeholders, and the fear of expending resources only to disprove a hypothesis. This risk-averse mentality can stifle the willingness to experiment—regardless of the available technical infrastructure—leading to incremental rather than transformative improvements in final deliverables.

---

2 "Overcoming a Bias Against Risk" by McKinsey & Company (www.mckinsey.com/capabilities/strategy-and-corporate-finance/our-insights/overcoming-a-bias-against-risk)

Cultivating a higher risk tolerance in an organization begins at the leadership level and requires a fundamental shift in how employees perceive and approach their roles. It involves embracing the role of a change agent, empowered to push boundaries and innovate, understanding that sometimes these forays into the unknown may retract. For individuals navigating low-risk tolerance environments, a practical starting point is to engage in low-risk experiments that demonstrate the value of a more adventurous mindset. This is why conducting a FIA using historical data is often recommended as an initial step.

A **fixed mindset**, which is closely linked to risk avoidance, is a belief that once something is broken, it's irreparable. This mindset can permeate an organization, obstructing the vision of a continuously evolving product. Experimentation is intrinsically tied to fostering a *growth mindset*,[3] the belief that any future iteration of oneself or one's product can be achieved through hard work and dedication. Organizations that reward the creation of "working" products without recognizing the importance of iterative development and continuous improvement are discouraging the pursuit of enhancements and the identification of mistakes. They are, in essence, promoting the elusive goal of getting it right the first time—a rarity in our dynamic and complex world—and dissuading reassessment and revision.

Democratizing evidence creation is the enabling of all employees, regardless of seniority, to create new insight to assist with decision-making. The hurdle occurs when individual employees are open to the concept of experimentation, but their leadership is not ready to relinquish the control of directing the questions answered by research.[4] When employees at all levels are empowered to experiment and contribute to the product experience, they become agents of knowledge generation, which necessitates a shift in organizational dynamics. Every piece of evidence generated by an employee has the potential to challenge the status quo, gradually redistributing decision-making power away from the top. This shift requires a deliberate choice by leadership: maintain a centralized control over decision-making knowledge or empower employees to generate new insights, accepting that the collective wisdom of the organization might surpass that of its leaders. As with fostering risk tolerance, if you find yourself

---

3 *Mindset: The New Psychology of Success*, by Carol S. Dweck
4 "Building a Culture of Experimentation" by Harvard Business Review (https://hbr.org/2020/03/building-a-culture-of-experimentation)

in a setting with limited encouragement for evidence creation, the onus falls on you to demonstrate the value and potential of democratized insights.

Organizational Hurdles

Addressing organizational barriers is the second crucial component in cultivating a culture of experimentation.

Perceived complexity and effort are significant impediments to conduct experiments. For many, the concept of experimentation is daunting, often perceived through the lens of academic rigor. It's vital for teams to understand the spectrum of experimentation methods available—not every test needs to be a complex, randomized control trial. Applied experimentation can range from sophisticated, statistically significant methodologies to simple A/B tests that help choose between design elements and copy versions. Recognizing the variety of testing methods and acknowledging that even limited data is preferable to purely intuition-based decisions can demystify the process and make it seem less formidable.

Restrictive rules and regulations are a closely related hurdle that can stifle experimentation. Although it's essential to safeguard customer experience and minimize risks, an overly cautious approach can inhibit innovation. Experimentation, by its very nature, involves exploring uncharted territories, which can sometimes lead to unexpected results or even failures. When organizations prioritize risk avoidance, they inadvertently create a culture where time constraints are frequently cited as reasons not to experiment. However, this short-term risk aversion can lead to long-term vulnerabilities, particularly from more agile competitors who are willing to experiment and innovate rapidly. Striking the right balance between risk mitigation and the freedom to test new ideas is crucial.

Lack of collaboration is a third common hurdle that stifles experimentation. Even in situations where teams possess the requisite skills and support for experimentation, they may lack a deep understanding of the products they are testing. This issue is particularly prevalent in larger organizations, where the team skilled in experimentation may not be closely aligned with the design and product teams. As with the challenges in metric creation, there can be a disconnect between those with functional knowledge and those with technical expertise. If the experimentation team operates as a shared service, they must navigate the delicate balance of proactively suggesting tests while also promoting their services and demonstrating the possibilities they can unlock.

Whether you're in an organization where experimentation is ingrained in the company culture or in a company that is just beginning to embrace this mindset, adopting an Impact Mindset positions you as a catalyst for change. Implementing a FIA and its constituent steps can initiate a shift toward a more agile and adaptable organizational approach. It starts with the realization that a feature's usage does not necessarily equate to its effectiveness, followed by testing to understand its true impact on users.

The framework for the FIA is designed as a guide for organizations to develop their experimentation capabilities. Reviewing features based on historical data provides a clear demonstration of the potential value of this approach. As more teams recognize the benefits of adopting an Impact Mindset, it can create a momentum that encourages leadership to endorse and embed experimentation at all levels, paving the way for a culture that thrives on evidence-based innovation and continuous improvement.

Experimenting in Applied Settings

As outlined in previous chapters, randomized control trials (RCTs) represent the pinnacle of high-quality research due to their robust ability to minimize noise and extraneous variables. These meticulously controlled studies are typically conducted in lab settings and involve extensive processes for participant recruitment and management.

However, in the realm of applied research, particularly in product development, such rigorous methodologies are often impractical. Applied research tends to engage directly with a product's user base, where participant recruitment often hinges on finding users willing to invest their time or those deeply invested in the product and eager to contribute to its enhancement.

In today's virtual and asynchronous world, the feasibility of creating controlled environments akin to lab settings is significantly reduced. Researchers and participants seldom share physical spaces, which poses unique challenges for conducting active studies. Consequently, many organizational tests lean toward using pre-existing data or data passively generated through user interactions. This approach, while different from the idealized scientific setups, can still yield highly valuable insights. The key for applied researchers is to shift focus from striving for perfect experimental conditions to generating evidence of adequate quality for the decisions at hand. This transition from seeking scientific precision to embracing practical, decision-oriented research is crucial in realizing value in an applied setting.

Teams that have mastered this balance become vital contributors to the product development process. Their experiments form a cornerstone of a culture that prioritizes evidence-based decision-making. This culture acknowledges that faster, more accurate decision-making is achievable through the generation and application of insights. Tech giants such as Google and Amazon exemplify this approach.[5] With centralized experimentation teams and skills distributed across the organization, they make decisions—from minute design changes to overarching product roadmaps—based on data rather than solely on intuition.

However, it's not just the technology behemoths that have embraced the power of experimentation. Companies like Booking.com routinely run over a thousand tests, most of which are not RCTs but rather A/B tests and other methodologies that enable quick, insight-driven decision-making. Similarly, Intuit has expanded its experimentation scope beyond product development to include marketing strategies, allowing teams traditionally reliant on creative intuition to refine their approaches for maximum impact. Even established brands like L'Oréal[6] are finding innovative ways to blend their time-honored business practices with a forward-thinking experimental culture.[7]

In essence, experimenting in applied settings is about finding the optimal balance between scientific rigor and the practicalities of the business environment. It's about understanding that while the perfection of RCTs might be unattainable in many business contexts, there is immense value in the insights gleaned from more pragmatic experimental approaches. This shift toward practical experimentation is a transformative step toward making more informed, evidence-based decisions that drive product innovation and business success.

---

5 "Why These Tech Companies Keep Running Thousands of Failed Experiments" by Fast Company (https://www.fastcompany.com/3063846/why-these-tech-companies-keep-running-thousands-of-failed

6 "How L'Oréal, a century-old company, uses experimentation to succeed in the digital age" by Think with Google (https://www.thinkwithgoogle.com/future-of-marketing/digital-transformation/lor%C3%A9al-cosmetics-beauty-brand-experimentation/)

7 "Building a Culture of Experimentation" by Harvard Business Review (https://hbr.org/2020/03/building-a-culture-of-experimentation)

Experimenting Across Teams

The essence of conducting a FIA lies in its interdisciplinary nature, necessitating the integration of both behavioral and attitudinal data. Ideally, this integrative approach should be the norm in applied research. However, in practice, teams tend to operate within their areas of expertise—UX research often focuses on generating deep qualitative insights, while data science predominantly concentrates on quantitative analysis. Although specialization in these domains is understandable, it often leads to a missed opportunity: the comprehensive understanding that emerges from combining knowledge about what happened (the quantitative aspect) and why it occurred (the qualitative perspective).

Embracing an Impact Mindset effectively bridges this gap. To measure the changes brought about by product use, it's essential to gather data on both the behavioral alterations users undergo and the subjective meaning of these changes to them. This approach redefines product success by establishing benchmarks across all five key dimensions: usage, usability, behavioral impact, user outcome satisfaction, and business outcomes. Achieving this comprehensive data collection inevitably requires collaboration across various teams, thereby breaking down silos that traditionally exist within organizations. Although initiating such cross-functional teamwork might initially be challenging, it plays a pivotal role in enhancing company-wide efficiency. By positioning your efforts as a catalyst for unifying the work of multiple teams, you not only facilitate cross-team efficiencies but also contribute significantly to the organization's overall effectiveness.

Although it falls outside the primary scope of this book, it's important to note the growing trend of centralizing insights efforts across firms that gained momentum in 2023. As funding for research and insights departments started to dwindle, leading to significant layoffs in these fields, the idea of amalgamating parallel efforts emerged as a viable cost-saving strategy. This concept recognizes that while different teams—including UX, data science, marketing insights, product analytics, and applied research—are engaged in similar work, they often operate in isolation due to their specialized approaches. The move toward a centralized insights model promises to augment the value these teams provide by creating robust, centralized insight repositories and reducing organizational redundancies. Although this concept is still in its nascent stages, by leading the way in the FIA, you position yourself as a key player in the evolution of this model. Your role in pioneering this initiative not only showcases your leadership in advancing interdisciplinary collaboration but also signals your capacity to contribute significantly to the strategic transformation of insight generation within your organization.

Balancing Rigor with Practicality

As has been mentioned earlier in the book and chapter, deviating from the stringent methodologies of RCTs inherently introduces a higher potential for noise and bias in research results, impacting their validity. Rather than perceiving this as an insurmountable obstacle, researchers must reframe their perspective to see it as a balance between feasibility and validity. Given the low probability of an applied research team conducting a clinical-grade RCT, this form of research represents one end of the spectrum—characterized by high validity but low feasibility as shown in **FIGURE 9.1**.

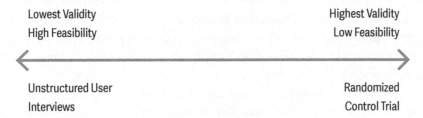

Lowest Validity
High Feasibility

Highest Validity
Low Feasibility

Unstructured User
Interviews

Randomized
Control Trial

FIGURE 9.1 The trade-off between validity and feasibility

At the opposite end of this spectrum lies a realm where studies are marked by high feasibility but lower validity. This could manifest in various forms, such as unstructured user interviews aimed at understanding usability or analyzing product session recordings to map out not just user actions but also their underlying motivations. These methods are comparatively easy to implement but often yield data that might not paint a fully accurate picture. In this context, there is no definitive right or wrong approach to deploying a study. The guiding principle should be to produce data that is, at the very least, superior to relying solely on product intuition.

As the orchestrator of the FIA experiment, the responsibility falls on you to determine the minimum acceptable standards for your experimental setup. Your deep understanding of your organization's unique culture, gleaned through the work conducted up to the experiment and analyze phase, will be instrumental in discerning what to advocate for and where compromises may be necessary. The next section, "Exploring the Components of Experimentation," will delve into the various components of an experiment, aiding you in making these crucial trade-off decisions. Meanwhile, it is pertinent to introduce four significant biases that can profoundly influence the outcome of a test. As you progress through the development of your experiment, aim to minimize these biases to enhance the validity and reliability of your results. This mindful approach to balancing rigor with practicality is not just a tactical decision; it's a strategic maneuver that acknowledges the complexities and constraints of applied research while striving to uphold the integrity and usefulness of the data collected.

Researcher bias encompasses a variety of influences stemming from an individual researcher's background, experiences, and personal beliefs, which can affect the decisions made during the setup of an experiment. This form of bias acknowledges that researchers, being human, invariably carry their own predispositions into the research process. These biases can subtly shape the design of an experiment, potentially leading to a setup that might not optimally address the research questions or objectives. For example, a researcher with a strong background in ethnographic studies might favor observational methods for data collection, valuing them above the use of passively collected behavioral data, even when the latter could provide more objective or comprehensive insights for the study at hand.

Mitigating researcher bias requires engaging in a collaborative review process with other researchers and stakeholders before finalizing the design of an experiment and its analysis approach. Soliciting diverse viewpoints helps in identifying and challenging any assumptions that may skew the experimental design. Additionally, reviewing established best practices for generating insights relevant to the specific research questions at hand can provide a more objective framework for designing experiments. This approach ensures that the chosen methods are not just reflective of a researcher's personal preferences but are also aligned with the objective of delivering reliable and valid insights.

Sample bias is a critical concern in research, arising when the sample chosen for a study does not accurately represent the broader population from which it's drawn. This discrepancy can lead to skewed results and conclusions that may not be applicable to the general population. Sample bias often results from non-random selection methods, where certain groups or individuals are more likely to be included or excluded from the study. For instance, a study focusing solely on recent purchasers of a product, particularly following a significant Instagram advertising campaign, may inadvertently bias its sample toward younger, more technologically savvy individuals, ignoring broader demographics of the product's user base.

Researchers should strive for diversity and randomness in their sample selection to decrease the likelihood of sample bias. Relying solely on participants who have engaged with previous research or who are followers of the company's social media channels can exacerbate bias. Instead, employing a variety of outreach strategies can help in approximating a random sample. Methods such as using Google ads, sending cold emails to a randomly selected group of users, or engaging with potential participants in LinkedIn Groups are effective in diversifying the sample. These strategies not only broaden the pool of potential participants but also reduce the likelihood of sample bias, ensuring the research findings are more representative and reliable.

Confirmation bias represents a cognitive shortcut that predisposes individuals to favor information or outcomes that reinforce their pre-existing views while dismissing or undervaluing evidence that contradicts those views. This bias is particularly problematic in research settings, where it can lead researchers to subconsciously seek out results that align with their hypotheses or beliefs, thereby skewing the study's outcomes. For example, a researcher interviewing users of a software-as-a-service (SaaS) product might frame questions in a manner that predisposes respondents to provide positive feedback. Similarly, they might unconsciously give more weight to responses that affirm their expectations about the product's benefits, while overlooking or minimizing critical feedback.

To counteract confirmation bias, it's essential to adopt neutral questioning techniques and maintain an open mind throughout the research process. Questions should be framed in a way that doesn't lead respondents toward a particular type of answer, such as avoiding prompts like "tell me why this mockup is good" or "share all the things you don't like about using this product," which inherently bias the direction of responses. Additionally, soliciting feedback on research designs from individuals not involved in the study can provide fresh perspectives. Asking them to assume a contrarian role can help identify potential blind spots or biases in the project plan. Furthermore, approaching data analysis with an exploratory mindset, without preconceived notions about what the findings should reveal, encourages a comprehensive examination of all emergent themes, thereby minimizing the influence of confirmation bias on the research outcomes.

The Hawthrone effect, a well-documented bias in research and evaluation, describes the phenomenon where individuals alter their behavior simply because they are aware of being observed or studied. This effect can manifest in various settings, including research studies, evaluations, or performance assessments, where participants modify their actions due to the knowledge that they are being monitored or measured in some manner. For example, individuals participating in a study on the effectiveness of a finance application to improve money management skills may exhibit heightened motivation and attention to their finances solely because they are aware of being observed. Consequently, any observed improvements in financial management skills may not solely reflect the impact of the application but could also be attributed to the Hawthorne Effect, leading to potential overestimation of its effectiveness.

Several strategies can be employed to mitigate the Hawthorne effect. Firstly, researchers can opt for studies that use pre-existing data where users have previously consented to data collection, thus reducing the awareness of being observed. Secondly, when active permission is required, refraining from informing users of the specific times of behavior measurement can help minimize the effect. Additionally, adopting an approach that fosters a relaxed and natural environment, such as dressing and behaving casually to create a sense of camaraderie rather than a formal research setting, can help alleviate participant awareness and encourage genuine behavior. Furthermore, comparing the experimental group with a similar control group not subjected to observation can provide valuable insights into the magnitude of the Hawthorne effect and its potential impact on study outcomes. These measures collectively contribute to a more accurate assessment of the true effects of interventions or applications under study while mitigating the influence of the Hawthorne effect.

Exploring the Components of an Experiment

Navigating the trade-offs inherent in the design of experiments involves a holistic examination of the experiment as well as its individual components. Making informed decisions about these components can significantly enhance the overall quality of the experiment while ensuring its feasibility. For instance, opting for a convenience sample drawn from regular app users becomes more justifiable if your advanced data science capabilities can effectively mitigate some of the inherent noise. Likewise, the ability to rapidly deploy a survey for attitudinal data can compensate for the absence of certain behavioral metrics. These individual component trade-offs are strategized with the dual objective of maximizing the experiment's quality and ensuring its timely launch. Adopting this granular perspective facilitates quicker decision-making and helps ensure that no critical elements are inadvertently overlooked.

By redefining the paradigm of an ideal experiment in an applied setting, moving away from the unattainable standard set by RCTs, and focusing on what is realistically achievable, you can establish a more practical benchmark for "good" in experimental design. This shift in perspective also aims to alleviate the reluctance often associated with making necessary trade-offs.

Let's dissect the ideal experiment into its key components, each of which will be explored in detail, providing a deeper understanding of their roles and importance.

Concluding the section are five experimental setups examples that are meant to serve as starting points, offering a glimpse into the array of possibilities rather than an exhaustive catalog of options. It's crucial to remember that the primary goal is to launch the experiment. Beyond that, it becomes a matter of making strategic decisions to acquire the highest-quality data within the confines of unalterable constraints. By focusing on the components of an experiment and understanding the potential trade-offs, you can effectively balance the demands of rigorous research with the realities of applied settings, thereby ensuring that your experiments not only are feasible but also yield valuable and actionable insights.

Reimagining the Ideal Experiment Setup

Recognizing that RCTs are not always feasible or even necessary in the context of applied research for business decisions, it's essential to envision a new ideal for digital experimentation. This model is inspired by the best practices of digital experimentation leaders and is not intended as prescriptive guidelines, but rather as an aspiration as you enhance your team's experimentation capabilities. The aim of the FIA is to develop features that drive real-world outcomes, and this necessitates testing whether the features actually influence user behaviors.

In an optimal scenario for a digital product, you would be able to conduct a highly controlled experiment directly on the product platform. Key to this is the ability to gather data at scale through various systems, such as passive data collection systems, in-product survey platforms, and an experimentation system that facilitates selective feature exposure to different user groups. For instance, consider a smart home device app: The ideal setup would involve the app automatically recording all user interactions (like adjusting light settings, setting schedules, and so on) and capturing feedback from users through an in-product survey tool when they seek help.

Assuming the presence of these data collection and experimentation systems, researchers would segment a random assortment of users into groups. These groups should be balanced across demographic factors and unrelated behavioral patterns. Taking the smart home device app example further, one group (the treatment group) would experience the new light "theme" feature, while another (the control group) would not. These groups would be homogeneously composed of users with varying interactions with the app, such as those using the device with different smart home integrations or those regularly using the app for light scheduling.

To enhance the experimental design, more than two groups can be included, with additional groups exposed to different variations of the feature. For our smart home app, a third group might receive both the light "theme" feature and a redesigned home screen. Once the groups are defined and the feature variations deployed, the next step is to monitor the impact over a set period. In our example, the smart home app would track behavioral metrics differences, conduct sentiment analysis on feedback, and analyze survey responses. Comparisons across all five success metrics (usage, usability, behavioral impact, user outcomes, and business outcomes) would then be drawn between the different groups.

This ideal FIA digital experiment framework is about more than just data collection; it's about setting up a controlled, yet practical, experimental environment that yields actionable insights. By aligning your experimentation strategy with this ideal model, you position your team to validate the effectiveness of new features and also to drive meaningful improvements in your product based on solid, evidence-based insights.

Examining All the Experiment Components

Fully executing the ideal experiment setup requires a collection of tools and capabilities. Taking the example of the smart home application team, a comprehensive toolkit is required, including an experimentation platform, mechanisms for participant randomization, passive behavioral metric collection, in-app feedback and survey tools, a data storage solution, and a skilled team to analyze the data. These, along with the capacity for real-time, digital implementation, comprise the seven primary components of a digital experiment: digital or in-person execution, experimentation platform, data infrastructure, data science capabilities, real-time or retroactive approach, attitudinal data collection, and participant pool. Let's delve into each of these components:

Digital or in-person: One of the most important choices you must make is whether you will be conducting your experiment digitally or in-person. If your product or service is digital, much of the data you need is already being generated; you just need to capture and get it into a usable state. If capturing the data is impossible or your product is not already digital, it makes more sense to conduct an in-person experiment. There are also times when an in-person component makes sense even with digital products. For instance, if the outcomes you are trying to measure are obtainable only through attitudinal metrics, it may be useful to have participants come to a physical location to collect this data. In these cases, usability studies or other ethnographic research may also provide the details you are looking for, even if the sample size needs to be greater for statistically significant results.

Experimentation platform: How will you get your feature to participants? Deploying new features is generally easier in a digital environment than in a physical one, but they do not immediately guarantee an open sandbox of potential. Instead, a team must have an experimentation platform or feature manager to quickly toggle feature or feature variants to be shown to different users. Only once this is in place is it quick and efficient to test different versions of a feature digitally. In a physical environment, it is much more difficult to rapidly release new versions or quickly change the product or service a customer is experiencing, but it can be done.

Data infrastructure: How will you collect and manage your data? As discussed previously, you must determine if you can passively collect data and where said data goes. An ideal situation will have the raw data sent to a system where the team can build metrics. After this, the team should send these metrics to an analytics system where an analyst can run basic statistics and where the team can easily export the data for further analysis. If this infrastructure is not in place, data may have to be collected manually, stored in more rudimentary systems such as Microsoft Excel spreadsheets or Google Sheets, and passed on into that statistical environment via batch transfers.

Data science capability: What resources do you have for analyzing data? Some studies, such as causal inference modeling, are experiments that the team can do on previously collected data using advanced statistics. You should assess what data science resources you will be able to use, such as people with statistical software knowledge (Python) and the ability to conduct advanced modeling (such as propensity score matching). Although not necessary, having these resources can add a layer of analysis, bringing you closer to statistical significance and the gold standard of causality.

Real-time or retroactive: Although the ability to run historical analyses is highly dependent on the data infrastructure and your team's data science capabilities, when available, you will have to determine if the experiments will be done with live or previously collected data. In a live environment, you'll recruit participants, onboard them, and then conduct the experiment. In contrast, studies done with previously collected data require that an individual has already given permission or you solicit that agreement before your analysis.

Attitudinal data capability: How will you collect attitudinal data? The fastest method for collecting this type of data is surveying participants. At a minimum, you should be able to access a free survey platform, such as Qualtrics or Survey Monkey. More advanced usage of these platforms includes automatically sending surveys and the deployment of surveys in user interaction. The first requires near real-time access to what a user is doing, followed by a system where you can create triggers that, when activated, send specific surveys. An example of this stack would be using Segment to collect behavioral data, using Chameleon to receive the data and recognize an event has happened, triggering a survey, then prompting Airtable to send the actual form. As a reminder, you can use a platform such as GetFeedback to get this job done.

Participant pool: Where are you getting your participants from? Although it is generally considered an afterthought, recruiting individuals to participate in a study can become the most challenging aspect of conducting an experiment.

First, you must determine the overall population you can pull from, then decide how realistic it is to get a completely random sample. In many cases, experimenters will fall back on convenience sampling, where only those who respond to an email or in-app notification requesting participation are chosen. This works as an appropriate last resort but inherits bias, as these participants have self-selected to join the research. A better solution is to have a fully digital system where the team can run tests on the interface that live customers are using. This approach decreases the need to actively recruit users. For intimate testing and surveys beyond one or two questions, the research team works with a group of users who have indicated they would like to participate in future research. Companies can also develop insider groups who participate in research for monetary and non-monetary rewards.

Determining the Correct Setup for the Experiment

Teams who are not able to replicate the ideal approach are not without the ability to execute a digital experiment. The smart home example and the breakdown of the ideal approach were offered to establish a new gold standard of experimentation to represent the art of what is possible when companies strive to build the best types of digital experiments. Teams requiring one or more of these systems can find ways to deploy high-quality research; still, it will require more creative thinking and, in some cases, manual alternatives.

While kicking off the process of setting up your experiment, the best first step is to review which of these systems you have in place. You can leverage the technical partners that you have worked with to create new metrics to assist you in determining your current capability for launching features to select groups, technically called *feature flighting*. If you haven't already, now is the time to engage with UX research and market insights teams to understand their methods for collecting attitudinal data and participant compensation strategies. As with the process of building new metrics, your aim is to understand what you already have in place, what components there is an appetite to build, and what is likely, or unlikely in the future.

At this point, you might feel overwhelmed regarding how you might build data collection systems for so many metrics. To reduce this, you should revisit the metrics you previously determined to be the most important for properly understanding your feature. Ideally, you will ultimately be able to capture and compare metrics across all five levels your aim is to ultimately determine if the feature is impacting users' desired outcomes, so be sure to include at least one behavioral and user outcome metric.

From that point, unless you are at a company with a highly mature experimentation culture, you will likely find that you do not have the capabilities required for the ideal setup. In many cases, the collection of attitudinal data is not in place, and the engineering team has not yet set up the infrastructure to properly deliver different features to separate audiences. Participant recruiting is another common challenge, whether because of a lack of the right data to find a random selection or because of rules against outreach to certain groups. For example, many B2B companies do not want researchers to contact customers who are in the sales process, which for many is a continuous cycle!

When components are inadequate or missing, the trade-off begins. If you wait for the systems to be built, you risk the results not being useful to the product team, but the quality of data might yield significantly better insights. For example, consider a dating service that is conducting research on a new feature intended to increase the quality of matches. In this situation, the user's perception of quality is highly important as behavioral metrics, such as conversation length, will only get one so far. The researcher leading this study must decide whether waiting for the technical team to implement an in-product survey is worth the risk that the feature will still be fully implemented without any evidence of its effectiveness.

Encountering gaps in your experimentation systems should kick off the process of assessing the likelihood of these gaps being filled. From there, determine what resources you have at your disposal to make that happen. Does your team have a budget for hiring a vendor to help with the collection of data or recruiting participants? These trade-off decisions are the reality of doing applied research; becoming a strong researcher means identifying where to invest minimum resources. By building out a FIA, you at least have a framework to work backward from. Through the definition of new success metrics, you know what is needed to determine effectiveness of a feature. From there, ensure you are investing your resources toward what will get you as close as possible to two groups: one of feature users and one not, that you can compare the most important metrics between.

Illustrating this further, imagine a company with a product that matches users with life coaches. The new feature is an assessment intended to yield better matches between users and coaches. Although there are many ways to evaluate "better," the researcher has determined this is based on how frequently the user meets with their coach, the rating of the session, and most importantly, the number of goals they set in the platform after sessions. After an audit of their experimentation systems, they learned there is no passive data collection system. Building a product analytic system for usage data, a surveying platform for attitudinal feedback, and a passive behavioral data collection system would be great, but this would demand too much time and too many resources. Triaging for the most important metric to determine success as they have defined it, they can confidently encourage their engineering team to focus on building an event-tracking system to understand how many goals they have set.

You may differ significantly from the ideal experiment model throughout these trade-off decisions. This is a natural concern but reflects the reality of operating within an organization with limited resources. Shift your benchmark from the perfect scenario to whether the insights generated are superior to decisions made purely on intuition. This approach ensures that your research, though perhaps not perfectly aligned with the gold standard of experimentation, is still grounded in evidence and contributes meaningfully to informed decision-making.

Understanding the Spectrum of Experiments

Acknowledging the trade-offs inherent in experimental design, it becomes clear that there is a spectrum of experiment quality and, correspondingly, the caliber of evidence each type can yield. On one end of this spectrum is the ideal experimental setup, closely aligned with the rigors of RCTs. This setup is anticipated to produce high-quality data, potentially yielding statistically significant results that could even meet the stringent criteria for academic publishing but requiring significant infrastructure and resources. The strength of evidence generated from such experiments is considerable, often providing robust, actionable insights.

Contrastingly, at the opposite end of the spectrum lies a setup akin to ethnographic studies. Although these studies provide valuable qualitative insights into user behavior and outcomes, they typically lack the scale required for advanced statistical analysis. Consequently, the quality of data derived from these studies is inherently limited but can be created quickly with little data infrastructure. This approach can still yield insights superior to having no data at all, but it is generally considered a fallback option when more controlled, quantitative methods are not feasible.

Understanding this spectrum of experimental quality is essential in making informed decisions about the type of study to conduct, based on the resources and capabilities available. Within this range, we will explore five distinct types of experiments, employing the seven components previously outlined (**TABLE 9.2**). These examples are not exhaustive but serve as foundational templates that can be adapted and expanded upon depending on your specific research goals and constraints.

TABLE 9.2 Components of Five Types of Experiments

	TYPES OF EXPERIMENTS				
COMPONENT	IDEAL	DIGITAL BEHAVIORAL	RETRO	UNMODERATED SCALED	NEAR ETHNOGRAPHIC
Fully digital	(✓)	(✓)	(✓)	✓	✓
Feature rollout system	(✓)	(✓)	✓	✓	✓
Data infrastructure	(✓)	(✓)	(✓)	✓	✓
High data science capability	✓	(✓)	(✓)	✓	✓
Real-time	(✓)	(✓)	✓	(✓)	(✓)
Survey capability	(✓)	✓	✓	(✓)	(✓)
Participant pool	Completely Random	Before vs. After	Users vs. Non-Users	Panel	Convenience Sample

These experiment types, each with their own strengths and limitations, provide a framework for applied researchers to navigate the complex landscape of digital experimentation. By carefully considering the trade-offs between the quality of evidence and the feasibility of each experimental type, researchers can choose the approach that best aligns with their objectives, resources, and organizational context. Whether aiming for the rigor of an ideal setup or adapting to the constraints of more qualitative methods, understanding this spectrum enables you to tailor your experimental design to deliver the most meaningful and reliable insights possible in your given circumstances.

TABLE 9.3 shows the component breakdown of each experiment type.

TABLE 9.3 Experiment Types and Their Components	
COMPONENT	**DESCRIPTION**
Ideal experiments are fully digital, deploy a new feature to a random sample, and include a collection of attitudinal and behavioral data across all four levels of success metrics.	
Digital or in-person	This is a digital experiment where all participants interact with the feature on a mobile application.
Real-time or retroactive	This is deployed in real-time in the product flow, capturing data as users engage with the feature.
Feature rollout system	The team has a feature management system in place, so at the start of the experiment, each of the three groups receives differing versions of the new feature with just a few clicks.
Data infrastructure	When users engage with the product, it automatically creates behavioral metrics that are tied to the specific behaviors outlined in the user outcome analysis.
Data science capability	The team has adequate statistical skills to perform the inferential statistical analysis, a t-test, to determine that a statistically significant effect was captured between the feature variants and the control groups.
Surveying capability	In-product surveys are deployed to users via an automatic trigger that occurs after the feature's setup process is completed.
Participant pool	Random samples are pulled from a master list of users done by a data analyst. These users are then placed into an Excel spreadsheet with a random placement model built in it such that each is placed into one of three variants (one control and two feature versions).

continues

COMPONENT	DESCRIPTION
TABLE 9.3 **Experiment Types and Their Components** *(continued)*	
Digital behavioral experiments are fully digital and completed in real-time with a random sample, but without any attitudinal data.	
Digital or in-person	This experiment is fully digital in a way that a user may not even know that they are a part of the test.
Real-time or retroactive	It is real-time such that users are actively engaging with the feature in their live experience.
Feature rollout system	This requires a feature flagging system where users will be greeted with different options.
Data infrastructure	This requires the ability to capture behavioral data.
Data science capability	The ability to manage all the behavioral data will require someone trained in data science.
Surveying capability	Not required for completion.
Participant pool	This group of product users is where participants are drawn from.
Fully retro experiments are digital, and the experimental groups are constructed using historical usage of a feature. Given the passive nature of the study, they can use only behavioral data.	
Digital or in-person	This is a digital experiment where all participants interact with the feature on a SaaS application.
Real-time or retroactive	Deployed on behaviors that already occurred and thus done retroactively.
Feature rollout system	The feature was rolled out to everyone, but not all users have engaged.
Data infrastructure	Behavioral data is tracked on users who engage with the feature, and metrics are created to align with the specific behaviors outlined in the user outcome connection.
Data science capability	Using the propensity score matching statistical technique, the study compares the feature users against a group of non-users who share similarities in all relevant metrics (for example, demographic characteristics, types of behavior on SaaS products, months of experience with the product). This enables an experiment in a completely retroactive sense.
Surveying capability	Since this is completely retroactive, no surveying occurs.
Participant pool	This study is completed on a random sample of current users.

COMPONENT	DESCRIPTION
Unmoderated scaled experiments are a collection of interviews completed through a platform that allows a user to respond to questions in an asynchronous manner.	
Digital or in-person	It is digital and hosted on an unmoderated interview platform such as userinterviews.com.
Real-time or retroactive	This is performed in real-time as people will be interacting with it in a live setting.
Feature rollout system	Run as two separate studies with one group, getting one version and the other the other version.
Data infrastructure	All data will be collected within the vendor platform system or homebrew solutions such as Google Forms.
Data science capability	The data created will not be highly technical, and therefore basic statistical tests should suffice for insights to be generated.
Surveying capability	Survey can be given to users after their engagement.
Participant pool	Recruited within whatever platform that the test is run.
Basic moderated experiments include physically showing prototypes to users and then actively collecting behavioral and attitudinal feedback, only hypothetical outcome metrics.	
Digital or in-person	Physical experiments done with users in the headquarters office.
Real-time or retroactive	This is performed in real-time as people will be interacting with it in a live setting.
Feature rollout system	Participants can interact with different types of prototypes.
Data infrastructure	A note taker is present in each interview to record how the participants interact with the feature. All data is collected through this note-taker.
Data science capability	Limited data science skills on the team limit the results to comparisons of averages and other basic descriptive analytics.
Surveying capability	Participants respond to a basic survey after the study.
Participant pool	Interviewees are chosen from a pool of users who responded to a random solicitation regarding the study.

Launching the Experiment

With your experimental setup meticulously planned and constructed, the stage is set for launching the experiment. The preparatory steps you've followed provide not just a roadmap for what needs to be done, but also a clear rationale for each chosen step. It's beneficial to document this process for future reference and for other team members. A comprehensive experiment launch plan, encompassing each of the seven components and detailing roles and responsibilities, is recommended. An example of such a plan is in the supplemental materials accompanying this book.

Launching an experiment involves meticulous program management, a topic that extends beyond the scope of this book. For those interested in delving deeper, resources like *The Experimentation Field Book* by Columbia Business School Publishing and materials from the Project Management Institute are invaluable. Within the context of this book, your execution strategy should focus on three key areas: securing stakeholder buy-in, ensuring accurate data collection and validation, and preparing contingency plans.

By now, you will have collaborated closely with your technical team for metric creation and experimental setup. Keeping them continuously informed about the experiment's progress is crucial. Additionally, any product or design changes necessitated by the experiment should be communicated to the respective teams, including any potential downstream impacts. Whether or not the experiment has an executive sponsor, this phase presents an excellent opportunity to pique the interest of leadership in the experiment and its possible outcomes. This is also a timely moment to involve any other potential stakeholders who may benefit from or contribute to the experiment's results.

Revisiting and validating the newly created metrics is an important step at this juncture. The reliability of the data collected during the experiment forms the foundation for the validity of your insights and the strength of the evidence supporting the connection between variables. Therefore, the higher the quality of the metrics, the more robust your findings will be. Implementing a monitoring system to keep track of the data throughout the experiment is best practice.

Preparing for unforeseen challenges is an integral part of any project. While it's impossible to anticipate every potential issue, having contingency plans for the most probable problems is essential. Critical considerations include plans for data flow interruptions and strategies for managing participant drop-outs or customer feedback related to new features being tested. By asking yourself relevant questions and crafting action plans for each scenario, you can preempt many common issues.

Generative AI (GenAI) in Practice

Trained on a large collection of human knowledge, GenAI can provide a list of potential challenges that an individual may face when accomplishing any sort of task. When building an experimental setup, these tools can provide assistance choosing the right methodology on top of highlighting potential areas of challenge. In this prompt, instructions are given to identify potential issues with the experimental design, and ChatGPT is able to offer a few potential concerns.

User Prompt

You are an expert in experimental design who commonly helps others plan out potential issues with their experiment and prepare contingency plans. Today you will help me with an experiment I am building.

I am launching a test of a new feature to a random collection of users and then finding a comparable group of users who won't get the feature to match them. I will collect behavioral data using my event data provider Segment and then send an in-product survey to users 1 minute after usage for the group that gets the feature and 15 minutes into usage for the group that doesn't.

Please share three potential issues that might arise in this design and what I should do to prevent them. Provide each issue in no more than one paragraph.

ChatGPT

Certainly, designing an experiment to test a new feature requires careful consideration to ensure that the results are reliable and valid. Here are three potential issues with the described experimental design and suggestions for prevention:

continues

Timing of Survey Deployment: Sending an in-product survey 1 minute after usage for the group that gets the feature and 15 minutes into usage for the group that doesn't could introduce bias based on the timing of feedback collection. Users' immediate reactions might differ significantly from their reflections after a longer period of use, affecting the comparability of responses between the two groups. Prevention: Standardize the timing of the survey deployment relative to the user experience with the feature. Either delay the survey for both groups to a time when users have had enough interaction to form a considered opinion or send it at the same short interval after exposure to the new feature for both groups.

Selection Bias in the Comparison Group: Randomly selecting users to receive the new feature and then finding a "comparable" group for the control might introduce selection bias, particularly if the comparability is based on criteria that do not fully account for factors influencing users' behavior or their reaction to the new feature. Prevention: Use a truly randomized control trial (RCT) where both the test and control groups are randomly assigned without any post-selection matching. This method ensures that both observed and unobserved variables are equally distributed across groups, minimizing selection bias.

Survey Response Bias: The act of responding to a survey, especially with different timings, might itself alter user behavior or perceptions. For example, receiving a survey could make a feature more salient to users or interrupt their natural usage patterns. Prevention: Minimize the intrusiveness of the survey by ensuring it is as unobtrusive as possible, and consider deploying it after a standardized usage period for both groups. Additionally, triangulate survey findings with passive behavioral data (e.g., usage metrics, engagement rates) to verify that survey responses align with actual behavior.

In each case, the goal is to ensure that any differences observed between the test and control groups can be confidently attributed to the new feature itself, rather than to extraneous variables or biases introduced by the experimental design.

As you proceed with the execution of the experiment, adhere to your plan but also maintain the flexibility to adapt as needed. When challenges arise, assess them quickly, devise solutions, and continue with the execution. Your goal is to complete the experiment with the highest quality data possible, as this will set a strong foundation for the subsequent analysis. The next chapter will delve into how to approach analyzing the data collected from your experiment, transforming it into powerful evidence to inform decision-making and future product development strategies.

Taking the Experimentation Leap

Setting up an experiment can be intimidating and even after completing this chapter, you may still feel lost as to where to start. The supplemental information, especially the template provided should offer you a strong foundation to build upon, but recognize that you are not alone. While some companies run hundreds of experiments a week, most are stuck in stagnation, running only a few a year. Building a true experimentation structure requires time, effort, and the confidence to go and do it. I see this difference in the companies that I work with when it comes to building out their first Feature Impact Analysis. Only the ones who have at least one stakeholder who wants to bring the vision to life are the ones who actually do.

One example of this is the company FocusMe, which runs a productivity application focused on assisting knowledge. Their powerful platform has a variety of science-backed tools that help their users get into focus mode, including the blocking of social media apps, a Pomodoro timer, among others. The founders are bought into the Impact Mindset, desiring not to just build something that people use but to create a solution to help people do their best work. With this passion, they sought out to run their first FIA, and together we set up a solid experiment.

Building on the science of establishing intentions to increase goal attainment, the FocusMe team created a feature that allowed users to establish intentions before going into a focus mode.[8] They hoped this would build a greater sense of motivation for users to get work done in their allotted time. To test this, they set out a FIA (**TABLE 9.4**) with the intent of validating that their new addition was

---

8 https://psycnet.apa.org/record/2007-19538-002

creating better outcomes for their users as measured by multiple factors. From a behavioral view, they hope they would see higher levels of focus as rated by their proprietary focus metric. When looking at attitudinal data, they hoped to see higher levels of productivity, commitment to focusing, and feelings of ability to finish work in the allotted time. Beyond their altruistic desires, the team hoped that their product would be retained for greater periods if they were successful in driving these user outcomes.

Although a new experience for the team, their passion for creating an impactful product drove them to continue pushing for the maximization of their feature's effectiveness. Together we determined what systems they had in place and what they could easily create. Their custom event tracking, product analytic software allowed for the creation of usage metrics and their model for the focus level metric was already in place. For surveying they were most comfortable with deploying a survey via email. All this data would then be analyzed by the core team who were comfortable with advanced statistical analysis. With this experiment setup, the FocusMe team was ready to deploy the study, generating raw data for analysis.

TABLE 9.4 FocusMe Experiment Component Descriptions

COMPONENT	DESCRIPTION
Digital or in-person	This is a completely digital experiment, with users not knowing they are participating in the experiment.
Real-time or retroactive	This is conducted in real-time soon after the feature is launched.
Feature rollout system	This is deployed as a 50/50 random split to users.
Data infrastructure	This is behavioral data captured by a custom event-capturing solution.
Data science capability	This is a traditional survey deployed via email to users.
Surveying capability	The team already had data science capabilities.
Participant pool	This is the users of the feature, as determined by those who set an intention during the setup of their focus plan.

CHAPTER RECAP

- **Creating a culture of experimentation:** Launching a FIA is the first step toward encouraging more tests to be done and increasing evidence-backed decision-making.

- **Trade-offs in applied research:** While the RCT is supreme in academia, the reality in an applied setting is that you must find the balance between rigor and actually getting the study done.

- **New ideal experiment:** Replacing the RCT, a new ideal setup is one where two similar groups are given separate experiences, and their behaviors and attitudes are compared.

- **Components of an experiment:** Two main questions need to be answered when setting up an experiment. Is it digital or in-person and real-time or retroactive? Additionally, there are five main components of the experiment that must be decided upon: feature rollout system, data infrastructure, data science capability, surveying capability; and participant pool?

- **Choosing the right setup:** It is up to the researcher to determine the level of evidence quality that is needed and whether it is possible to create that given the available resources.

- **Launching the experiment:** Before executing a study, it is important to think through potential roadblocks and establish contingency plans such that the study can go on.

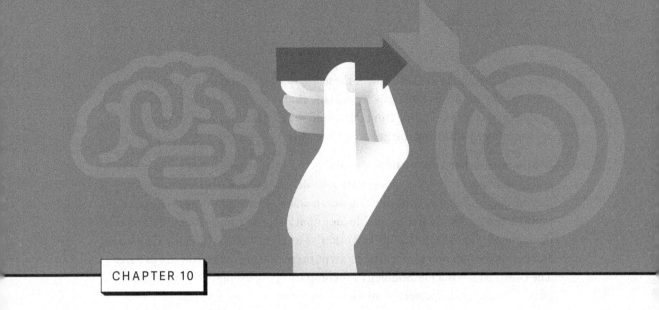

CHAPTER 10

Generating Insights from Experiment Data (FIA Step 4, Part 2)

A significant milestone in the Feature Impact Analysis (FIA) is the conclusion of the experiment. It marks a transition from the intricate task of establishing new technical capabilities and processes to the generation of meaningful insights and their effective dissemination. Armed with the raw data collected from the experiment, the focus shifts to converting this data into evidence that either validates or refutes the hypotheses formulated during the FIA's validate phase.

The potential for analysis stemming from any experiment is directly influenced by the nature of the data obtained through its design. Statistical analyses, inherently quantitative, necessitate data that quantifies variables of interest; the richness and scale of data determine the sophistication of analytical techniques that can be applied.

However, the practical execution of these analyses is bound by the expertise and capacity of the data analysis team. This chapter explores a spectrum of analytical methods, ranging from quantitative to qualitative, and examines their applicability in affirming the impact of a feature as intended.

Distinguishing between quantitative and qualitative analysis mirrors the differentiation in data types. Qualitative analysis delves into the realm of subjective perceptions and sentiments, offering depth and context rather than definitive proof. These methods are invaluable for unpacking the reasons behind observed phenomena. On the other hand, quantitative analysis deals with numerical data and definitive outcomes, essential for hypothesis testing in the context of FIA. The t-test, which is a methodology for comparing the averages of two groups, often emerges as the preferred method of analysis. It is powerful for its ability to provide a structured means to examine the relationship between variables within the user outcome connection framework.

Understanding Qualitative Analysis

For millennia, humans have thrived on stories, passing down narratives that bridge time and space. This innate inclination toward storytelling provides researchers with a potent tool for communication, transforming complex data into memorable and engaging narratives. When armed with rich qualitative data that encapsulates user behaviors and the reasoning behind them, researchers are poised to weave these disparate threads into a coherent story. Taking a narrative approach not only guides the audience through the data in a relatable manner but also helps embed the information in memory through vivid imagery and context.

Qualitative analysis opens a window into the minds of users, offering insights that transcend mere numerical data. Although it may not directly validate hypotheses or enumerate user facts, it unravels the nuanced layers of user experience—unearthing themes and patterns that remain obscured within quantitative confines. This form of analysis delves into the subjective realm, where the emphasis is on understanding the "why" behind user actions and sentiments rather than just the "what."

The subjective nature of qualitative data means that its analysis is not a one-size-fits-all endeavor. Thematic analysis stands out as a preferred method, wherein researchers dissect and digest verbal or written feedback into actionable insights. This process involves categorizing insights, identifying overarching themes, and pinpointing recurring patterns. Although seemingly straightforward, the depth of understanding derived from this analysis is directly proportional to the time and effort invested in looking beyond surface-level insights to grasp the underlying motives driving user sentiment.

Emerging from thematic analysis are mental models—comprehensive insights into how users perceive, interpret, and anticipate the world around them. These models, reflective of users' assumptions and expectations about a product, become invaluable resources for design and product teams. They guide the creation of solutions that resonate closely with user needs, thereby enhancing product development.

As researchers continue to collect data, qualitative analysis becomes increasingly rich, paving the way for constructing journey maps and personas.

A *persona* is a detailed description of a fictional target user's key traits. These documents embody a customer's characteristics, desires, actions, and expectations. Good personas place a person in the middle of a relevant context such that the product team can imagine how their solution would fit directly into that person's life. Teams can use personas to remind themselves of who they are building for and assist in properly recruiting an "ideal user" while conducting research.

A *journey map* is the other main output of qualitative analyses. If a persona is a single snapshot of a customer, a journey map is the series of actions the persona takes to solve a problem. Two types of journey maps can be constructed depending on where in the product development cycle a team finds itself. The first is a journey map describing what the person does in the current state without the addition of a company's solution. Think of this as the "natural state." It can also be the series of steps that a person takes while engaging with a company's offerings, which is the "product interaction state." Journey maps are useful for thinking through how to create a holistic experience, factoring in the state a person is bringing to a situation and the potential downstream impacts of a solution.

Turning Qualitative into Quantitative

Although qualitative analyses offer a rich tapestry of user experience and context, they often fall short of directly validating the connections within your user outcome connection. Their strength lies not in proving hypotheses with hard facts but in enriching our understanding of the environment in which a feature operates. However, there's a bridge between the qualitative and quantitative realms through content analysis. This process involves human or AI coders reviewing qualitative data and quantifying it by assigning scores based on pre-defined criteria.

Consider, for example, user feedback on a feature designed to enhance focus during work. This feedback could be systematically assessed by reviewers who score each piece of feedback on effectiveness, satisfaction, and the likelihood of future use on a scale from one to ten. Despite the subjective nature of this task, content analysis offers a structured approach to bring qualitative insights into the quantitative fold, enabling statistical analysis that can further validate hypotheses.

It's important to tread carefully when leaning on subjective data for quantita-tive analysis. The inherent biases in subjective assessments can pose threats to the validity of your findings. This step, while bridging gaps between qualitative understanding and quantitative validation, requires a mindful approach to ensure that the insights gained do not stray from objectivity and reliability.

Generative AI in Practice to Categorize Survey Data

Coding data at scale is a valuable use of ChatGPT. The following prompt pro-vides an example of giving ChatGPT a set of responses to a survey regarding a new workout feature. It uses a one-shot approach, since it gives the system one example to work with. This is just the beginning of what is possible, and a prompt can be enhanced by providing more context on the product, the survey, and the classifications.

User Prompt

You are an experienced coder of qualitative data, who has many times turned written feedback into classified categorical data. Today you are going to be assisting me and running a coding analysis on the following data. I will give you the raw responses and you will classify them into one of the following categories: "effective," "ineffective," and "unsure." Please respond only with the classification.

Examples of each are as follows:

"effective" = "Thrilled with the app's progress tracking, keeps me motivated!"

"ineffective" = "The subscription fee seems high for the value provided."

"unsure" = "Enjoy the flexibility of workouts, but the app sometimes lags."

1. "Love the personalized workout plans, definitely seeing results!"

2. "Frustrated by constant crashes in the middle of workouts."

3. "Wish there were more variety in the workout routines, feels repetitive."

4. "As a beginner, the instructional videos are clear and very helpful."

5. "Not sure if it's effective; been using it for weeks with little to no progress."

ChatGPT

effective

ineffective

ineffective

effective

unsure

Understanding Quantitative Analysis

Omitting the importance of qualitative analysis would be an oversight, given its crucial role in fostering a comprehensive insights ecosystem. However, within the confines of FIA, quantitative analysis takes center stage. It's this analytical approach that equips us with the means to definitively determine the existence of relationships within the user outcome connection. Recall the essence of a randomized control trial (RCT). It isolates a single variable in an otherwise uniform environment, comparing the outcomes of two groups subjected to a distinct change. Such comparisons are inherently quantitative, with methodologies that compare average differences across groups being commonly used, as they are respected in both academic and practical research spheres. The strength of quantitative analysis lies in its ability to reveal unequivocal differences between groups, providing a factual basis for observations.

Before delving deeper into quantitative methodologies, let's address a common challenge for product teams: the pursuit of statistical significance. Although achieving statistical significance—the probability that an observed effect is not due to chance—is a noble and often necessary goal in academia, it's not always imperative in applied research contexts. Statistical significance helps minimize the risk of being misled by data noise, but it doesn't inherently resolve all interpretative challenges, such as assessing how large the effect is or if it even matters to the greater context. The real-world impact of statistical findings is commonly called the *practical significance*.

To illustrate this, consider a hypothetical scenario involving a dating app testing a feature designed to enhance conversation starters. Suppose the analysis reveals a statistically significant increase in response rates for users employing the feature. Although initially promising, the practical significance may diminish if the effect size is minuscule, offering negligible real-life benefits to users. Moreover, if the feature, despite increasing initial responses, leads to superficial conversations or fewer in-person meetings, its practical value in achieving the desired outcome becomes negligible or even counterproductive.

Although statistical significance enriches the analysis with a degree of confidence, it's not the be-all and end-all. When feasible, pursuing statistical significance adds rigor to the research, but it's crucial not to overemphasize its importance. For a robust statistical analysis, a sample size of at least 30 participants per group is generally recommended to ensure sufficient statistical power. However, for any claims of a legitimate difference between groups without seeking statistical significance, a minimum of 10 participants per group is advisable to avoid mistaking mere noise for genuine effects.

Types of Data

The nature of data significantly influences the scope and depth of quantitative analysis possible in the context of the FIA. The characteristics of the data, including its size, type, and the quality of its organization and completeness, are critical factors determining the feasibility and complexity of the analyses that can be undertaken. To navigate the landscape of quantitative analysis, it's essential to understand the four primary categories of data. This foundational knowledge is pivotal in deciding which statistical techniques are applicable and beneficial. Although a deep dive into statistics is beyond this book's scope, a brief overview of common statistical methods is provided to arm you with the knowledge necessary for targeted discussions with data experts.

Nominal data (categorical data) categorizes data without a natural order or ranking among the categories. It classifies information into distinct categories that lack a natural order or hierarchy. Although such data can be used in statistical analyses, it necessitates specific approaches, primarily serving to determine group memberships. Categories such as gender, nationality, race, or living arrangements are examples where each category stands alone without any ranking.

Ordinal data organizes data with a clear order or ranking, but without consistent intervals between categories. A step above nominal data, ordinal data categorizes while introducing a clear order or ranking among the categories. However, the intervals between these ranks aren't uniform. Educational levels, satisfaction ratings, and disease severity stages are instances where a sequential order is evident, yet the distance between stages isn't equal or quantifiable.

Interval data scales data with meaningful intervals between values, but without a true zero point. It is numerical, where the sequence and the precise difference between values carry meaning. However, they lack a true zero, preventing the computation of ratios. Operations like addition and subtraction are valid, making interval data suitable for measuring temperatures or dates, where zero doesn't indicate an absence of the quantity.

Ratio data measures data with both a true zero point and equal intervals, allowing for a full range of mathematical operations. The most comprehensive data type, ratio data inherits interval data's properties with the addition of a true zero, enabling the calculation of differences and ratios. This data type is ideal for FIA, facilitating detailed comparisons between groups. Height, weight, age, and income are examples where zero signifies the absence of the quantity, providing a full spectrum of analysis possibilities.

Understanding these data types lays the groundwork for selecting appropriate statistical techniques, from basic t-tests to more complex analyses, depending on the data's nature and the analysis's goals. This section aims to equip you with the foundational knowledge to engage effectively with data professionals, ensuring that your discussions are informed and productive.

Understanding the characteristics of the data you've collected is a cornerstone in determining the suitable methodology for analysis in the FIA framework. Most behavioral data, in its initial form, is categorized as ratio data, making it highly suitable for sophisticated statistical analyses. For instance, consider a to-do tracker app. The number of tasks a user sets possesses a definitive zero point, and the increment between tasks is consistent, whether moving from one to two or six to seven tasks. This type of data allows for a broad range of analytical depth.

When categorizing tasks from a predefined set, this data typically falls under nominal data, useful for distinguishing between groups during deeper analysis. Surveys present a more complex scenario, offering data across all four categories and requiring nuanced interpretation. Many attitudinal questions yield ordinal data due to their subjective nature and the non-uniform intervals between responses. For example, a 2 out of 5 rating on usability may significantly differ in meaning from one respondent to another. Contrastingly, questions about concrete quantities or preferences can generate interval or ratio data, such as preferred vacation temperatures or average meeting durations.

A fundamental awareness of these data types allows you to better articulate your analytical needs to the data team, setting realistic expectations for the insights that can be derived. This chapter guides you through three analytical approaches applicable in a FIA: descriptive, inferential, and causal techniques. *Descriptive* methods provide an overview of your user groups, offering initial insights into a feature's impact. *Inferential* techniques delve deeper, testing whether observed effects in a sample are indicative of the larger user base, making them vital for hypothesis testing. *Causal* methods, the most advanced, pinpoint the specific reasons behind observed effects, offering precise understanding. Although other statistical methods exist for prediction and understanding, they fall beyond this book's scope. **TABLE 10.1** includes a description of these three most common approaches, along with the common tests used to present the results and the drawbacks of each.

TABLE 10.1 Three Most Common Technique Types for FIA			
TECHNIQUE TYPE	**DESCRIPTION**	**COMMON TESTS**	**DRAWBACKS**
Descriptive	Summarizes basic data features, highlighting patterns or trends without testing hypotheses	Mean Median Mode Variance Standard deviation Percentiles Quartiles	Cannot infer or predict beyond the data presented Does not establish causality
Inferential	Generalizes or predicts information from a set of collected data, testing hypotheses the team has created	t-test Chi-squared test Analysis of Variance (ANOVA)	Requires assumptions about data distribution Has potential for misinterpretation if the sample is not representative
Causal	Determines cause-and-effect relationships between variables, showing how changes in one affect another	Combined exact match Difference in differences (DiD) Regression discontinuity design (RDD)	Is often complex and resource-intensive Requires careful design to avoid confounding factors and ensure validity

Descriptive Techniques

Descriptive statistical methods are the foundational tools for data analysis, enabling you to condense and illustrate the essential attributes of a dataset succinctly. These methods help to transform voluminous data into comprehensible summaries, unveil patterns, and elucidate trends without extending into hypothesis testing. Descriptive statistics are particularly effective at organizing and presenting data, offering a snapshot of its characteristics and behaviors. For instance, in the context of e-commerce, these techniques convert the vast arrays of user interaction data into actionable insights.

Taking the example of time spent on a webpage, which is a critical metric for gauging user engagement, you can employ central tendency measures to uncover the typical duration of a visit. This includes calculating the mean (average time), median (middle value in an ordered list), and mode (most frequently occurring time). Imagine a scenario where users spend 55, 60, 65, 65, and 70 seconds on a particular page. Here, the mean time is 63 seconds, giving a general idea of visit length. The median, at 65 seconds, indicates that half the visits are shorter and half longer, offering a balanced view even in the presence of extreme values. The mode, also at 65 seconds, points out the most recurrent duration, suggesting a common engagement length.

Furthermore, measures of variability such as the range, variance, and standard deviation help assess the dispersion of visit times. The range, calculated by subtracting the shortest visit time (55 seconds) from the longest (70 seconds), provides a 15-second spread, revealing the extent of variation. Variance and standard deviation further detail how much individual visit times deviate from the average, offering insights into the consistency of user engagement.

Positional measures like percentiles and quartiles rank individual data points in the dataset, providing a clearer picture of distribution patterns. For example, the 25th percentile might show that 25 percent of visits are 60 seconds or shorter, highlighting quicker interactions. Quartiles divide the dataset into four equal parts, aiding in understanding whether visit durations are tightly clustered or spread out.

Correlation analysis, another facet of descriptive statistics, examines the relationship between two variables, such as webpage visit duration and customer satisfaction. If analysis shows a positive correlation, indicating that longer visits correlate with higher satisfaction, it suggests that more in-depth engagement with a page correlates with a more positive user experience.

These descriptive methods paint a detailed portrait of user interactions, laying the groundwork for deeper analysis. However, they are limited to describing the data at hand and do not infer causality or predict outcomes. To complement these insights, it's recommended to use descriptive statistics alongside inferential methods, ensuring a comprehensive understanding of the data before proceeding with further experimentation.

Inferential Techniques

Inferential statistics act as the bridge between the collection of data and the impactful decisions that shape product evolution. This analytical domain empowers researchers to extend insights derived from a subset of data to infer patterns, behaviors, and outcomes applicable to a broader user base. By leveraging sample data, inferential techniques facilitate hypothesis testing, prediction, and the estimation of true population parameters, offering a robust foundation for evidence-based decision-making.

Contrary to descriptive statistics, which aim to neatly summarize data characteristics through metrics like averages or distributions, inferential statistics delve deeper, probing the underlying relationships and causations that drive user interactions and business outcomes. These methods are pivotal in the FIA process, where the primary goal is to discern the actual impact of product features on user behavior and business metrics, transcending mere observations to uncover the statistical significance of findings.

Key inferential methodologies include hypothesis testing, confidence interval estimation, and regression analysis, among others. Each plays a vital role in validating assumptions, quantifying the strength of relationships, and predicting future trends based on current data. For instance, a t-test might be employed to compare the pre- and post-implementation effects of a new feature on user engagement, providing statistical evidence on its efficacy. Similarly, regression models could elucidate the degree to which various user actions contribute to overall satisfaction or conversion rates, guiding targeted improvements and innovations in the product.

In the realm of FIA, the application of inferential techniques is indispensable. It allows product teams to move beyond guesswork, grounding feature development and refinement in statistically validated insights. Whether assessing the impact of a user interface redesign on app engagement or evaluating the effectiveness of a recommendation algorithm in boosting sales, inferential statistics illuminate the path from data to actionable knowledge.

By adopting inferential techniques within the FIA framework, teams can confidently navigate the complex landscape of product development. This approach ensures that every feature addition, modification, or retirement is not just a stab in the dark but a calculated step toward enhancing user satisfaction, engagement, and, ultimately, business success.

Causal Techniques

Causal techniques represent the pinnacle of statistical analysis by providing a sophisticated framework that transcends mere description and inference. These methods allow you to not only characterize and infer from data but also decipher the intricate web of cause-and-effect relationships. Causal analysis is pivotal when the objective transcends understanding patterns and extends to unraveling the direct consequences of specific actions, interventions, or changes.

Crafting a causal narrative demands a more nuanced approach, often involving resource-intensive methodologies that hinge on deep expertise. Among these, three stand out for their ability to dissect the intricate cause-and-effect relationships within the user outcome connection: combined exact match, difference in the differences, and regression discontinuity design. Each offers unique insights that will be further illustrated through the following example of a hypothetical data pipeline company keen on evaluating the impact of a newly introduced user interface on integration implementation rates.

When pursuing a causal technique in FIA, the combined exact match is the most common technique, because it isolates the effect of a specific intervention by matching units (for example, individuals, companies) in treatment and control groups based on identical characteristics, except for the intervention. For our example data pipeline company that is rolling out a new user interface, this method could involve comparing users who have switched to the new interface with those who haven't, while ensuring both groups are identical in terms of usage patterns, industry, and size. By identifying pairs or groups with exact matches across these characteristics, the company can more accurately attribute differences in the number of connected integrations directly to the new interface, minimizing the influence of non-related, external factors, commonly called confounding variables.

Another technique, difference in differences (DiD), offers another causal inference approach, particularly useful for observational data over time. It compares the pre-and post-intervention changes in the outcome variable between a treatment group and a control group. Applying DiD, the example data pipeline company could compare the change in the number of connected integrations before and after introducing the new interface for users who adopted it (treatment) against those who continued with the old interface (control). This method helps in isolating the effect of the new interface by controlling for time-invariant unobserved heterogeneity and any trends affecting both groups equally.

A third valuable technique in causal analysis is regression discontinuity design (RDD), which identifies the causal effect of an intervention by assigning a cutoff or threshold for treatment assignment. For instance, the data pipeline company might introduce the new interface only to users above a certain threshold of data usage, assuming those with higher data usage are more likely to benefit from and use advanced features. By comparing users just above and just below the threshold, RDD can reveal the causal impact of the new interface on the number of connected integrations, assuming all other factors are held constant around the cutoff.

Each of these techniques—combined exact match, difference in differences, and regression discontinuity design—provides a unique lens through which to view and understand causal relationships, moving beyond mere associations or correlations. For the data pipeline company, employing these methods can unveil not just whether the new user interface is associated with higher levels of connected integrations but whether it directly causes this increase, a critical insight for strategic decision-making and future product development.

Choosing the Right Analysis

Selecting the appropriate analysis for your data involves a nuanced decision-making process that extends beyond simply matching data types to analytical methods. You should consider three main factors when choosing a methodology: the data you have collected, your team's resources and capacity, and the specific analytical needs of your project. This choice becomes even more critical in the context of a resource-limited organization, where the cost and complexity of certain analyses may outweigh their potential benefits. As the project lead, navigating these decisions is a key part of your role in fostering helping your team understand the importance of evidence-based decision-making, the foundational of an Impact Mindset culture shift.

Data—Start with a clear-eyed assessment of the data you have, setting realistic expectations for what can be achieved. The nature and quality of collected data fundamentally guide the choice of analytical techniques, impacting the depth and validity of insights derived.

Team capacity—Understanding the technical skills of your team members is next, recognizing their strengths and limitations in handling different types of analyses. The team's technical expertise and resource availability are crucial in determining the feasibility and scope of analysis that can be conducted.

Expectations—Equally important is gauging the level of analytic rigor required to meet or exceed stakeholder expectations without overextending your resources. Stakeholder expectations and the significance of the feature under study shape the analytical approach, balancing the need for rigor with practical constraints. This involves discerning which analyses are essential for validating your hypotheses and which might be deprioritized or simplified without compromising the integrity of your findings.

Ultimately, the choice of analysis reflects a strategic decision that aligns with both your project goals and the operational realities of your team. By thoughtfully navigating these considerations, you position yourself as a leader capable of guiding your team through the complexities of data analysis, ensuring that your efforts contribute meaningfully to the broader cultural shift toward impactful, data-informed decision-making.

The Data

Once the data is collected and formatted for analysis, the initial step is discerning the nature of each metric collected. Running elementary statistics on these metrics not only deepens the understanding of each variable but also verifies that their collection methodology hasn't introduced significant bias. With a foundational grasp of the data at hand, you and any team that is assisting you with the data analysis can assess the feasibility of conducting a t-test, a versatile and commonly used statistical method in FIA for hypothesis testing across various data types.

For data collected through qualitative methods, such as interviews, the scope of analysis may be limited to qualitative insights and basic quantitative descriptions. This limitation doesn't diminish the value of the data; rather, it necessitates a pragmatic approach to the insights it can provide. For example, correlating user satisfaction ratings with qualitative feedback can show how different aspects of a scheduling app meet user needs, suggesting potential areas for deeper investigation despite not conclusively validating a hypothesis.

Conversely, large datasets signal the opportunity for comprehensive quantitative analysis. Navigating big data can initially feel daunting due to its sheer volume, making manual review impractical. However, understanding basic descriptive statistics of the data you have collected sets the stage for more intricate analyses. This step is crucial for assessing data quality, including the presence of missing values or its distribution pattern, which influences the suitability of advanced statistical methods for causal inference.

The decision to employ sophisticated causal techniques hinges on their potential to yield highly valid insights. Such methods can definitively establish the existence of cause-and-effect relationships, significantly boosting confidence in the findings and informing user understanding and product development strategies. However, the resource-intensive nature of these analyses, both in terms of time and the learning curve for advanced methods, necessitates careful consideration. Just because the data supports the use of complex causal methods doesn't automatically make them the best choice for every situation.

Ultimately, selecting the right analytical approach involves balancing the depth and rigor of the analysis with the practical constraints and goals of your project. This critical decision-making process underscores your leadership in driving the Impact Mindset culture shift, guiding your team through the complexities of data analysis to achieve meaningful, data-informed outcomes.

The Team's Capabilities

In this complex dance of rigor and realism, possessing advanced data is only one part of the equation for successful analysis. Having a team equipped with both the time and the skills necessary to leverage this data effectively is crucial. Ideally, throughout your journey of metric development, a partnership with your data team would have been fostered, allowing for an understanding of their capabilities and available bandwidth. If such discussions have not occurred, it is imperative to initiate them, inquiring about your team's familiarity with conducting experimental analyses.

A foundational requirement for your team is the capacity to conduct basic statistical tests, such as t-tests or chi-squared analyses. Should your team lack these fundamental skills, it's crucial to consider whether they can acquire them, as these abilities are necessary to fostering an experimentation culture. When internal skill development is not feasible, software solutions such as IBM's

Statistical Package for Social Sciences (SPSS) and Stata are available. These tools, especially SPSS with its user-friendly graphical interface, enable individuals with a basic understanding of statistics to execute simple analyses, provided they select the appropriate method for their data.

As your team's proficiency in data analysis grows, so too will the demand for their expertise. Consequently, even if your team possesses the requisite skills, it's essential to confirm their availability to undertake the analysis within your timeline. This necessity underscores the importance of crafting a comprehensive launch plan for your FIA, as discussed in Chapter 13, ensuring alignment with partner teams' schedules. Often, the analytical phase is what prolongs the completion of FIA.

Understanding the tools your data team will employ in the analysis is also critical. This knowledge is crucial not only for replicating the analysis, should stakeholders request it, but also for recognizing potential limitations and how to navigate them. For instance, R, a powerful statistical programming language, may encounter difficulties with large datasets. Similarly, SPSS, while user-friendly, can lead to errors if users are not well-versed in selecting the appropriate statistical tests.

The Expectation

The final piece of determining the correct analysis is ensuring the results match the needs of the team. Even if you may have a highly effective team that has the bandwidth to support you in any fashion needed, you should determine if you need to utilize their full potential. The underlying question here is what level of fidelity do you need to gain the support of your team and for you to feel comfortable with releasing the results? The answers to these questions likely stem from your core stakeholders and the importance of the feature.

In general, the more technical the lead drivers of the study are, the higher the quality of the data and insights they will demand. Engineers and data scientists are likely going to appreciate statistically significant results. Meanwhile, designers and market analysts may be more open to simpler descriptive statistics. Assess the way that these groups communicate within themselves and the common metrics that they use to do so to determine what their expectations are, and then operate from that starting point. Similarly, think about what level of fidelity the team is likely to comprehend without too much time being spent explaining the study. The last thing you want to do is have an advanced study that ultimately detracts from the impact because no one wants to take the time to understand what was actually done.

I was a co-author on a paper that was published in *Nature Human Behavior.* Although the difference-in-difference model that was constructed for this paper was outstanding and yielded a highly valid outcome, it came with the condition that whenever the results were shared, a full explanation of the technique was required. In front of academic audiences, this was applauded; in front of product teams it would sometimes cause them to lose interest, even though the results were more powerful at confirming a relationship than a simple t-test would have been.

After formulating a baseline of expectations based on your understanding of the core stakeholders, the other element is the importance of the feature being assessed. For large-scale decisions that will impact millions of users, you will likely want to bring out the best analysis that you can form. An iterative test that will impact a prototype likely doesn't warrant an advanced statistical analysis. Matching the team is the most important factor, as every team has its own expectations and needs, but be sure to lean toward more advanced methods for those features that have a large audience or impact and opt for more agile methods for those that are less vital.

Considering the data available, the analytical team's resources and capabilities, and the expectations of your stakeholders is essential in choosing the right technique to turn your raw data into insight.

Expanding on the Analysis

Once you have completed a digital experiment complemented by a survey, you possess both behavioral and attitudinal data from both users and non-users. Running t-tests across these metrics enables you to identify statistically significant effects, providing solid evidence on the existence of connections within your user outcome connection. This achievement is commendable. However, there's room to broaden your analysis through complementary studies.

Adopting a mixed-methods approach, which integrates both qualitative and quantitative methods, enhances understanding. Although t-tests excel at comparing quantitative variables between user groups, they only hint at the specific outcomes' differences. Enriching this with qualitative analysis of open-ended feedback or detailed descriptive statistics paints a more comprehensive picture of the observed changes.

Before diving into your analysis, consider what additional studies could augment your approach and if other teams possess data that could enrich your narrative. For instance, insights from teams such as customer solutions, which ensure that users are getting the most value from the product, or themes from customer support interactions could offer valuable context. Reflect on any metrics that might further articulate the story you aim to convey through your analysis. It's beneficial to ponder this before and after completing your analysis, but doing so beforehand minimizes bias influenced by your initial findings.

Potential mixed-methods approaches include:

- Conducting a thematic analysis highlighting the main reasons users appreciate a feature, providing context to the positive effects identified through t-tests.

- Exploring correlations between two behavioral actions in an app, further elucidated by survey-derived attitudinal ratings on related user outcomes.

- Analyzing social media feedback from users in conjunction with their app usage patterns.

These approaches serve as starting points for incorporating qualitative data to augment your quantitative analysis, not just validating the user outcome connection but also creating excitement around measuring the impact of features.

Executing the Analysis

Once the preparatory stages are completed, including data consolidation and identification of the appropriate analysis method, the focus shifts to the practical execution of the analysis. This phase is about transforming planning into action, akin to adhering to a recipe while remaining open to adjusting as needed. As with the intricacies of conducting an experiment, the analysis phase is prone to unforeseen hurdles, ranging from data inconsistencies and shifting team priorities to unexpected feedback from stakeholders.

Facing these challenges necessitates a strategic pause to reassess the situation, considering the new dynamics of data availability, team capability, and stakeholder expectations. The absence of a one-size-fits-all solution places you, the project leader, in a decisive position to navigate these challenges effectively.

Adaptability becomes a key asset during this phase. It's about striking a balance between striving for empirical rigor and recognizing the pragmatic need to progress with the available resources and insights. However, it's crucial to maintain the integrity of the analysis, ensuring that the outcomes will withstand scrutiny and meet the anticipations of key stakeholders. This often involves tough decision-making, grounded in a thorough understanding of the impediments at hand and exploring all viable alternatives to surmount them.

Upon resolving the optimal course of action, it's imperative to realign the data team to the revised plan and communicate the rationale behind any significant changes to stakeholders. This ensures transparency and maintains trust in the process, illustrating your commitment to deriving meaningful insights despite the obstacles encountered.

Circling Back to the User Outcome Connection

After completing the analysis, it's time to revisit the hypotheses formulated in the second phase of FIA. Now equipped with sufficient data, you can evaluate the existence of relationships between the variables within your user outcome connection. This review can lead to three potential outcomes for each hypothesis: validation (confirming a relationship), refutation (disproving a connection), or the need for more information (suggesting mixed results and the necessity for additional exploration).

Armed with these insights, you're now prepared to update the user outcome connection. This updated version should serve as a guide for the product team, outlining the next steps based on empirical evidence. Before presenting this refined connection to your stakeholders, the last phase of the FIA awaits, focusing on translating these insights into actionable directives for your team. Chapter 11 is designed to transition these analytical findings into a strategy for fostering an Impact Mindset culture in your organization.

Determining the Effectiveness of Tasky

With metrics defined and ready to be collected for Tasky, the chatbot intended to help users begin using ChatGPT in their work, the next step was to design and execute the experiment. I was optimistic that measuring these metrics, and comparing them before and after a user's interaction with the chatbot, would reveal effects instrumental in deciding whether to scale it. Furthermore, given the emphasis on business outcomes, substantial insights were expected from surveys and interviews.

As this product was proactively built, experimentation occurred in real time, with data collection constrained by the platform I used. The infrastructure for attitudinal data collection was minimal, relying on a feedback form attached to the prototype for core metrics, including crucial business metrics. Usage data was tracked through the hosting platform. Without the capability for staggered feature releases, all participants engaged with a uniform experience. User recruitment was done by leveraging my personal and professional network, mainly through LinkedIn.

A target of at least 100 users marked the experiment's completion, with the hope that over 50 percent would report increased confidence in using generative AI in their workflows. On the business metrics front, the goal was for users to express willingness to spend a minimum of $5 monthly for such a product. Contingency planning addressed potential user recruitment challenges and technical issues within the chatbot experience, outlining strategies for mitigation.

I've detailed what I actually did given resource constraints, but let's explore the possibilities that would have existed had I had further access to more sophisticated data. In a fully resourced product development setting, detailed event data and chatbot conversation transcripts would provide richer attitudinal insights. Ideally, connections to downstream systems would reveal whether chatbot interactions genuinely altered task completion behaviors.

A more complex experiment would have compared my chatbot against a less effective variant and a control group receiving a less intricate solution such as a form to go through with similar instructions. Users, sourced through paid channels to ensure randomness, would be randomly assigned to these groups for a comparative analysis. Such a detailed study, necessitating greater resources, is warranted when more substantial investments are being contemplated.

After the Tasky chatbot's public launch, I observed considerable usage but minimal feedback, a challenge often faced in experimental research. Typically, I anticipate a 10 percent survey response rate; however, this experiment saw only a 5 percent response. Coupled with a data infrastructure ill-equipped to capture detailed event data, I navigated these constraints to extract meaningful insights from the available data, while also contemplating an optimal approach.

The data primarily consisted of usage metrics and a handful of survey responses. The usage data revealed high initial engagement with the chatbot, yet a notable drop-off before completion suggested the chatbot's value was unclear to users. The survey feedback mirrored this, with users finding the chatbot intriguing but unclear in purpose. The limited scope and depth of the data necessitated a qualitative analysis, concluding that further refinement was needed for the chatbot to effectively serve users.

In an ideal scenario, a more robust response rate would enable a t-test to compare the Tasky chatbot users against those using ChatGPT with a similar task, specifically aimed at integrating generative AI into their workflows. This analysis, feasible with the expected interval data from an expanded survey response, would focus on comparing the effectiveness ratings between the two user groups. A sufficiently large sample would likely reveal statistically significant differences, offering insights that, when combined with qualitative analysis, would clarify the comparative effectiveness of the Tasky chatbot against a known solution like ChatGPT.

CHAPTER RECAP

- **Qualitative analysis:** Used primarily to understand more about user's perceptions and expectations, these techniques provide complementary information to the FIA.

- **Quantiative analysis:** Focused on the measurement of characteristics about a group, these techniques are most useful for creating evidence to complete the FIA.

- **Types of data:** There are four types of data each that allow for different types of analyses to be conducted with them. Nominal data is best for categories, ordinal and interval data are useful in some statistical techniques, and ratio data is the best form for completing statistical techniques.

- **Different technique:** Three primary techniques were covered. *Descriptive*, which describes information about the groups; *inferential*, which depicts differences between groups; and *causal*, which identifies how changes to variables yield predictable outcomes.

- **Choosing the right technique:** Determining the best technique for a FIA depends on the data that was collected, the capabilities and bandwidth of the team, and what type of data is best suited for stakeholders.

CHAPTER 11

Actions Based on the FIA Results (FIA Step 5)

Consider a consumer application you've frequently used lately, perhaps related to well-being or entertainment. Think about one feature that you often engage with. Suppose the product team has completed their first Feature Impact Analysis (FIA) and found it successfully achieves its intended purpose. This insight might explain your frequent use; the feature effectively meets your needs. Reflect on how this revelation should influence the team's next steps. How might this knowledge shape your future interactions with the app?

Conversely, consider the outcome where the FIA reveals that the feature falls short. It fails to engender the desired behavioral change or, worse, prompts unintended behaviors unlinked to positive user outcomes. What actions should the team take considering these findings? Is the mere acquisition of these insights valuable, or does their true worth lie in the subsequent actions taken?

This chapter argues that actionable responses to FIA findings hold the key to unlocking their real value. It delves into the take action stage—the culmination of the FIA process. By its conclusion, you'll be equipped to convert insights from the experiment and analyze phase into compelling evidence. This evidence will validate or refute your initial hypotheses, guiding you to communicate your discoveries persuasively and motivate stakeholders to make informed decisions based on these insights.

Preparing for the Share-Out

Before you rush to broadcast your analysis findings, pause for strategic preparation. Although prompt dissemination is valuable, ensuring you possess the correct communication tools is paramount. No matter the outcome of the analysis, you are sure to have some who are excited and some who will challenge it, and surely a lot of questions. Crafting comprehensive materials in advance will help you steer the conversation effectively.

Consolidate your findings and related documents in a centralized digital workspace, leveraging your organization's suite of productivity tools such as Google Docs, Notion, or Coda. This centralized hub should offer easy access to all project stakeholders, facilitating swift retrieval of information to address any questions or feedback. This approach is not just about maintaining order; as is discussed later in the chapter, it's a project management strategy that promotes efficiency and responsiveness to stakeholder interactions, regardless of their nature.

Having organized your project's documentation, the focus shifts to the implications of your findings. Remember that the true measure of applied research lies in its ability to spur meaningful action. The insights from your FIA gain significance through the practical steps they prompt among your stakeholders. Therefore, interpret your feature's redefined purpose and the FIA outcomes to articulate clear recommendations. That is the entire point of the fifth and final stage of the FIA, take action, as shown in **TABLE 11.1**. Your guidance, informed by the evidence you have created, should illuminate the path forward, signaling whether and how a feature should be evolved or refined.

TABLE 11.1 Feature Impact Analysis, the Take Action Stage			
STEP	ACTION	PROCESS	OUTCOME
1	Define	Identify the specific behaviors that a feature alters to impact user and business outcomes.	Completed User Outcome Connection(s) for the feature
2	Validate	Validate User Outcome Connection assumptions and document evidence gaps.	Validated User Outcome Connection and hypotheses to be answered
3	Collect data	Scope metrics at each level of the success metric framework and determine how to collect.	Identified metrics and strategy for how each will be collected
4	Experiment and Analyze	Compare users versus non-users to generate data to support or deny hypotheses.	Determined whether a feature is creating its intended impact
5	Take Action	Share the results of the analysis and determine the next steps based on findings.	Identified next steps based on the results of an analysis

Determining Actions Based on the Findings

Recall where the FIA started—a User Outcome Connection was created during the define phase. This critical stage outlined a user outcome to be influenced, pinpointing specific behaviors the feature aimed to modify and business outcomes that would benefit from achieving the user outcome. In the validation phase, the assumptions between these variables were identified, and data was sought to determine how much evidence already existed to ensure a match. As a reminder, **FIGURE 11.1** shows three User Outcome Connection assumptions. Where evidence fell short, hypotheses were crafted, setting the stage for targeted research to bridge the gaps.

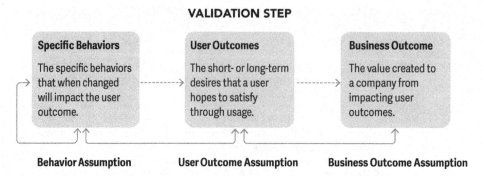

VALIDATION STEP

Specific Behaviors

The specific behaviors that when changed will impact the user outcome.

User Outcomes

The short- or long-term desires that a user hopes to satisfy through usage.

Business Outcome

The value created to a company from impacting user outcomes.

Behavior Assumption   User Outcome Assumption   Business Outcome Assumption

FIGURE 11.1 Three User Outcome Connection assumptions

With the experimental phase concluded, it's time to reassess every assumption under the lens of your newfound data, categorizing each hypothesis as:

- **Validated:** Data confirms a relationship exists between the variables.

- **Refuted:** Data indicates no discernible relationship.

- **Needs more information:** Experimental limitations or other factors render the evidence inconclusive.

Consider an app designed to deliver daily affirmations, hypothesized to prompt users toward gratitude breaks, enhancing happiness, and, consequently, retention. Upon analyzing existing data, the team confirms that heightened happiness correlates with increased retention. However, the effectiveness of daily affirmations in prompting gratitude breaks and boosting happiness remains untested. Thus, the team creates three hypotheses, two targeting behavioral changes and one assessing the impact on user outcomes.

Generating evidence to determine the effect of their platform, the team conducts a study sending daily affirmation notifications to a group of users and daily notifications with fun facts to another comparable group. For the specific behaviors, the team measures the screen time three minutes after the notification is sent and sends in-app surveys to ask about the sense of gratitude on the same day. Unfortunately, the team found that there was no difference in screen time between groups. Additionally, there is no difference in the gratitude-sharing ratings of the groups. But through this approach, the team identifies a connection between sharing gratitude and self-reported happiness in the app.

Looking at the three hypotheses, each has a different outcome:

- **Behavioral Assumption Hypothesis 1:** "Use of the daily affirmation feature will increase ratings of gratitude sharing."

  Refuted: Given that the best approach possible was taken—surveying users in-app on the same day of the alert, there was no noticeable difference between groups—the team can confidently say their feature is currently not increasing gratitude sharing.

- **Behavioral Assumption Hypothesis 2:** "Use of the daily affirmation feature will increase breaks from the user's phone."

  Needs more information: Due to the method used to gather behavioral data—the focus of three minutes of usage after the notification is sent—the team considers this hypothesis inconclusive. Users may see the alert, finish their task, and then log off their phone. Due to this and other similar situations, the team is not confident enough to thoroughly refute the hypothesis.

- **User Outcome Hypothesis 1:** "Increased sharing of gratitude increases self-reported happiness."

  Validated: The team confidently believes that when users increase their sharing of gratitude—as measured by the in-app survey—they also increase self-reported happiness. This outcome ensures the team continues building features that increase sharing of gratitude.

In this scenario, while the team validates the positive impact of gratitude on happiness, the current strategy to foster gratitude through affirmations proves ineffective. The next step involves reevaluating and refining the approach to fully realize a successful User Outcome Connection. The intrinsic value of these findings lies not merely in their academic interest but in the actionable insights they offer. Each outcome dictates a distinct course of action, guiding the team toward the most beneficial interventions. Consolidating these insights and aligning on recommended actions are preparatory steps for sharing the results broadly, ensuring readiness to engage a wider stakeholder audience.

Let's take a closer look at the three hypotheses.

Validated Hypotheses

When the evidence from your experiments confirms the hypotheses, indicating a clear relationship between the targeted variables, it's a significant win for the team. Such validation provides the assurance needed to scale the feature, understanding its direct benefit to both users and the business. The focus shifts toward leveraging these positive outcomes: amplifying their impact and ensuring they inform future product development.

The first action is to share the findings with the product team. In cases where all three assumptions in the User Outcome Connection are now validated, the team should rejoice in the accomplishment of building a successful product. Empowered by these findings, the team can invest in increasing usage, knowing that the feature will create a business impact. If there are still assumptions to be validated, then having partial success with one validated hypothesis should be used to make a case for further investment in validating the others or making the necessary changes to get to a completely validated User Outcome Connection.

The revelations do not stop with the product team; they hold substantial value for marketing and sales teams as well. Demonstrating the tangible benefits of a feature that is supported by hard data empowers these teams to communicate the product's value more effectively to potential customers. It's essential to go beyond simply presenting these findings; sharing the meticulous research process behind them enhances credibility. In the best case, they will become significant supporters and encourage further similar studies to be created. If your company has an insights team or a similarly market-focused team, they would also be a great stakeholder for positive impact outcomes.

Deepening the analysis, conducting a post-mortem review with the product and research teams can unearth the key drivers behind the feature's success. This understanding enables the identification of replicable elements that can inform the design and implementation of future features. For instance, discovering that a successful feature taps into the behavioral science principle of ownership bias offers a proven strategy for engaging users in subsequent projects.

Taking this a step further, the data can be sliced based on certain demographic and behavioral factors to move beyond averages and determine whether there are certain user groups that are benefiting the most from the feature. In these cases, there is an opportunity to begin targeting this feature toward similar users with a message that they are likely to experience increased benefits. By diving further into the results, there is also the potential that some user groups will be discovered to have a lesser effect; this presents the opportunity to take similar actions to a refuted hypothesis but only for the certain subgroups. This nuanced analysis lays the groundwork for personalizing the product experience, a strategy that will be explored further in Chapter 16.

Refuted Hypotheses

Discovering that a feature isn't achieving its intended impact is a natural, albeit challenging, aspect of the experimental process. This realization—rooted in a well-structured study—signals it's time to dissect the feature's shortcomings. It's crucial to discern whether the feature's premise is flawed, whether it needs refinement to fulfill its purpose, or whether it's misaligned with user needs to the extent that its continuation is questionable.

Initiating this introspective journey begins with a candid conversation with the owners of the feature. Although this might be a difficult discussion, it is best to let them know of the findings before they find out themselves. Approach this dialogue carefully, framing the findings not as failures but as stepping stones toward refinement and growth. Propose organizing a workshop to unravel the root causes of the feature's ineffectiveness, and brainstorm potential enhancements. The product and design community offers numerous methodologies for diagnosing and addressing such challenges, and although I will highlight a couple of my favorites, this list is by no means exhaustive.

When it comes to understanding why a feature is not creating the desired behavior or the behavior assumption, an examination of the design is required. As shown in **FIGURE 11.2**, the CREATE framework, developed by Steven Wendell in his book *Designing for Behavioral Change,* should be your go-to. This diagnostic tool dissects the user engagement process into a series of six checkpoints, identifying where users might disengage or fail to achieve the intended behavior. Users might not notice it, which would be a fault of the *cue*; they may not be able to take the action in the moment they are prompted, delineated by the *ability check*. Each step must be satisfied for someone to engage in a feature and to yield proper behavioral change.

FIGURE 11.2 The CREATE framework can be used to evaluate why a user isn't following through with a behavior. Credit to Stephen Wendel.

The CREATE framework is especially useful because once the team has determined the steps where users are getting lost, they have already identified clear directives for design improvements. It becomes a design question, but each step has a corresponding threshold to be met before a user can continue. For example, if a user is not engaging in a behavior because they don't feel they have the time to do it, the team can focus on choosing a better time or creating a sense of urgency.

Should the feature fail to impact user outcomes, the focus shifts to the solution's suitability. This demands more focus on the chosen solution than on the specific design. Using the Double Diamond Design process, as shown in **FIGURE 11.3**, is especially useful here. It encourages the team to reassess what they are trying to solve for their customers by understanding their problem and then scoping down the focus to what precisely a solution is attempting to do for them. When diagnosing why a feature doesn't change an outcome, the team should revisit what that specific problem is and why they believe the chosen approach should work. From there, new techniques can be tested according to the second diamond.

When a feature meets user outcomes without influencing business metrics, it's time to reassess the chosen business metrics and their connection to user satisfaction. A team can use a process like the double diamond to assess why they believe satisfying a problem will propel customers to increase their positive interactions with the company. They can also use a pricing tool such as Conjoint Analysis, which presents participants with multiple bundles of attributes, to determine what customers are willing to pay. Taking one of these approaches might reveal misaligned expectations about what benefits users are willing to support, suggesting a need to realign or redefine the metrics of success.

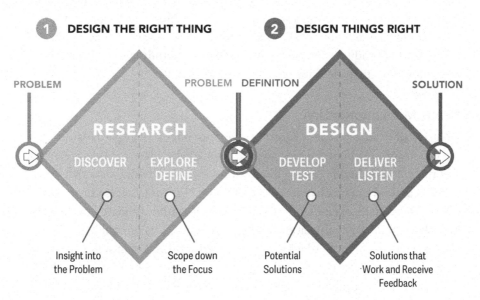

FIGURE 11.3 The Double Diamond Design approach consists of two primary phases, research and design.

Bringing to the table actionable recommendations in response to refuted hypotheses fosters a constructive dialogue, demonstrating the intrinsic value of the FIA. It's not just about identifying what's not working; it's about charting a course for improvement or reevaluation to unlock the feature's true potential. Along the way, you will be sure to uncover interesting insights about your users, which may point toward the need to update the User Outcome Connection.

As you continue to explore the feature's effectiveness, it also might point toward the reality that the feature is not having its intended effect and that updating it to do so would be a costly endeavor. All hope is not lost in these situations, as you have still identified that this feature likely contributed to feature bloat and that should begin discussing whether to deprecate the feature. All this points toward ways to use experiment results that may not be desired, positioning your research team at the center of an effort to better understand the product and its customers.

As the exploration progresses, it might become evident that adjusting the feature to meet its original goals is impractical. This insight, while disappointing, highlights the opportunity to address feature redundancy and contemplate its removal, thereby streamlining the product offering. It also addresses a common challenge faced by product teams: having too complex a product due to an abundance of features, commonly referred to as feature bloat. In essence, leveraging less-than-ideal outcomes as catalysts for advancement places the research team at the heart of product evolution, enhancing understanding of user interactions and guiding strategic decisions for the product's future.

Needs More Information

Occasionally, the outcomes of a study might not offer a clear path forward, leaving you uncertain about the next steps. This could be a late-breaking realization that the sample is highly biased, filled with skewed behavioral data that causes concern around too much noise, or other issues that compromise the reliability of the results. In most cases, you should choose to either validate or refute the hypothesis with the qualification of whatever concern you might have. This allows you to move forward with the suggested actions. Yet in some situations, it may be appropriate to classify the hypothesis as "needs more information," signaling a need for further investigation or a repeat of the study.

Addressing these concerns requires a methodical approach. For data collection issues, reassess and possibly redefine your metrics, improve data gathering methods, or identify corrective measures for the original concern. If the problem lies with the feature's definition, collaboratively reexamine and refine the User Outcome Connection. Should the overall experiment design be at fault, consider redesigning the study or acknowledge that available resources may be insufficient to generate insights that meet your ethical standard.

The decision to label a hypothesis as needing more information should not be taken lightly. While validating and refuting hypotheses create a potential for positive value generation, they can lead to the belief that resources were wasted. If you opt for this course, emphasize the learnings acquired during the process and how they inform future attempts to avoid similar pitfalls.

Reminder of a Complete User Outcome Connection

A User Outcome Connection reaches completion only when all underlying assumptions have been validated. This validation ensures confidence in the feature's ability to positively influence user behavior, thereby impacting the business. If the study results in a combination of validated and refuted hypotheses, achieving a completed User Outcome Connection necessitates at least one validated hypothesis for each assumption. The absence of this validation means you have generated valuable insights yet are still on the journey to a completed User Outcome Connection. Depending on your strategy, you may choose to share these preliminary findings or quickly pursue additional testing to address the gaps.

Building Your Feature Impact Analysis Report

By now, you've centralized all information regarding your experiment, encompassing its rationale, outcomes, and proposed next steps. The natural next step is to distill these insights into a comprehensive presentation or document, ready to communicate, or *share out,* your team's findings effectively to all pertinent stakeholders. Preparing this documentation in advance guarantees that as interest in your team's endeavors grows, you're well-equipped to engage anyone who might influence or benefit from the study's conclusions.

A presentation enables you to craft the narrative you aim to convey about your experiment. Echoing the earlier sentiment "applied research is only as valuable as the impact it creates," this presentation should not only detail the experiment but also, more crucially, bias toward action. Your goal isn't merely to report on an experiment but to catalyze a broader shift toward an Impact Mindset.

A compelling narrative around the Impact Mindset integrates themes explored throughout this book. It highlights the shortcomings of traditional measurement practices, underscores the significance of incorporating behavioral and user outcome metrics, and champions experimentation as the cornerstone of effective impact assessment. Furthermore, weaving this experiment into a broader strategic framework—which will be elaborated on in Chapter 13—enhances the narrative.

By embedding this storyline within your shareable content, you ensure the integrity of the message through the collected data. This approach is crucial for maintaining your team's pivotal role in this transformative journey and securing continued support for future initiatives. Position yourself as the leader of the Impact Mindset initiative or frame it within the context of fostering an evidence-based decision-making culture—or any other terminology that resonates with your audience. This presentation is more than a report; it's a manifesto for change, advocating for a new direction in how your team will perceive and act on research insights.

Structuring Your Share-Out

Crafting an influential narrative that fosters an Impact Mindset during your presentation involves several key components. Each of the following sections should be included to develop the most impactful readout, biasing the reader toward action while ensuring they have the background knowledge to do so confidently. You will find further insight on these sections in the template included as a complementary resource to this book.

Introducing the Impact Mindset: Begin by contextualizing the Impact Mindset philosophy, highlighting the pitfalls of over-relying on traditional metrics like usage and usability. Emphasize your initiative to pioneer metrics centered on behavioral changes and outcomes for users and the business, underscoring the shift toward a more nuanced understanding of feature impacts. This section should lay the groundwork for why experimentation empowers the development of more effective solutions that your team will be able to invest in confidently with knowledge it will positively impact the business.

Feature overview: Offer a concise overview of the feature in question, detailing prior research and evidence that suggest its potential impact on users and business outcomes. Introduce the User Outcome Connection framework and the level of validation for each assumption, setting the stage for the hypotheses evaluated in your study.

Experiment and analysis details: Share insights from your recent research, balancing detail with clarity to ensure comprehension without overwhelming the audience. The results should be shared from the study in a way that represents the outcome with enough context to guide readers on how people interpret it. Here is where the use of mixed-methods can be beneficial, creating both quantitative data to showcase what has happened and qualitative data to provide detail.

Results interpretation: Connect the dots between the experiment's outcomes and the User Outcome Connection framework, illustrating how the feature's role and effectiveness have evolved based on your study. Discuss the analysis of your hypotheses here, demonstrating how the research has refined your understanding.

Recommended next steps: The most critical section of the deck is the actionable recommendations derived from your study's insights. You want to ensure that everyone, whether they agree or not, develops an understanding of what you believe should be done based on the insights. Bolster your case with potential follow-up studies and workshops. Additionally, highlight opportunities to integrate new metrics into regular reporting and KPIs, weaving your efforts into the team's operational fabric.

Using your understanding of your organization, you can adopt these sections in addition to whatever else you believe your stakeholders will desire. The initial share-out you build should be built for all audiences, a go-to resource to share with anyone interested. Yet the data for each section should be presented three times at different scopes. Doing so ensures that readers of all types will find the level of detail they are looking for to gain buy-in.

Executive summary: Intended for the business audience and leadership who want to stay informed, this scope should be no more than three slides, and it should summarize the key points from all the sections above plus what you deem most important.

Main deck: Intended for the product team and any additional core stakeholders, this is the primary information as suggested above plus anything additional you believe your audience will want to know. You want to find the right level of detail here; this balance is unique to each culture but essential to creating a compelling narrative.

Appendix: Intended for other researchers and those who are especially skeptical, the appendix can include additional detail that you believe makes the case that your approach was the correct one and that the suggested next steps are the most valuable based on the insights the experiment created.

Increasing the Effectiveness of Your Share-Out

The effectiveness of your research presentation can determine whether your insights inspire action. These tips, distilled from your experience presenting to diverse audiences, are designed to maximize the impact of your share-out.

Tailor for different audiences: Adapt your presentation to match the specific audience you're addressing. This strategic approach significantly enhances the likelihood of your recommendations being implemented. Modern productivity tools, including AI assistants, can streamline the process of tailoring your presentations for different groups.

Incorporate existing research: Integrating findings from previous studies enriches your presentation. This demonstrates thoroughness, builds your credibility, and engages the original researchers, fostering a sense of collaboration and investment in your findings. Recognizing others' contributions can create a sense of shared ownership, making your insights more compelling.

Leverage proven frameworks: Use established presentation structures to create a coherent and persuasive narrative. The "What? So what? Now what?" framework effectively outlines the discovery, its implications, and actionable recommendations. Alternatively, the repetition in "What I'm going to tell you. Now I'm telling you. What I just told you" ensures your main messages are understood and remembered. Choose a framework that resonates with you and suits your data best.

Supplement with strategic communications: Extend your influence beyond the presentation itself by preparing accompanying communications. This approach primes your audience, setting the stage for how they should perceive and interpret your findings. Careful framing can significantly influence the reception and comprehension of your insights. Moreover, it makes it easy for viewers to identify the creators and offer feedback, fostering an environment of open dialogue and continuous improvement.

Sharing to Generate Action

With your compelling share-out in hand, the final task is devising a strategic plan for its distribution. The goal is to circulate the document as widely as is appropriate, ensuring recipients grasp its context and correctly interpret the findings. Develop a targeted strategy for where and how the document will be disseminated, tailoring your approach to each audience segment for maximum impact.

A direct presentation in a group setting is ideal for your primary stakeholders, allowing you to guide the narrative and address questions in real time. This interactive format ensures that your research's core message and implications are clearly understood. Reaching broader audiences where a live presentation isn't feasible requires them to comprehend your work within the correct context. Plan how to introduce each audience to your findings, determining which preparatory materials or communications will accompany the share-out to clarify its relevance and significance.

Consider diverse platforms for sharing your insights, such as inclusion in company-wide reports that summarize recent research activities or during periodic business reviews of the features analyzed in your FIA. But don't restrict dissemination to research-centric forums. Your findings likely intersect with various aspects of the organization, making them relevant across departments. The key is to bridge the connection between your insights and each department's specific interests or functions.

By thoughtfully planning the distribution and presentation of your share-out, you ensure that the right people receive your message in a context that resonates, increasing the likelihood of inspired action across the organization. Generating action from the FIA doesn't end with this single share-out. You should continue to think about how to spread the insights, progressing your organization toward an Impact Mindset. Central to this endeavor is the creation of what I call the "Insight Hub," an easily accessible repository for all generated evidence. Establishing such a hub will be detailed in Chapter 13.

Driving Action

Throughout this chapter we've covered various strategies to prompt action based on your research findings. This section encapsulates these strategies, emphasizing the significance of implementing both the novel metrics and the insights derived from your study. These recommendations should be prominently featured in your share-out, accompanying communications, and stakeholder discussions.

Emphasize novel metrics: Introducing new metrics based on your study offers fresh insights into feature performance, representing a significant advancement in the team's analytical capabilities. These innovations in measuring user behavior and outcomes deserve recognition for contributing to the team's growth. To maximize their utility, incorporate these metrics into existing dashboards and review processes, such as usage and satisfaction monitoring. Setting goals related to these new metrics and revisiting them in structured settings like sprint planning meetings can solidify their value and ensure ongoing attention.

Create actionable insights from the experiment: Beyond generating insights, the aim is to translate these findings into concrete actions. One approach, albeit demanding, involves assigning specific tasks to stakeholders, emphasizing the study's purpose to enlighten and enact tangible improvements. Whether it's applying insights from a successful feature elsewhere or discontinuing an ineffective one, the key message is that the research directs us toward definitive action.

As we wrap up the FIA, you're now armed with evidence-based insights to enact meaningful improvements—both to the focal feature and to the broader product strategy. Whether you've been following along with an actual feature in mind or you're imagining a hypothetical scenario, this process has prepared you for substantive, data-driven decision-making. If uncertainty about selecting the right feature for analysis has held you back, Chapter 12 addresses precisely this concern, guiding you toward initiating your own FIA with confidence.

Taking Action on Tasky

Given the lackluster feedback collection in the study I conducted on Tasky, I decided to classify my hypotheses as "need more information." Taking this approach was easier given that I had no team to report my finding to, but it also captures the reality of early product testing. The study setup was sound for the type of data I was attempting to create, but the lack of responses made the data collected too limited to make any strong decisions.

With this determination, I decided that further upgrades were in order before a full decision on whether to go forward was made. Taking this approach allows for the likelihood of creating a more captivating experience that would in turn generate higher usage and more intention to provide feedback by those users. The end goal would be to stick to a similar study but be able to generate enough feedback to properly classify the hypotheses as validated or refuted.

CHAPTER RECAP

- **Transforming insights into actions:** Emphasizes turning FIA results into actionable improvements for both product features and business outcomes.

- **Validating hypotheses:** Focuses on leveraging confirmed hypotheses to replicate success, guiding teams to scale impactful practices across product development.

- **Addressing refuted hypotheses:** Stresses the importance of diagnosing and addressing the root causes of disproven hypotheses, encouraging revisions or discontinuation of ineffective features.

- **Tailored sharing for impact:** Advocates for custom presentations to different stakeholders, ensuring insights lead to informed actions across the organization.

- **Novel metrics adoption:** Highlights the importance of integrating new user behavior and outcome metrics into team processes for deeper insights.

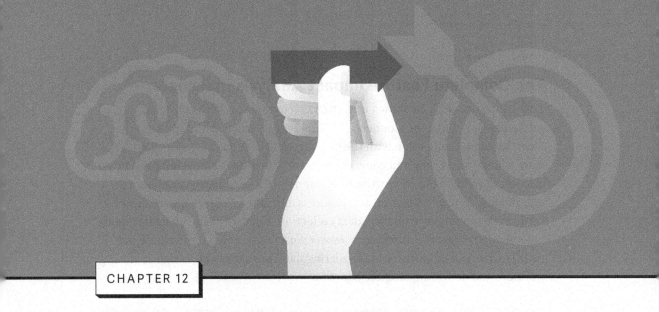

CHAPTER 12

Starting a Feature Impact Analysis Today

After familiarizing yourself with the intricacies of Chapters 5 through 11, you're well equipped to embark on your inaugural FIA. This journey empowers your team with invaluable insights and presents distinct challenges, each phase sharpening your evaluative acumen. In applied research aimed at enhancing your product's impact, the path to success is marked not by clearcut answers but by informed decisions, agility, and the readiness to adapt as new insights emerge.

As you stand on the threshold of initiating your FIA, the pivotal question often revolves around selecting the most suitable feature for analysis. Although you might already have a candidate in mind, and it could indeed be the optimal choice, a preliminary evaluation of potential features is advisable. This chapter delves into an overview of the FIA process and outlines a strategic approach for identifying the ideal feature to kickstart your FIA journey.

The Complete Feature Impact Analysis in Review

Embarking on a FIA, as shown in **TABLE 12.1**, commences with constructing a detailed User Outcome Connection. Your venture starts with filling out the User Outcome Connection with the best guesses that you can come up with from a literature review and conversations with the team. This is followed by an attempt to validate the connections between the three primary variables: specific behaviors, user outcomes, and business outcomes. When gaps are discovered in the supporting evidence, data collection is outlined, and an experiment is conducted to test the differences between users and non-users in these metrics. The journey culminates in translating data into actionable insights, closing the loop, and delivering tangible benefits.

TABLE 12.1 The Feature Impact Analysis Process

STEP	ACTION	PROCESS	OUTCOME
1	Define	Identify the specific behaviors that a feature alters to impact user and business outcomes.	Completed User Outcome Connection(s) for the feature
2	Validate	Validate User Outcome Connection assumptions and document evidence gaps.	Validated User Outcome Connection and hypotheses to be answered
3	Collect data	Scope metrics at each level of the success metric framework and determine how to collect.	Identified metrics and strategy for how each will be collected
4	Experiment and analyze	Compare users versus non-users to generate data to support or deny hypotheses.	Determined whether a feature is creating its intended impact
5	Take action	Share the results of the analysis and determine the next steps based on findings.	Identified next steps based on the results of an analysis

Walking through an end-to-end example based on an amalgamation of work completed, this entire process would go as follows for a team building a grant completion tool. First, the context: imagine a company that desires to construct an AI assistant that aids with establishing context regarding money grants and then uses that information to write tailored applications. Anticipating that this feature would enhance application quality and quantity, the team posits that streamlined content creation and enhanced personalization will foster user loyalty and promote organic growth.

Deciding to conduct their first FIA, the team began with creating a User Outcome Connection filled with the user outcomes of increased grant application output. They believe that the specific behaviors will decrease the time to complete a page of content and increase tailored responses; in return, they believe satisfying this outcome will yield loyal users who contribute to the organic spread of the product. From there, the team completes a review of all previous research along with the documents that contributed to the creation of the feature and finds little evidence to support a relationship between these variables.

Responding to this discovery, the team designs a digital experiment that classifies users as those who input at least three documents for their AI assistant to use in the personalization of content. Users of the product are bucketed into one group of 150 members, and then the averages of a few demographic factors, including gender, industry, and professional level, were calculated. A non-user group was then constructed to have similar averages within all the demographics of interest. From there, metrics for the specific behavior and user outcomes—which included both behavioral, as previously described, and attitudinal, as measured by a deployed survey—were compared using the appropriate type of t-test based on how the sample was developed, called the *pooled t-test*.

With raw insights, the team identified that they had created a functioning feature that changed behaviors as desired and impacted user outcomes. Subsequently, they ran a test to ensure that user outcome changes did impact retention and were pleased to find that they did. Armed with these revelations, the team presents their findings across the organization, starting with product development and extending to marketing teams, illustrating the FIA's role in fostering an evidence-based approach to product innovation. In these presentations, this work not only validates the feature's success but also sets a precedent for adopting a data-driven mindset company-wide.

You Are Ready to Launch

In Chapter 9, we explored the ideal scenario for a digital experiment: deploying a feature to a random subset of users while withholding it from a similar group for comparison. This setup allows for the collection of behavioral data and the deployment of surveys directly within the product. The team can conduct their own inferential statistics to determine if there is a statistically significant effect. This ideal model is proposed as an alternative to the more traditional, academically inclined randomized control trials, serving as a benchmark rather than a prerequisite for undertaking a FIA. It is not intended to prevent anyone from moving forward if they don't meet all components.

You don't need to wait for the perfect conditions to start your FIA. Consider a hypothetical company lacking all the essential tools for experimentation—no data collection systems, survey tools, or analysis capabilities. Even in such bare-bones conditions, initiating the development and validation of user outcome connections is possible, setting the groundwork for the initial phases of the FIA. These early efforts can effectively argue for the necessary investments in experimentation infrastructure.

With even minimal resources for qualitative or elementary quantitative research, insights can be garnered to advocate for further investment in experimental capabilities. Although these conditions might not support completing the User Outcome Connection in its entirety, they represent strides toward that objective. The aim is to gradually equip the team with the means to execute experiments in the envisioned ideal setup.

If you're debating whether to start now with what you have or wait for more sophisticated tools, the advice is typically to begin with your current resources. Any effort, if it transparently acknowledges its assumptions and constraints, contributes valuable insights to the team. The exception might be if an imminent upgrade in capabilities is expected, such as the near completion of a behavioral data capture system by the data science team, which would significantly enhance your experimentation framework.

Creating momentum, you are getting the team to move toward a desired future of generating evidence that will then be used to make informed decisions. Your main goal is to get something moving and then ensure all actions are plotted into a larger strategy that is communicated to all interested parties. Chapter 13 will delve deeper into creating a cohesive roadmap to ensure alignment of various initiatives toward fostering an Impact Mindset. For now, any effort toward building projects supporting this mindset is progress, moving your team closer to developing more impactful products.

Factors to Consider When Choosing a Feature

Feature selection is essential, especially for your team's first FIA. It can as easily create undue challenges as set up your team for an easier experience. Before you jump into the first feature that is pitched or even one that feels right, evaluate as many options as possible to identify trade-offs that might come from each. Taking this approach yields insights into your team's experimentation mindset and clarifies key considerations for feature selection. There are four primary factors to consider when choosing the first feature for your FIA, as shown in **TABLE 12.2**.

TABLE 12.2 First Feature Decision Factors

FACTOR	DESCRIPTION
Feature importance	How connected is the feature to the core value proposition of the product?
Team	How bought-in is the feature team to the idea of an experiment?
Timing	Where in the product development cycle is the feature, and has the team undergone any recent significant changes?
Executive stakeholder visibility	How much attention are senior leaders giving to the feature?

As suggested in Chapter 5, the first question that should be asked about a feature when determining if it is a good candidate for FIA is whether it is a defining feature of the product. It is recommended that the feature be an essential part of a greater product rather than a standalone solution. This equates to features that make a product stand out or provide real value to users. Think about those features that connect most closely to your company's mission statement and what would drive the product to be closer to fulfilling it. This is compared to generic functionalities that are standard across similar products, such as admin panels in SaaS products or hamburger menus in mobile apps.

One framework that began to gain traction in the early 2020s and is helpful in identifying the feature of most importance or unique value to your customer is the identification of the "aha moment."[1] Defined slightly differently by various groups, at its core it's when a user understands how the product will help them

---

[1] "How to Identify Your Product's Aha Moment," by ProductLed https://productled.com/blog/how-to-identify-your-products-aha-moment

or the value they will get using it. For a ride-sharing application such as Uber, the aha moment for a rider would be the first time a car arrives to pick them up after they clicked the button to hail a ride. In an expense tracking application, it is the first time a user scans a receipt, and it automatically uploads the content. These moments underscore the product's capability to meet user needs.

Understanding the aha moment aids you in identifying essential features that facilitate this realization. Again, for the ride-sharing app, these necessary elements include the feature that enables the car to be called, the feature that displays the ride, and the feature that locates the user's car on the maps and estimates their remaining before arrival. Each of these features is core to the primary value offered by the product and is an outstanding place to begin contemplating a FIA.

As will be touched upon with all the factors that go into choosing a feature, you should find the right balance of importance but also those that do not have too much riding on them already. Especially for your first FIA, opt for a feature that excites the team and promises valuable insights yet isn't overshadowed by marketing campaigns, tight deadlines, or complex existing processes. Aim for a grassroots approach, selecting fertile ground for growth and dissemination of findings rather than immediately targeting the most prominent feature.

From there, three additional factors are essential to the assessment you conduct with each feature for which you are contemplating conducting a FIA. The first is the level of buy-in that the team has expressed. Next is where the feature is in the development cycle, the timing. The final factor is how visible the feature is to executive stakeholders and those who need additional funding.

Feature Team's Perspective and Structure

Gathering initial information for filling in a User Outcome Connection is crucial in laying a solid foundation for a FIA. This task can range from being straightforward and enjoyable, offering a chance to revisit the rationale behind a feature's design and development, to being arduous and emotionally taxing. The variance in this experience often hinges on the product team's level of engagement and willingness to participate in the study. Teams may range from supportive to indifferent or even opposed, significantly influencing the required effort.

Your goal should be to identify a feature backed by a team that is either supportive of or neutral toward the FIA. Opting for a feature with a hesitant team is advisable only as a last resort or when other compelling reasons outweigh the potential challenges. Engaging with less enthusiastic or neutral teams necessitates additional effort in conducting the FIA and fostering supportive relationships. The challenge lies in not only delivering a meaningful study but also building rapport with stakeholders to ensure they are receptive to the findings and recommendations.

Another critical consideration is the team's operational tempo. Teams that progress too rapidly might have shifted focus away from the feature under study by the time the FIA concludes, mainly if developing new metrics introduces significant delays. Conversely, teams operating too sluggishly could excessively prolong the analysis, undermining its potential impact. Ideally, you want to collaborate with a team that strikes a balance: agile enough to avoid becoming a bottleneck in gathering foundational information but patient enough to allow for a thorough and impactful study.

Phase of Product Development

The timing of a feature's inclusion in a FIA is critical. It can be dissected into two main elements: the product development phase and alignment with significant company goals. Understanding where a feature sits within its lifecycle is essential, and for simplicity, this can be categorized into four stages: pre-design, design, development, and post-launch, as shown in **FIGURE 12.1**. Each stage of carrying an idea—from an opportunity to solve a user's problem through deploying a feature built around a solution—presents unique opportunities and challenges for the team, necessitating careful consideration and balancing what's achievable.

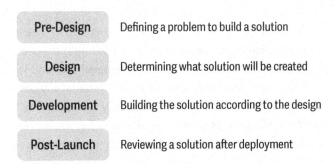

FIGURE 12.1 Four product development steps in the framing of solution identification and creation

Engaging with a feature in the pre-design phase offers unparalleled potential to shape and significantly influence its final form. However, this stage requires a forward-looking FIA approach, which might be feasible for only some organizations, particularly those with established experimentation practices. Initiating a User Outcome Connection during the pre-design and proceeding into the design phase ensures that the feature's intentions are clearly aligned before development begins. Although this represents an ideal scenario, achieving it is often challenging due to ongoing foundational research. Chapter 13 will delve deeper into the proactive execution of a FIA.

In many instances, FIAs commence during the development or after the launch of a feature. Conducting a FIA during development offers a proactive yet constrained opportunity, as the feature's blueprint is mostly established. This timing permits the simultaneous creation of new metrics as the feature rolls out, integrating them into launch KPIs and directly linking them to critical product decisions.

Alternatively, when the FIA is done on a launched feature, it is a retroactive study. As has been discussed, this allows for much more leeway regarding the time taken and the data available. Conducting the studies in a retroactive function also allows for using pre-collective data and statistical techniques to create mock experimental setups. All this freedom is why it is suggested that most teams start with this setup style.

Beyond development phases, the overall timing within the organization plays a pivotal role. Leadership-driven initiatives can significantly sway the FIA's feasibility. For instance, a corporate push for enhanced experimentation or broader success metrics could increase resource allocation to your FIA. Similarly, periods of process auditing present opportunities to propose the Impact Mindset as a fresh strategy.

However, not all initiatives are conducive to launching a FIA. The close of financial quarters or performance evaluation periods might deter the introduction of new metrics due to concerns over their manageability and impact on performance evaluations. Similarly, data collection and privacy concerns may run counter to any effort to fill out new metrics. Any restructuring can open the opportunity for new changes to be made, but ideally, you will have laid the groundwork of conducting your first FIA before the change began.

Ultimately, the most favorable scenario for a FIA is to engage with a feature from its inception, maintaining involvement through its launch and integrating outcomes into success metrics. This approach allows for the most opportunity to influence underlying beliefs around the purpose of the feature and connects to broader product measurement practice changes. Doing so is ideally done within a stable organizational climate with no recent upheavals.

Visibility to Senior Stakeholders

The visibility and engagement of senior leadership constitute the final crucial factor in selecting a feature for your FIA. Although previous considerations significantly influence this aspect, certain features inherently draw leadership's attention, due to either their enthusiasm for the idea or its potential impact on the business. Features that garner significant interest from stakeholders are prime candidates for analysis. However, it's essential to discern the root of this interest. If a feature is deemed too critical, it may warrant a pause, as heightened scrutiny could impose tight deadlines, potentially constraining the FIA's scope. Striking the right balance is key.

In cases where stakeholder interest isn't directly apparent, identify features that could influence key performance indicators (KPIs) prioritized by leadership. Such features are more likely to secure support, as they align with business outcomes critical to the company's success. By ensuring these outcomes are integral to your User Outcome Connection, you link your FIA directly to areas where leadership is already inclined to allocate resources.

Embarking on your first FIA entails navigating a complex landscape. You aim to showcase this endeavor as a blueprint for future initiatives, ensuring it's feasible within a manageable timeframe. Starting with features that resonate with the product's core mission sets a strong foundation. This should be balanced with the team's commitment to the FIA's potential impact and timed to align with organizational dynamics to foster success. Lastly, understanding and incorporating senior leadership's focus into your feature selection ensures that your FIA not only yields significant insights but also champions the adoption of an Impact Mindset across the organization. Evaluating these four dimensions—feature importance, team, timing, and executive stakeholder visibility—positions you to select a feature that promises meaningful outcomes and fosters a culture of evidence-based decision-making.

The Process of Selecting a Feature

When it comes time to sift through potential features for your inaugural FIA, specific options will naturally emerge as front-runners. Each option will bring its own set of resources and unique challenges. Your task is to navigate these waters, balancing the importance of each feature—which likely promises more support but also increased pressure—against the practicalities of executing the project.

A structured approach to this decision-making process is advisable. I recommend creating a comparison table incorporating the previously outlined key factors: feature importance, team engagement, development phase, and visibility to senior stakeholders. Additionally, based on these factors, three specific callouts should be included: potential impact, available team resources, and any unique constraints. This structured comparison facilitates a holistic view, aiding in an informed decision-making process. **TABLE 12.3** illustrates such a table based on our discussions of FocusMe in Chapter 9.

TABLE 12.3 Comparison of the Primary Factors in Choosing a Feature			
	FOCUS PLAN	FOCUS SCORE	INTENTION-SETTING
Feature importance	Flagship feature	New feature	New feature
Team engagement	Interested	Very interested	Very interested
Development phase	Post-launch	Design	Development
Senior leadership visibility	Equal given the size of a company		
Potential impact	Medium	High	High
Available team resources	Medium	High	High
Unique constraints	None	None	None

FocusMe, dedicated to enhancing workplace focus, faced a choice among their established plan feature, a newly developed focus score, and an intention-setting feature grounded in behavioral science. To choose the feature, a review of each, along with the crafting of a comparison table to assist with the decision, was performed. The established plan feature, closely tied to the company's mission, was already launched, making any FIA here retroactive. Despite its proven positive impact on users, its established status and existing data lessened the appeal for further exploration.

Both the focus metric and the intention-setting feature had not been launched yet, and they were both highly visible to the founding team. The founders were excited to conduct a FIA but were more willing to invest in something that was focused on their new features.

The primary plan feature posed limitations due to its integral role in the product, precluding the option of disabling it for a test group. This issue was not present for the newer features, which could be assessed through A/B testing. With equal resources allocated to each feature but heightened founder interest in the newer additions, the decision narrowed.

Although the primary plan feature had demonstrated user benefits, the novelty and potential insights were greater with the new features. The focus score, though pervasive and significant, was tied to a complex model, suggesting that insights could be multi-factorial and less direct. The intention-setting feature, by contrast, offered a focused opportunity for a compelling, evidence-based marketing narrative.

A comparison table was created, and a trade-off discussion was held. The core focus plan feature was quickly decided to be set in the backlog, as there was more potential for the new features to be successful. Although the focus score feature had the greatest potential if shown working, it was also a multi-step feature that was based on a novel model. Thus, any insight created could be due to many factors and less immediately actionable. While the team knew that it would be important to do a FIA for this feature, we ultimately decided that the intention-setting feature was the best for their first experiments of this kind. The impact of an evidence-backed marketing story around this feature would be ideal.

This process exemplifies a comprehensive approach to selecting a feature for a FIA: dissecting core variables, weighing them against one another, and ultimately choosing based on a balance between potential impact and project feasibility. The responsibility of making the final call rests with the FIA lead, guided by a strategic evaluation of impact versus practical execution considerations.

Additional Tips

As we wrap up the concluding chapter of Part 2, I'd like to share additional insights drawn from my experiences in deploying FIAs.

Communication is fundamental: The essence of conducting a FIA transcends mere testing; it heralds a shift toward an impact-focused mindset. Achieving this paradigm shift hinges on your ability to engage stakeholders effectively, encouraging them to embrace and act on the insights derived. Paramount to this endeavor is maintaining transparent communication with key stakeholders right from the FIA's inception. Regular updates, ideally weekly, should be communicated to your immediate team. Furthermore, ensuring that those poised to receive the results are well informed and that any arising concerns are promptly addressed is crucial. Being prepared with easily shareable materials for newly interested parties is also vital.

Manage overwhelm: Delving into the depths of FIAs, it's natural to feel daunted, particularly in environments with nascent experimentation cultures. The prospect of building numerous components for an optimal experimental setup can seem daunting. However, it's crucial not to let the ideal vision of future experiments deter you from starting with what you have now. Set achievable goals for yourself and your collaborators and focus on executing them. There will always be opportunities to enhance your testing infrastructure and refine your methodologies. For now, the priority is to initiate the process, leveraging initial findings to foster a culture of continuous experimentation and improvement.

Leverage other researchers: In many organizations, a diverse array of professionals is tasked with generating insights, including user research, data science, and market insights teams. These individuals are instrumental in informing product development to ensure both efficacy and profitability. Depending on your approach, these groups might view your FIA efforts as either a valuable partnership or potential competition. This underscores the importance of communication once again. Your goal should be to demonstrate how your FIA complements their ongoing work, thereby transforming potential rivals into allies. Collaborating with other researchers can open new avenues for problem-solving and enrich your analysis with a broader spectrum of insights.

Embrace a mixed-methods approach: Augmenting your quantitative FIA findings with qualitative insights is crucial. Whenever possible, integrate observations, user interviews, or open-ended survey responses into your analysis. This combination not only enriches your understanding of the data but also provides a more nuanced view of how and why features affect user behavior and outcomes. Qualitative insights offer compelling narratives that resonate with stakeholders and can bridge gaps in quantitative data, facilitating a more comprehensive and relatable presentation of your findings. By employing a mixed-methods approach, you make your work more accessible and relevant to a broader audience, encouraging cross-disciplinary engagement and collaboration.

Maintain an impact-oriented perspective: The goal of any FIA should be to ascertain the tangible impact your work will have on stakeholders and the product itself. From the outset, focus on identifying the potential actions and decisions that your analysis will inform. This impact-driven approach ensures that your FIA is not just an academic exercise but a strategic tool that drives product improvement and innovation. Celebrate incremental achievements throughout the process and share preliminary insights to generate interest and maintain stakeholder engagement. By consistently highlighting the real-world relevance of your findings and framing your analysis around its implications, you'll not only foster a sense of anticipation but also underline the value of adopting an evidence-based approach to product development.

By adhering to these guidelines—prioritizing communication, setting realistic goals, and collaborating with fellow researchers—you can navigate the complexities of initiating and conducting effective FIAs, paving the way for a more data-driven and impact-oriented product development culture.

CHAPTER RECAP

- **Complete Feature Impact Analysis review:** A reminder of the complete Feature Impact Analysis process encapsulated the five-phase process that focuses on completing a User Outcome Connection.

- **Factors for choosing the first feature:** The four primary factors to consider when determining which feature you should conduct a Feature Impact Analysis on are the feature's importance, the team's buy-in, the timing of development, and the visibility by senior leadership.

- **Specific considerations for each feature:** Based on the four factors, three primary considerations must be determined for each feature: the potential impact that can be created by conducting the FIA, the resources available, and any unique constraints.

- **Process for selecting the first feature:** A comparison table should be created with any contending features to determine the best feature on which to start a Feature Impact Analysis.

- **Additional tips:** A collection of tips was offered to help with finding success when starting your first Feature Impact Analysis, including communication, managing overwhelm, leveraging other researchers, taking a mixed-methods approach, and staying impact-oriented.

PART 3

EXPANDING FROM A SINGLE PROJECT TO A PHILOSOPHY CHANGE

With the foundational groundwork laid through your engagement with the initial features and the Feature Impact Analysis (FIA), you are now strategically poised to launch your inaugural experiment. For some of you, the instructions from Part 2 will be sufficient to launch the first phases of the FIA immediately. If so, do it; then circle back to Part 3! However, for those in larger organizations, garnering the necessary resources and organizational buy-in might entail a more detailed project plan.

Regardless of your situation, the essence of the FIA is to catalyze the adoption of an Impact Mindset across your company. This endeavor extends beyond simply repeating the analysis; it involves cultivating a culture grounded in evidence-based decision-making. Creating such an environment requires a path to get from where you are today to that ideal future, including finding a home for all the insights generated from your analyses that are easily accessible by all product team members.

Part 3 of this book is structured as a guide to building out the components of the Impact Mindset. It starts by introducing the concept of an "Insights Hub," which you can consider the home for all the efforts associated with completing the FIA and adopting the Impact Mindset. Then, you are introduced to the concept of a strategic roadmap to assist with the project planning of the culture shift and its three main components: systems, people, and vision. The goal is to craft a vision of embracing an Impact Mindset that aligns your team's efforts, identifies potential barriers, and outlines the necessary project management strategies to achieve your objectives.

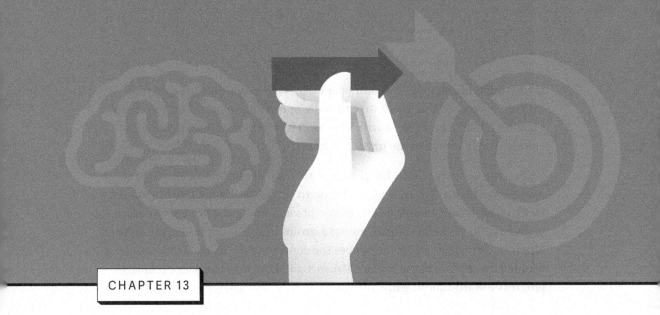

CHAPTER 13

Establishing a Path to the Impact Mindset Future

O nce a FIA is complete and its findings are documented, the real challenge begins: ensuring these insights catalyze continuous improvement rather than gathering digital dust in forgotten archives. The dynamic nature of digital products demands that insights from one FIA inform not just the immediate feature adjustments but also future iterations and related features across the product ecosystem. To anchor these insights into the daily rhythm of product development, I advocate for the creation of a centralized Insights Hub. This is the final piece of building an Impact Mindset culture shift.

This dedicated repository serves as a collective brain, archiving the wisdom from completed FIAs and making it accessible and actionable. As more FIAs are performed, the hub becomes richer, transforming into a robust decision-support tool that continuously feeds into the product development process. This ensures that every team member—from product designers to marketing professionals—has immediate access to a wealth of user-driven insights. By embedding this hub within the operational workflows, you create a feedback loop where past learnings inform future innovations, fostering a culture deeply rooted in the Impact Mindset.

Embracing this centralized Insights Hub not only streamlines knowledge management but also positions your team to act on the cumulative learning of all FIAs, ensuring that insights translate into action. It provides a single place to serve as the home base for all efforts surrounding the adoption of the Impact Mindset. This chapter first introduces the concept of the insights followed by a detailed description of the Impact Mindset and how to assess your company's progress toward adopting it.

Activating Research for Impact

At its best, research acts as a guiding beacon, illuminating the path through the complex landscape of product development. To fulfill this vital role, research must not only be conducted rigorously but also be actively integrated into the decision-making processes. Although the methodological rigor of research is a staple of academic programs and professional discourse, its integration into product strategy is less straightforward yet crucial for achieving a tangible impact. Surprisingly, nearly half of all companies lack a formal system to weave research findings into their product decisions, highlighting a significant gap between insight acquisition and application.

In response, a growing number of research professionals are formalizing their efforts into structured programs. These research programs, often documented in widely used productivity suites like Microsoft Office or Google Workspace, detail the purposes of various features, pose pertinent research questions, and consolidate learnings across teams. Such frameworks not only clarify the research agenda but also provide a comprehensive reference that helps product teams understand and leverage insights effectively.

Concurrently, there is a rising trend toward the creation of research repositories. These centralized databases are designed to archive the output from multiple research initiatives, making them readily available for future reference and use. Today, almost half of all companies report that they systematically channel research outputs into such repositories, underscoring a commitment to better organization and accessibility of insights.

Product managers, who often serve as the nexus of various product-related activities—from development to marketing to design—rely heavily on these insights. The challenge and opportunity here is clear: Research is just one of many inputs influencing the product's trajectory. For research to truly resonate and influence product strategy, it must be meticulously broken down and presented in a manner that is accessible and specifically relevant to each stakeholder's needs.

Establishing a research repository is a step in the right direction. It provides a structured environment where insights can be stored and accessed, bridging the gap between data collection and application. However, such systems often remain underutilized unless they are seamlessly integrated into the tools and workflows already familiar to the product teams. Innovative solutions by companies like Dovetail, UserTesting, Aurelius, and Marvin offer advanced functionalities for managing and analyzing research data. Nonetheless, the ultimate effectiveness of these tools often hinges on their adoption by the broader product team, not just researchers.

For research to truly impact decision-making and product strategy, it must become a core element of the daily operations within product teams. This integration is pivotal to cultivating an Impact Mindset and embedding evidence-based decision-making within the organizational culture. Only through such deep integration can the full potential of research be realized, ensuring that insights do not merely inform but actively drive business impact.

Establishing the Insights Hub

To fully embody the Impact Mindset, the creation of an Insights Hub is essential. This hub serves a dual function, acting as a research program and a research repository. It is designed to centralize all pertinent information about a collection of features, including their definitions, associated research questions, and all related research insights. This consolidation helps clarify the purpose and effectiveness of each feature, supporting ongoing and future product developments.

The Insights Hub is structured around three primary components:

- **Feature definitions:** Clear descriptions of what each feature is intended to do

- **Connected research questions:** Specific queries that guide the research agenda related to each feature

- **Research insights:** Consolidated findings from various teams that provide evidence and context for each feature

At its heart, the Insights Hub is the definitive source for comprehensive information on features and User Outcome Connections, backed by supporting data that illustrates the relationships between various variables. This resource is dynamic, allowing for the addition of new research questions and insights as they develop, ensuring that all relevant information from any team conducting research is included.

Creating a central location for this crucial information encourages frequent utilization by product stakeholders, who can rely on finding the most current data in a single, easily navigable location. This eliminates the need for stakeholders to independently track down the latest insights or rely on potentially outdated reports. Instead, a clear taxonomy based on future definitions and user outcome connections guides them, integrating the Insights Hub into regular review processes for feature success.

By centralizing all unanswered questions, the Insights Hub also becomes a primary resource for researchers planning new projects. This setup helps streamline the identification of common themes and knowledge gaps, facilitating efficient prioritization of research efforts. The presence of the Insights Hub thereby stimulates ongoing demand for investigative work, reinforcing commitment to the Impact Mindset.

As a practical example of the Insights Hub in action, consider a SaaS platform designed to help users create data profiles of their customers. Multiple teams contribute to this product, each responsible for different features crucial to the overall user experience—from data integration managed by the UI team to profile portability handled by the use case team, and security features overseen by the admin team. Each feature is cataloged in the Insights Hub, complete with its User Outcome Connections and a list of pertinent research questions and supporting data.

This organized repository allows the product team to quickly identify existing gaps, such as the lack of evidence showing that certain features enhance customer purchases. This visibility increases the urgency for targeted research, making it easier for researchers to design and execute experiments that either substantiate or refute the hypothesized impacts. As results from various feature impact analyses are collected, the insights within the hub are updated, providing all stakeholders with up-to-date, actionable information.

As familiarity with the Insights Hub grows, product teams begin to rely on it not just for information but as a crucial tool in their decision-making arsenal. For instance, validated user outcomes, like the proven impact of usable profiles on upselling, might prompt the development of new features to further exploit these findings. Over time, the hub not only informs but also shapes strategic decisions, with its comprehensive and centralized data becoming indispensable in driving product innovation and effectiveness.

Reviewing the Impact Mindset Cultural Shift

Navigating the competitive landscape of product development demands continual innovation. Product teams regularly grapple with the evolution of technology, which mandates changes to tools and processes and necessitates a fresh approach to task management. Often, the lack of progression toward more experimental and evidence-based decision-making is not due to a deficiency in leadership willpower but stems from the relentless challenges and shifting priorities that cloud the pathway to refining product development methodologies.

Enter the Impact Mindset, led not by theory but by practical experimentation. As the leader of the FIA, you serve as the catalyst for change, illustrating the advantages of focusing on behavioral changes and their effects on outcomes through tangible examples that reflect your organization's unique context. By establishing the User Outcome Connection, you've already achieved an immediate gain: redefining your feature. The development of new metrics marks another stride forward, broadening your team's toolkit. Completing an experiment provides a replicable model for assessing feature impacts, showcasing immediate value and setting the stage for broader discussions about the long-term benefits of adopting this new approach.

Building the path from the current state to the vision requires a thoughtful approach, strong project management, and a growth mindset to learn and adapt continuously. Steering your company along this transformative path is a formidable but worthwhile endeavor. Adopting an Impact Mindset offers more than just a quick fix; it addresses pervasive challenges faced by product teams.

It proactively applies the principles of the FIA to foster the development of more effective features with measurable impacts, cultivates a culture of inquiry and evidence-based action, and empowers employees to work in ways that are more aligned with customer needs and the company's mission. This paradigm shift, while substantial, will likely gain wide acceptance as team members experience firsthand how it enhances their capacity to deliver meaningful, impactful work.

Four Components of an Impact Mindset

Adopting an Impact Mindset fundamentally revolves around understanding how product features initiate behavioral changes that then influence both user and business outcomes. This shift necessitates a cultural transformation within product teams and the development of systems essential for evidence-based decision-making. Culturally, this means fostering an environment where every team member views their role as pivotal in creating tools that drive meaningful actions aligned with user needs. By delivering products that meet these needs, teams enhance customer retention and encourage positive word of mouth.

On the systems front, implementing an Impact Mindset requires establishing robust processes and tools to facilitate experimentation, capture insights, and make informed decisions based on these findings. Without the proper infrastructure, even the most committed teams can struggle to translate theory into practice, from defining features to executing data-driven actions.

User Outcome Connections: Throughout this book, the continued return to the User Outcome Connection highlights the importance of this framework. It is the core that the Impact Mindset rests within, offering a new lens to view each feature. Most people will have heard of user outcomes and addressing needs; this has become common knowledge in product development. Fewer will ensure that these user outcomes connect to business impact. This oversight often relegates research to a secondary status rather than recognizing it as integral to sustainable product development. Even fewer will have thought about user outcomes as the output of a behavioral change. The novel addition of the Impact Mindset aims to find a validated thread between behavior changes, user outcomes, and business impacts.

A company that has wholly adopted an Impact Mindset will establish a User Outcome Connection for each of its core features. This foundation will provide a detailed understanding of what a feature is attempting to do for users. With each User Outcome Connection validated, the team will feel more confident in their investment in specific behavioral change. The features without validation will provide opportunities for new FIA projects to be completed, and new features will have User Outcome Connections completed concurrently with their development.

Experimentation: The only way to move a User Outcome Connection from filled out to validated is to test data to ensure a connection between each variable of the framework. Although this does not always demand a full experiment, it does require the organization and analysis of data to ultimately generate insights that can be used to establish confidence that said connection exists. All this demands systems that collect data, make it accessible, and generate new information from it.

Beyond the tools and processes required to experiment, a team must be able and empowered to go and do it. Ability means that a team has the technical skills to use the available tools to create and deploy experiments, turning raw returns into actionable insights. Empowerment equates to that team feeling they can run those tests without extreme amounts of administrative burden, making the process laborious or so costly that resources would be better devoted elsewhere. Meeting systems and culture requirements positions a company to generate real value from its experiments.

Insights Hub: As discussed in the previous chapter, it is beneficial to centralize all the User Outcome Connections for all features along with the results from the completed research and experimentation: a home for all team members to visit to be quickly brought up to speed on the point of a feature, what is known about it, and any gaps that might be filled with further metric development and testing. The transparency created by such a place enables all product team members to feel ownership in what is understood about a feature and, thus, what level of confidence they should have in further investing in it.

Centralizing this information significantly bolsters the importance of research on the product team, too, as any gap is now seen not as an error but as an opportunity. Unknowns can be scary, and they require a team to become comfortable with the openness surrounding the gap tracking. Yet they are much less detrimental than the unknowns that the team does not know about, where teams believe something is working without any correct evidence. The availability of this insight is also helpful in decreasing the error of replicating previous work, as insights are more accessible by all parties. At the same time, it enables those doing research to have more information to assist in the prioritization of new efforts.

Evidence-based decision-making culture: With systems in place to do experimentation, an Insights Hub, and a team ready to act, an Impact Mindset necessitates a move toward decision-making processes that prioritize data over intuition. Even the most valuable evidence is without merit when a decision-maker ignores it, relying on their original beliefs. Creating an evidence-based decision-making culture requires overcoming the biases that plague everyone, especially the pursuit of evidence that aligns with one prior belief, also known as confirmation bias.

Establishing processes that demand stoppages in decisions to ensure relevant evidence has been consulted is the most powerful way to ensure the investments in the other components are actually made valuable. Although sometimes draconian, these processes ensure that all team members have a written policy or procedure to identify when they see leadership defaulting toward their intuition rather than following the data. As the culture changes toward an evidence-based one, these processes can be lightened, but the implementation of these types of processes is the only way to complete the Impact Mindset feedback loop.

Benefits of Impact Mindset

Embracing the Impact Mindset necessitates understanding its benefits explicitly linked to your organization's unique needs. By adopting a step-by-step progression through the FIA, each phase contributes valuable deliverables. Completing the FIA with a validated User Outcome Connection offers significant advantages, setting the stage for a shift toward evidence-based decision-making. Shared this way, it highlights again how starting with a FIA and expanding to a philosophy change offers both short- and long-term benefits, which should be spelled out to encourage immediate buy-in that can be sustained through the adoption of such a mindset.

Enhanced feature understanding: The first and most immediate impact of starting a User Outcome Connection is a systematic way to view the features your team creates. Although it sounds intuitive to have a single lens to evaluate all core components of a product, the reality is few companies have this in place. If there is any standard process, it is generally done through the lens of KPIs or success thresholds—metrics that measure outcomes rather than defining what a feature is intended to do.

Building a User Outcome Connection forces the discussion surrounding what a feature is intended to do for users and how it is attempting to make that change. Additionally, it asks how a feature is connected to the business goal of making a profitable product. Having this enhanced understanding of a feature allows for easier communication between teams and a single definition upon which to assess success. As features are experimented with, patterns of effective features will begin to be identified and able to be replicated, moving the team closer to better understanding how to craft features for your target audience.

New metrics: Most teams lack no desire to measure more. Instead, they lack the functional ability to expand their toolset; conducting a FIA breaks them free from this trap. The next significant benefit is the creation of new metrics, especially those to measure behavior, user outcomes, and business impact. Adding these new variables offers an extended way to assess a feature in any process already established by the team. They can be embedded in monitoring dashboards revisited during quarterly reviews, and their maximization can be tied to performance bonuses.

Expanding the definition of success beyond usage and usability will also empower the team with a new set of variables to use in churn and upsell analyses. For example, they might predict when a user will likely abandon usage or suggest that users who meet specific criteria are good candidates to be encouraged to upgrade. Additionally, making these new metrics well known to any teams associated with product development can generate benefits that might not even be immediately apparent.

Improved feature quality and marketing: Completing FIAs will yield validated User Outcomes Connections, confirming that features are working as intended. At the time, they will identify features not meeting the mark and require additional work to become fully functioning or the decision to remove them altogether. In the beginning, this will help a team be sure that the core components of their product are working as intended. As it scales, it will ensure that a product is turning into a powerful behavioral-changing tool. The benefit of improving the quality of the product is not just good will but, if done right, increased sales and decreased costs.

One of the main ways that it achieves this is through the ability to market the product as one that is effective at satisfying user needs. Instead of using vague, unproven language to paint a rosy picture, your marketing team can share validated benefits created for users through product engagement. Doing so will position your company uniquely among the competition and is also likely to assist with attracting top talent.

Investment confidence: As an Insights Hub is formed, collocating User Outcome Connections and corresponding evidence, the team will identify themes among the behaviors and user outcomes most connected to the business impact. This understanding empowers the team with the knowledge of what they are driving to change. It shifts from "what to build" to "how to design the best solution." Although still a significant challenge, resources are available to assist teams in moving toward the best feature design.

Natural gaps will be identified by surveying the list of behaviors connected to user outcomes. If a weight loss app is helping people eat fewer calories and burn more calories through working out, the additional behavior of encouraging less calorie burn or intake before bed could be a natural next feature to test. Whether through rapid prototyping or user research, having the foundation of functional behaviors to start will provide the team a head start in finding the most critical behaviors for driving an impact on the user outcome, which, being a part of a validated User Outcome Connection, will also mean a business impact.

Adaptive agility: Having built out all four components (User Outcome Connections, experimentation, Insights Hubs, evidence-based decision-making culture), the team will be greeted with the final benefits and increased agility to adapt to environmental changes. By shifting new feature design from addressing the surface needs expressed by customers or those expected to drive the most engagement to what will change behavior most significantly, the team will constantly transcend the need to catch up with the latest fad. Instead, the team can stay focused on the gaps that need to be addressed. Focusing on the design of a solution, new technology might be used. Still, it will not be a technology-first approach, but one that chooses the new modality only when it is expected to drive the most impact on the user outcome.

Respecting Advances in AI

As I write this, in 2024, the generative AI space continues to flourish. Although many people attempt to predict how it will change products, I avoid falling into the trap of planning for an unknown future. Instead, I rest in the certainty that one thing is sure: change is accelerating and sure to continue. Instead of guessing each next turn, I try to find what will remain constant. One sure thing is that people will continue to use products to satisfy needs, regardless of the format in which they are presented.

Why did AR/VR and the Metaverse not take off during the pandemic, even as companies poured money into them? In most cases, they could have been better at satisfying user needs than their alternative products. As soon as the novelty of the experience wore off, the cost of use was realized and abandoned for a more straightforward experience. Chatbots could easily fall into this trap, seeming very valuable to start, only to be discovered to be more convoluted than the process they attempt to replace.

All this is shared to highlight the power of subtracting oneself from the noise and focusing on the more stable dynamics. Starting with the user outcomes a person is driven to satisfy, and followed by the behaviors that will achieve the change, a team can build features that drive real user value, regardless of the technology used. This form of agility allows quick iterations to stay constant with trends while ensuring investments are not made in a fad purely because it is "hot."

Addressing Common Challenges

What we are talking about here is a significant effort, and I respect that you might be questioning whether it is worth it. This is the first common challenge and the one that underpins everything else. If you are reading this and cannot believe your organization can make the changes necessary to fully embrace the Impact Mindset, it will be impossible to inspire others that it is worth it.

I faced considerable doubt when I initially explored these concepts and advocated for behavior measurement within my organization. How could one employee effect such change in a large company? I put my pride aside and embraced what I felt (and still do) was true: measuring behaviors is essential to building sustained, valuable products. Fully leaning in, I talked to the product and engineering team with the confidence that this approach would move the team to a more informed understanding of our users. This initial effort garnered enough support for our first FIA.

Once it was complete and we had proof that measuring behaviors provided a new perspective, I was not the only person who believed that this was a valuable new way to think about our features. Was it a panacea? Did the team relinquish all its prior beliefs on product development and measurement and reconstruct itself around the Impact Mindset? No. If this book were a much more detailed case study, you would have heard of me because I had a keynote at leading tech conferences. Rather, it initiated a gradual cultural shift that continues to evolve, underpinned by a growing appreciation for comprehensive product analytics and data-driven decision-making. It kicked off a cultural change that is still ongoing, and this outcome all started with me believing it could happen.

Lack of belief that you can be the catalyst of this change is the biggest hurdle, but the one that you have complete control over. Once you have built that belief and kick-started the process, you will face many additional challenges, which you cannot directly influence as quickly. Standing on your belief, you will be positioned to do what is needed to keep the process in motion. Others will notice, and the change will continue. A few of these common hurdles that you will face are listed next. Remember, they are yours to influence, highlighting the importance of winning others over to support your effort. You are the catalyst, but cultural change cannot occur alone.

Conflicting philosophies: One common initial hurdle is reconciling the Impact Mindset with existing development philosophies. Questions like "How is this different from [insert philosophy]?" are frequent. The Impact Mindset is not a design process, but a philosophy focused on identifying necessary behavioral changes to fulfill user needs and create value. It complements frameworks like jobs to be done (JBTD) by enhancing them with specific behavioral insights that are crucial for fulfilling identified user jobs. Although the Impact Mindset can stand alone and often does so effectively, integrating it with known frameworks can ease the team transition.

Lack of investment: Another significant challenge is the need for more resources, especially in organizations prioritizing short-term financial metrics over long-term strategic investments. When economic forecasts look challenging, the research and development efforts are commonly slashed first. When one is removed from the people building or selling a product, they are less likely to have direct business value. Yet that same principle can be applied in reverse. In any work that is done to encourage an Impact Mindset, it is essential to think through how it can tie back to those who are creating the product or getting it into the hands of the customer. From there, ensure you generate both short-term wins that can satisfy the gains demanded by business leaders while progressing toward the long-term vision.

Privacy issues: A growing discussion across the tech field involves the proper handling and use of customer data. Let's start with the reality: this book espouses increased data collection about users' actions and sentiments. But the goal of the Impact Mindset is to enhance user satisfaction, not to foster dependency. It's crucial to navigate this fine line responsibly. What must be ensured is that all data is handled according to laws and regulations that are nuanced and require proper investment to ensure compliance. Handling this data should be done following industry standards. Collecting attitudinal data from customers should be done such that what is used will be collected and kept only for as long as necessary. Beyond that, having a solid relationship with the legal team and gaining their guidance and approval for the new processes is essential.

Getting to the Ideal State

When setting up an experiment as part of the FIA, defining an ideal state provides a visionary target to aim for, serving as a motivational benchmark. Similarly, for adopting the Impact Mindset, establishing a "North Star" helps guide the team's efforts, breaking down the journey into manageable components. This ideal state is delineated into three primary focus areas as outlined in **TABLE 13.1**, which also structures the assessment for gauging a team's progress toward fully embracing the Impact Mindset.

TABLE 13.1 Three Main Aspects of the Impact Mindset to Assess	
ASPECT	**ASSESSMENT**
System aspect	The technical infrastructure for FIAs enables experimentation and analysis and provides a centralized repository for easy access and maximum utility of data.
People aspect	Adopting the Impact Mindset requires a cultural shift toward evidence-based decision-making, supported by continuous leadership endorsement and education.
Vision aspect	Integrating the Impact Mindset into a company's strategic planning allows for the continual adaptation of culture and systems to enhance product impact and guide development.

System aspect: The technical dimension involves all systems and processes necessary for defining features, developing metrics, conducting experiments, analyzing results, and ensuring actionable follow-through. In its ideal state, the technical setup would enable teams to proactively conduct FIAs that are fully digital and include scaled attitudinal feedback mechanisms. Insights generated from these activities should be systematically categorized and stored in a centralized repository, readily accessible to all team members. This setup not only streamlines the data handling process but also ensures that every piece of information is leveraged to its fullest potential.

People aspect: This aspect focuses on the cultural shifts necessary to successfully adopt and sustain the Impact Mindset, alongside building the team's capability to use the technical infrastructure effectively. The ideal state here is characterized by a robust evidence-based decision-making culture. In this environment, the team proactively seeks out new data and creates it independently when needed. Support for the Impact Mindset from leadership is crucial, as is ongoing education and communication of its principles across the organization. This ensures that all members understand and are committed to the philosophy, fostering a unified approach to innovation.

Vision aspect: The vision aspect pertains to the holistic incorporation of the Impact Mindset into the company's product development ethos. Ideally, strategic planning would leverage insights derived from FIAs and the centralized Insights Hub to inform and guide product roadmaps. This vision-driven approach encourages continual cultural adaptation and the development of necessary experimental systems. It ensures that every employee comprehends the significance of the Impact Mindset, with established feedback loops to continually refine insight generation and implement effective actions.

These three pillars—system, people, and vision—collectively form a comprehensive framework for realizing the full potential of the Impact Mindset. By aiming for this ideal state, teams can ensure that their efforts are not only aligned with the company's strategic goals but also embedded in a culture that values and uses evidence-based insights to drive product development. This approach not only enhances product quality and user satisfaction but also positions the company as a leader in innovative, data-driven practices.

Assessment for Impact Mindset

Before delving into detailed plans for what should be constructed next within your organization, it's crucial to understand the current state. To facilitate this, a diagnostic tool should be used that categorizes essential components into three key areas: system, people, and vision. These areas should be assessed using a maturity scale—low, medium, and high—with the goal of progressing toward high as you advance toward fully adopting the Impact Mindset.

As you review the list, you will identify many elements that have been touched on in previous chapters. Don't look at this list as separate from the work of the FIA. Instead, it is a superset of components that are needed not just to complete FIAs across the company but to ensure the results make their intended impact. In an ideal Impact Mindset organization, insights are in demand. It becomes a problem of how to do all the work rather than devoting efforts toward how to get stakeholders to act on the findings. All the components, which will be introduced in more detail across the next few sections, are intended to make the Impact Mindset shift feel less like an amorphous change and instead like a collection of pieces that can be worked upon individually.

Presented without a detailed evaluation scale, this framework is intended to provide guidance rather than a true maturity curve where meeting certain factors qualifies a company to consider itself as meeting a level. Instead, due to the unique nature of each company's culture and desires, different needs must be prioritized in different contexts. Thus, it aims to centralize all the factors that one should consider and allow the architect of the Impact Mindset to make informed decisions based on their tailored knowledge while still ensuring they are on the path to the ideal state.

This assessment tool is not isolated from the principles discussed in earlier chapters or from the FIA process. Instead, it should be seen as an extension of these concepts, encompassing a broader set of requirements essential not only for completing FIAs effectively across the organization but also for ensuring that the outcomes of these analyses achieve their intended impact. The aim in a mature Impact Mindset organization is to shift the challenge from getting stakeholders to act on findings to managing the workload required to generate these insights.

This maturity framework is provided without a detailed evaluation scale to avoid the prescriptive imposition of a one-size-fits-all maturity curve. Instead, recognizing the unique cultural and operational nuances of each company allows for flexibility in prioritizing different needs. This approach enables the architect of the Impact Mindset within your company to make informed decisions about which areas to prioritize, based on a nuanced understanding of the organization's specific context and objectives. By considering all relevant components, as shown in **TABLE 13.2**, this tool ensures that strategic decisions are well aligned with the path toward the ideal state, facilitating a balanced and effective transition to a comprehensive, evidence-based organizational culture.

TABLE 13.2 Evaluation Components for Assessing the Impact Mindset

SYSTEM	PEOPLE	VISION
Experimentation platform	Buy-in on vision	Connected to company strategy
Behavioral data collection system	Demand for evidence	A North Star
Survey collection systems	Experimentation democratization	Average employee's knowledge of Impact Mindset
Access to participants	Evidence-based decision making	
Insights Hub	Leadership support	Overall system feedback mechanism
Project management	Communication plan	
Monitoring systems	Education and training	

System Aspect

Evaluating systems is the first piece of assessing the Impact Mindset and one you are likely familiar with by now. The technical infrastructure within your organization plays a crucial role in enabling scaled experimentation. In addition to these core systems, project management tools are vital for orchestrating tests and generating progress reports that bolster the cultural shift toward an Impact Mindset. As previously discussed, a centralized repository for storing all relevant definitions and insights is a critical system component. This system should also integrate monitoring tools that keep new metrics and user-product interactions continually updated and visible to teams. **TABLE 13.3** lists the seven system components along with their maturity rankings.

TABLE 13.3 The Seven Components of the System Aspect

	MATURITY		
	LOW	MEDIUM	HIGH
Experimentation platform: The set of tools and systems necessary for deploying various versions of a product feature and effectively gathering corresponding data.	The organization has no tools for controlled experimentation; feature rollouts and data collection are entirely manual and untracked.	Basic tools for deploying features are in place but are not integrated with data collection or analytics systems, necessitating manual intervention for comprehensive analysis.	There is a comprehensive, fully integrated platform that supports systematic testing, automatic data collection, and analytics, facilitating a seamless experimentation process.
Behavioral data collection: Systems and processes used to gather and analyze data on user behavior to inform product decisions and improvements.	There are no established systems for behavioral data collection; the organization relies on ad hoc methods that are incapable of supporting scalable metrics.	Basic data collection systems are operational; however, creating and processing metrics remains a manual and cumbersome process.	Advanced, automated systems are in place that not only collect extensive user behavior data but also facilitate the automatic creation and processing of metrics.

continues

TABLE 13.3 The Seven Components of the System Aspect *(continued)*

	MATURITY		
	LOW	MEDIUM	HIGH
Survey collection systems: Mechanisms and tools for collecting and analyzing user feedback to enhance product development and user satisfaction.	The organization lacks structured methods for collecting user feedback, relying instead on sporadic and ad hoc approaches.	A system for deploying surveys is in place, but it lacks a coherent, ongoing program to systematically gather and analyze user feedback.	There is an automated, continuous feedback collection system that is integrated with user engagement platforms, enabling real-time feedback analysis and responsive product adjustments.
Access to participants: The ability and efficiency of the organization to recruit and engage users for testing new features and improvements.	The organization struggles with accessing users for testing, with no established methods or channels for recruitment.	There are some methods in place for accessing participants, but they are not fully optimized for effective or scalable testing.	Robust and scalable systems are established, ensuring easy and efficient access to a diverse pool of users for testing purposes.
Insights Hub: A centralized repository where all data and insights related to product features are stored, managed, and made accessible for strategic use.	Data is scattered and poorly managed across the organization with no centralized repository for insights, leading to inefficiencies and missed opportunities.	There is a basic central repository that includes definitions and insights; however, it requires some manual effort to maintain and update.	A dynamic, fully integrated Insight Hub exists, and it is automatically updated with real-time data from across projects and departments, enhancing decision-making and strategy development.
Project management: The tools and methodologies used to plan, execute, and monitor projects, including the development and testing of product features.	Project management is ad hoc, with minimal formal structure or tools, leading to inefficiencies and challenges in tracking project progress.	Standardized project management tools are used but are not integrated with systems such as Insight Hubs or monitoring systems.	Advanced project management systems are in place that are fully integrated with all business systems, ensuring seamless communication, efficient resource management, and effective project tracking.

	MATURITY		
	LOW	MEDIUM	HIGH
Monitoring systems: Tools and processes used to continuously track and evaluate the performance of features in real time, adjusting strategies as necessary.	There is minimal to no real-time monitoring of projects or features, leading to delayed responses to issues and opportunities.	Basic monitoring tools are available; however, they provide limited insights and often require manual effort to analyze deeper metrics.	Sophisticated, automated monitoring systems are established, providing comprehensive, real-time insights into feature performance with minimal need for manual intervention.

People Aspect

Although we have discussed the importance of the team's buying into the experiment for making a smooth process and the ultimate use of insights created by a FIA, the macro cultural change required for an Impact Mindset amplifies the considerations. Rooted in evidence-based decision-making, an Impact Mindset leads development efforts based on research insights. Achieving this state typically necessitates fostering a demand for research among key product stakeholders and promoting the democratization of experiments across the organization, all supported by leadership that directs contributors toward this new vision. Effective change management in this context also relies on robust communication strategies and comprehensive education and training programs. **TABLE 13.4** lists the seven components of people aspects crucial to this transformation, along with their maturity rankings.

TABLE 13.4 The Seven Components of the People Aspect

	MATURITY		
	LOW	MEDIUM	HIGH
Buy-in on vision: The degree to which individuals and teams accept and support the Impact Mindset and its potential to enhance product development.	There is low awareness or acceptance of the Impact Mindset among team members, indicating a lack of understanding or skepticism about its benefits.	Some team members support the Impact Mindset, although it has not been universally adopted or understood across the organization.	There is strong organizational commitment to the Impact Mindset, with widespread understanding and support across all levels of the company.

continues

TABLE 13.4 The Seven Components of the People Aspect *(continued)*

	MATURITY		
	LOW	MEDIUM	HIGH
Demand for evidence: The inclination of individuals and teams within the organization to seek out and use data and research to inform decisions.	Decisions are predominantly made based on intuition or incomplete data, reflecting a lack of systematic approach to evidence-based decision-making.	There is a recognition of the value of data, but systematic implementation of evidence-based decision-making practices is inconsistent.	A strong culture of requiring rigorous data for decision-making exists, with comprehensive utilization of evidence across all departments.
Experimentation democratization: The extent to which individuals within the organization are enabled and encouraged to conduct their own experiments and contribute to evidence generation.	Individual experimentation is limited and centrally controlled, restricting innovative potential and personal initiative in testing new ideas.	Some teams are equipped to conduct experiments, but widespread capability and support for individual experimentation are not optimized.	All team members are empowered with the tools and support needed to conduct experiments, making it a core part of the organizational culture.
Evidence-based decision making: The prevalence of using data and evidence to make decisions within the organization, rather than relying on assumptions or hierarchical directives.	Decisions are often based on hierarchy or tradition rather than empirical evidence, which may hinder innovation and responsiveness.	There is a shift toward making decisions based on evidence, but old habits and non-data-driven approaches still dominate in some areas.	Decisions across the organization are consistently made based on clear, quantitative evidence, demonstrating a mature, rational decision-making culture.
Leadership support: The extent of encouragement and resource alignment from top management to foster a culture around the Impact Mindset.	Leadership is either unaware of or does not prioritize promoting an Impact Mindset, leading to a lack of direction and support for related initiatives.	There is sporadic support from leadership for Impact Mindset initiatives, which may not be consistent or fully effective.	Strong, consistent advocacy and resource allocation from leadership ensure the integration of the Impact Mindset into all business practices.

	MATURITY		
	LOW	MEDIUM	HIGH
Communication plan: The strategies and methods used to communicate the value and processes associated with the Impact Mindset within the organization.	Communication about the Impact Mindset is irregular or ineffective, often leaving employees unclear or uninformed about its value.	Regular communication initiatives exist but may not reach or effectively engage all parts of the organization.	Comprehensive and effective communication strategies are in place, ensuring that all stakeholders are well-informed and actively engaged in adopting the Impact Mindset.
Education and training: The resources and programs available to enhance understanding and skills related to the Impact Mindset among employees.	Minimal training is available on the Impact Mindset and related processes, leaving most employees unprepared to contribute effectively.	Some training programs are available, but they are not comprehensive or required, resulting in uneven knowledge and application among employees.	Extensive, mandatory training programs exist, supporting a deep, organization-wide understanding and implementation of the Impact Mindset.

Vision Aspect

Philosophical changes within an organization start with a push to build momentum and require a clear path to channel this energy. However, more than just a path, having an end goal—a North Star—is crucial, as it justifies the efforts and costs involved. Although this milestone need not be rigidly defined with a specific deadline, possessing a vision provides a powerful rallying point to garner support. Each company's North Star will differ but generally aligns with its mission and competitive strategy. Real change occurs when every employee understands this vision and sees their role in realizing it. This process is supported by flexible feedback systems that prevent the path to the North Star from becoming so rigid that it disillusions employees. **TABLE 13.5** shows the four vision components, along with their maturity rankings.

TABLE 13.5 The Four Components of the Vision Aspect

	MATURITY		
	LOW	MEDIUM	HIGH
Connected to company strategy: The extent to which the organization's long-term strategic planning incorporates and prioritizes the Impact Mindset.	The company's strategic plans do not include or align with the Impact Mindset, showing a lack of integration or prioritization.	There is some alignment with the Impact Mindset in company strategy, but it is either superficial or inconsistently applied across initiatives.	The Impact Mindset is deeply embedded in the company's strategic objectives, actively driving major initiatives and guiding overall corporate direction.
A North Star: The presence of a clear, overarching vision or goal that guides the organization toward continuous improvement and excellence in line with the Impact Mindset.	There is no clear long-term vision or strategic direction that aligns with the Impact Mindset, indicating a lack of purposeful guidance.	A defined long-term vision exists, but it is not fully aligned with the Impact Mindset or is not effectively communicated across the organization.	There is a clear, compelling long-term vision that fully integrates the Impact Mindset, continuously guiding all organizational efforts and decision-making.
Average employee's knowledge: The general understanding of the Impact Mindset among employees and how well it is perceived as beneficial to the organization's goals.	Most employees have little to no understanding of what the Impact Mindset entails or why it is important.	A fair number of employees have a basic understanding of the Impact Mindset; however, deep knowledge and its application are limited to specific groups or leaders.	A thorough understanding of the Impact Mindset and its benefits is widespread, reflected in the daily activities and strategic contributions of most employees.
Overall system feedback mechanism: The effectiveness of feedback systems in place for continually refining and improving the systems and cultural practices to better support the Impact Mindset.	Feedback mechanisms are either nonexistent or not utilized, resulting in stagnant or ineffective processes without continuous improvement.	Some feedback mechanisms are in place, but they are not effectively used to drive substantial improvements or process refinements.	Robust, systematic feedback loops are actively used to continuously refine systems and practices, supporting the dynamic development of the Impact Mindset across the organization.

Starting Points and Strategy Recommendations

Embarking on a philosophical change within an organization requires a well-structured plan and flexibility to adapt to unique circumstances. Your initial task involves launching the transformation by conducting the first FIA. This effort lays the foundation and must be supported by a strategic plan that mobilizes team support toward a clearly defined future state. We covered how to initiate a FIA in previous chapters, and this chapter outlined strategic considerations for assessing your company's current position toward adopting an Impact Mindset and planning the actual steps to achieve it.

The journey from your current state to the envisioned future should be meticulously detailed in what we call "the roadmap." This document will outline the logistics and strategies for developing the necessary systems to support the Impact Mindset, with further details in the next chapter. After system development, the focus will shift to the cultural changes required for an Impact Mindset. Chapter 15 will explore ways to generate buy-in from key stakeholders and collaborators and discuss how to create effective support materials that facilitate the adoption of this new philosophy, ensuring that all team members are aligned with the change.

Finally, the overarching vision that all these efforts aim to achieve will be addressed in Chapter 16. Starting with a bottom-up approach might seem counterintuitive, but it's essential to remember that this is a grassroots movement you are building. The strategy should start with practical, tangible actions that directly contribute to real business impact and gradually build toward broader strategic goals. By methodically planning and executing each phase and ensuring that all organizational layers are aligned with the change, your efforts will lay the groundwork for a sustainable shift that enhances decision-making and product development through data-driven insights.

CHAPTER RECAP

- **Four components of the Impact Mindset:** The Impact Mindset is structured around four key components—User Outcome Connections, experimentation, Insights Hub, and evidence-based decision-making culture—each crucial for fostering a comprehensive, evidence-based decision-making culture within the organization.

- **Main benefits of the Impact Mindset:** Adopting the Impact Mindset enhances feature understanding, introduces new metrics, improves feature quality, boosts investment confidence, and enables adaptive agility, leading to better overall business outcomes.

- **Three categories of assessment:** The assessment for adopting the Impact Mindset divides into three categories—system, culture, and vision—each evaluated on a maturity scale from low to high to guide progression toward fully embracing this philosophy.

- **Collection of components:** This is a collective approach to understanding the various systems, processes, and cultural elements that need to be integrated and enhanced to fully support the adoption of the Impact Mindset.

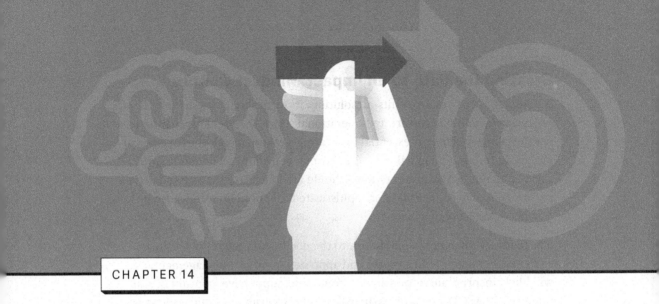

CHAPTER 14

Building a Strategic Roadmap

Think about your greatest professional achievement. Consider the steps that set the stage for this success. How could you repeat such a triumph? What would it take to make such effective processes or outcomes more common at your workplace? The key to scaling your efforts starts with a clear vision of what you want to achieve and a plan to get there. In project management, this plan is known as a roadmap.

The previous chapter highlighted the essential components needed to evaluate an organization's current state and what it would take to fully adopt an Impact Mindset. The systems in place are crucial; even the most dedicated teams need the right tools to carry out large-scale experiments. This chapter explores how to build this roadmap in more detail, starting with the initial steps. The following chapters will guide you through the rest of this journey.

Creating the Path to an Impact Mindset Culture

A roadmap is not a one-size-fits-all solution; its form should resonate with your organization's unique culture and operational style. The previous chapter laid out the primary elements essential to creating a roadmap, but the specifics of designing your roadmap will vary. The format you adopt—a dynamic spreadsheet or an interactive presentation—should facilitate easy sharing and collaboration. Tools like Asana can offer sophisticated functionalities for those seeking advanced project management features.

The roadmap's contents should cater to the needs and preferences of your audience. For teams with a more rigid approach to project management, you will likely incorporate responsible, accountable, supportive, consulted, and informed (RASCI) charts to clarify roles and responsibilities and use status indicators to track progress. Other, more agile cultures might find these aspects of a roadmap too restrictive. It is up to you to select elements that maintain the document's usability and relevance. Remember that the roadmap's complexity can affect its maintainability—aim for a balance where detail does not hinder the document's functionality.

Regardless of your structure, it is strongly recommended that you build the roadmap around milestones achievable every couple of months. Establishing milestones that mark progress, such as completing the first project, collecting user feedback from 100 unique customers, or doing whatever feels like an accomplishment for your team, will provide a strong sense of progress. With defined milestones, the next step is identifying key stakeholders critical for achieving each milestone and outlining the principal risks and contingency plans. Including these well-defined milestones ensures that the roadmap is a strategic document. Done right, your roadmap will be treated as a source of truth, organically making it a required visit for most of the team.

Moving from the structure of the roadmap to its vision, systems, and people are the three pivotal aspects of fostering an Impact Mindset and thus will be the main categories you will be building toward. The *vision* is your guiding star, setting a clear objective that unifies and motivates the team. *Systems* are the technical backbones that support data-driven insights and their accessibility. *People* are at the heart of the cultural shift, which is essential for nurturing an environment that values and uses these insights. You will guide the vision for as long as you own the effort, even if that vision is not shared beyond its reference at the top of the roadmap. Charting changes needed to the systems and people components will be the primary content of the roadmap.

Ultimately, your roadmap should function as a timeline and a checklist. It should outline a clear sequence of steps to achieve your vision and enumerate the specific needs that must be addressed to reach each milestone. This dual functionality helps track progress and integrate the roadmap into regular operational planning, such as quarterly reviews. By making the roadmap a central element of strategic planning, you ensure it becomes a vital tool in realizing the transformation toward an Impact Mindset.

Building the Roadmap

Embarking on a roadmap to foster an Impact Mindset represents a pivotal strategy for maintaining the momentum initiated by your first Feature Impact Analysis (FIA). While it can be started before you begin kicking off the define phase of the FIA, it is strongly recommended that you first create a User Outcome Connection. That will instantly move this effort from a theoretical philosophy change to a practical new view of features.

Create the first feature User Outcome Connection: The creation of the User Outcome Connection marks your first tangible deliverable under the Impact Mindset framework. With this cornerstone in place, you are well positioned to develop a roadmap that transitions from today's culture to one of evidence-based decision-making. The framework detailed in **FIGURE 14.1** guides you along eight steps of creating a roadmap. Although you are not required to adhere to every step in sequential order, this is intended to guide you through the specific elements in an intuitive order. The first step is the creation of the User Outcome Connection, which again is advised to ensure you can always direct curious stakeholders back to a destination.

Add first FIA components: The second step begins as you build out the FIA to validate that User Outcome Connection where you'll identify disparities between your current capabilities and the necessary infrastructure to succeed. Your aim is to focus resource allocation on the essential system components needed to execute this inaugural FIA, weighing the benefits of progress against the ideal conditions. This pragmatic approach involves outlining necessary infrastructure enhancements and assembling the right mix of team members and stakeholder support. Although a fully formed vision may still be evolving, completing your first FIA provides a significant milestone in this transformative journey.

FIGURE 14.1 Eight steps to creating a roadmap

Conduct systems fit-gap analysis: In this step, your aim is to conduct a fit-gap analysis of the systems components. If you are unfamiliar with fit-gap analysis, it is a technique that analyzes the gaps between an ideal state and the current reality. After identifying the gaps, the fit portion determines what needs to be developed to fill that void. While referenced in the remaining chapters as a "fit-gap analysis," you are welcome to plug in any framework you have for identifying organizational needs and working to fill them.

For the systems fit-gap analysis, you are moving beyond what is needed for the first FIA and thinking about what is required to help progress the faster and more effective deployment of future FIAs. You should triage these development efforts based on a mix of what is the least mature in its current state and what you believe is most important for building a more valuable FIA for your specific environment. For example, if your company has both limited behavioral data collection and no formal recruitment system, you will likely want to prioritize the passive collection systems, as they are pivotal for scaling up your efforts.

Conduct cultural fit-gap analysis: After updating the roadmap to meet your organization's systems needs, the next step is to conduct a fit-gap analysis of the cultural components. You may already have a few needs listed to ensure your first FIA can be completed, but here you will expand beyond that to think about what is needed to move the company's maturity forward. Generally, the resources needed to build out these elements are less technical and are separate from systems. However, if you find they overlap, you will need to determine which are more critical; the default here is that systems trump culture unless your company already has a well-established experimentation infrastructure.

Identify next FIAs: When you conclude these gap analyses, your FIA will ideally already be in flight. This is the perfect time to determine which feature should be added to the roadmap next. Following a similar approach to that shared in Chapter 12, the only additional factor to be considered is how closely the second and third FIAs are to the first. Ideally, you want there to be some connectedness to show how FIAs can expand on each other, highlighting the combinatory value of multiple FIAs.

Establish a vision: The next stage in developing your roadmap involves articulating a grand vision for adopting an Impact Mindset. Define the overarching reasons for this strategic shift and outline how you will keep the initiative aligned and focused. A good vision will connect to the company's mission and values, piggybacking on the investment already made in painting an ideal future. All of this is with the aim of creating a unifying mission to remind and motivate the team to push forward toward achieving a better version of themselves. Here it may be beneficial to break the overall effort into component parts following the System, People, Vision framework I have outlined or any other organization framework you see fit.

Prioritize momentum: With the vision set and an accompanying North Star to keep the team striving to improve, you should continue to identify where successes occur and double down in those areas, especially in the start. If you find that the engineering team is connecting with the infrastructure updates, invest in systems. If people love the philosophy even though the systems are not fully in place, prioritize building on the people momentum. Continue to triage the efforts to ensure that progress is felt.

Adjust and refine: As you continue down the path of building out varying aspects of the Impact Mindset, revisit the roadmap to incorporate new knowledge. Approach everything you do surrounding this effort with an experimental mindset; there are no wrong answers, just lessons learned. To do this you have to be willing to both accept feedback and try new things. With new insights, adjust the order of operations when simple tweaks are required to adapt to timelines or resource constraints. If you feel major stagnation, refine the entire roadmap attempting a new approach. Your roadmap should outline how you see getting from today to fulfilling the vision. When it begins to feel unrealistic, it's time for an update.

Executing the Fit Gap of Systems

Once the foundational needs for your initial FIA are pinpointed, the real task of constructing your roadmap begins. This phase kicks off with a fit-gap analysis, a critical evaluation of the maturity levels of your system components. By systematically reviewing the seven factors (**TABLE 14.1**) highlighted in the previous chapter using the maturity table, you will measure the readiness of each system involved in your experimentation and insights generation processes.

TABLE 14.1 THE SEVEN COMPONENTS OF THE SYSTEM ASPECT

COMPONENT	DESCRIPTION
Experimentation platform	The set of tools and systems necessary for deploying various versions of a product feature and effectively gathering corresponding data
Behavioral data collection	Systems and processes used to gather and analyze data on user behavior to inform product decisions and improvements
Survey collection systems	Mechanisms and tools for collecting and analyzing user feedback to enhance product development and user satisfaction
Access to participants	The ability and efficiency of the organization to recruit and engage users for testing new features and improvements
Insights Hub	A centralized repository where all data and insights related to product features are stored, managed, and made accessible for strategic use
Project management	The tools and methodologies used to plan, execute, and monitor projects, including the development and testing of product features
Monitoring system	Tools and processes used to continuously track and evaluate the performance of features in real time, adjusting strategies as necessary

Conducting this fit-gap analysis requires investigating what is currently available across the departments with whom you can reasonably work when conducting future FIAs. This could look like access to behavioral data from a data science team that you commonly work with, access to participants through your research team, or a contact on your company's project management team. You will have done some of this work when setting up the experiment as part of your first FIA, and that alone may be enough information to conduct the analyses. If not, seek out conversations with potential partner organizations to gain a better understanding of what is possible. You can also visit previous project documentation such as research plans and launch strategies to understand what data systems have been used in the past. With no strict benchmarks for each maturity stage, use the maturity ratings in Chapter 13 or the complementary material and make informed estimations when evaluating current system statuses.

It is recommended that you start with the four components most closely related to the ability to conduct experiments, connected to one of the four primary parts of the Impact Mindset. These include experimentation platform, behavioral data collection, survey collection systems, and access to participants. If you think back to the experiment and analyze phase, these components are needed to execute an experiment effectively. By doing the FIA, you are actively analyzing your current capabilities and what will be required to complete an experiment that meets your team's standards. In doing so, you must determine what is needed at a *minimum* and what should be achieved before feeling that you have succeeded.

Next, you should move toward the systems that are useful for ensuring that the insights from the FIA continue to be used. The first is the creation of an Insights Hub. Although sophisticated setups exist, even simple configurations using basic document management solutions like Microsoft Word, integrated with hyperlinks to existing research, can provide substantial value. Some research teams have been able to make valuable resources for their stakeholders that are purely text documents combined with links to all previous research. Look for wherever the primary team who was creating research stores their insights when auditing this. If there are none, you have an outstanding way to generate value with minimal effort.

A natural next step with the new metrics you created as part of your FIA is embedding them into the monitoring system. Doing so allows teams to track the effectiveness of the feature consistently, ensuring that design changes and external factors do not dramatically change the impact. A natural place to put these monitoring systems is the Insight Hub, but only after it has been established as a resource for the product team. Until then, monitoring systems should be located wherever current metrics are tracked.

Lastly, assess the project management tools and structures your team uses. The suitability of these tools will largely depend on the preferences and practices of the project management leaders. This step determines whether your Impact Mindset initiatives will seamlessly integrate into, or will require adjustments to, the existing project management frameworks.

Developing these systems is a balance between what is realistically achievable given your organization's investment appetite and the necessity for making progress toward your envisioned outcomes. Prioritize your roadmap's actions to build momentum and excitement strategically, ensuring each achievement not only meets a set goal but also propels your team toward the next milestone. This strategic progression is vital to maintaining enthusiasm and securing continued support for the Impact Mindset transformation.

Triaging System Needs

Effective allocation of resources in building out the aspects of the FIA hinges on strategic prioritization. Initially, you must focus on the necessities that will enable the completion of your first FIA. Demonstrating the tangible benefits of a well-executed FIA and a validated User Outcome Connection is crucial for justifying further investment and effort.

Subsequently, assess what systems are essential for your team to trust and act on the generated findings. If your team requires statistically significant results to proceed with recommendations from a FIA, then resources should be directed toward achieving this criterion. Likewise, if revisiting insights periodically is critical for maintaining operational relevance, investing in systems that facilitate this process is prudent. Often, team needs are not explicitly stated; probing with targeted questions will be necessary to unearth these requirements, allowing you to make informed decisions about where to allocate resources.

Once these primary needs are addressed, the direction of subsequent investments will largely depend on your strategic objectives and what you deem most critical for enhancing future FIAs. Identify any existing gaps in capability is a logical starting point. However, it's important to balance making progress with the need to fill these gaps. If addressing a particular gap does not critically enhance your organization's FIA capabilities or if it demands disproportionate resources, it may be prudent to defer this investment until it becomes essential.

After prioritizing the various system needs, the next step is to update your road-map with estimated timelines for developing each component. Depending on the granularity of your roadmap, consider breaking down each primary compo-nent into sub-components to provide a clearer view of each workstream. Once a preliminary version of the roadmap is drafted, circulate it among key stakehold-ers for feedback. This consultation helps refine your estimates and ensures the timeline reflects a realistic and achievable path forward.

Additional Considerations

Several project management components are critical to the success of any new initiative. While some of these were considered outside the scope of this discus-sion, it's important to address three key areas now, along with recommendations on who to engage for each.

Budgeting and financial planning: Developing each component of the FIA will inevitably require investments—whether in the form of direct financial resources or the allocation of time and other assets. Ideally, these efforts should be integrated into a broader project management framework that can oversee budgeting. If such a structure isn't available, aim to complete the first FIA using minimal resources. Demonstrating preliminary success can provide a solid foundation for justifying budget requests for subsequent milestones.

Legal and regulatory considerations: We previously discussed legal issues related to data collection, but other regulatory factors also demand attention. For example, some organizations face specific regulations governing experimen-tation with real customers or the retention of behavioral data. Early and regular consultations with your legal department are advisable. Establishing a dedicated legal contact can help navigate these waters efficiently, determining when issues need to be escalated or can be resolved at lower levels.

Connection to business metrics: Integrating business metrics into the experimentation process is crucial. While developing a functioning product is rewarding and essential, the ultimate viability of any project hinges on its ability to produce favorable business outcomes. These metrics may sometimes be developed internally in the product team, but often, collaboration with sales and business administration teams is necessary. Ensuring that your systems can capture and reflect these business metrics is vital for the continued funding and expansion of your initiatives.

CHAPTER RECAP

- **Strategic roadmap development:** This chapter outlines how to design a roadmap that delineates the journey from the current organizational state to the full adoption of an Impact Mindset.

- **Steps for creating a roadmap:** Introduced steps include establishing the first User Outcome Connection, adding necessary components for the initial FIA, conducting fit-gap analyses of system and cultural components, identifying subsequent features for analysis, and creating a vision to maintain momentum while expanding the roadmap.

- **Fit-gap analysis:** Performing a fit-gap analysis is recommended to identify and prioritize necessary improvements in system components to support effective experimentation.

- **Triaging system needs:** Detailed guidance is provided on prioritizing system updates that are essential for successfully executing the initial FIA, ensuring stakeholder buy-in for the results, and preparing for future FIAs.

CHAPTER 15

Creating a Cultural Change

Adopting an Impact Mindset involves more than just the integration of systems—it necessitates a profound cultural shift within the team. The initial step is conducting a thorough audit to establish the necessary infrastructure for proper experimentation. However, the mere presence of these systems doesn't ensure they will be used, a challenge frequently observed with large-scale technology integrations. Often, companies invest in cutting-edge technology only to see it underutilized, underscoring that cultivating an Impact Mindset is fundamentally about transforming culture.

The introduction of new tools to foster experimentation must be paired with a robust demand for their use to truly enhance product development. This requires everything from rethinking incentives for task completion to the cultural norms that shape solution-finding, all centered on the use and creation of evidence-based decision-making. A restructuring approach such as this is the clearest path to naturally generating a demand for insights and integrating their use organically.

Conducting the Cultural Fit-Gap Analysis

In the previous chapter, we explored the application of a fit-gap analysis to identify discrepancies between the current state and a desired higher level of maturity. The same analytical approach applies to assessing cultural elements, though with one significant difference: the components of culture are less tangible and cannot always be quantified directly. Instead, this evaluation will largely depend on engaging in discussions with stakeholders and observing organizational practices firsthand.

The goal is to develop a comprehensive understanding of your company's existing norms and expectations concerning experimentation and the generation of evidence. With this knowledge, you will be better equipped to establish the necessary foundations for a cultural shift toward an Impact Mindset. The human resources department, particularly the talent division, can be an invaluable partner in this endeavor. Collaborating with them is recommended, as they are likely to play a critical role in addressing the gaps identified through your analysis.

Assessing Current Culture and Tools of Change

The initial step in evaluating your organization's approach to evidence creation and use involves a comprehensive assessment of the current landscape among all stakeholders. Central to cultivating an Impact Mindset is the adoption of evidence-based decision-making. If this isn't currently practiced, it's crucial to understand the underlying reasons. Begin by gauging the level of buy-in from your stakeholders—are they enthusiastic and willing to engage in the Feature Impact Analysis (FIA), or are they reluctant? This will serve as a general indicator of what to expect as you evaluate other aspects of your organization's evidence culture.

Next, consider the demand for evidence. Does the product team express a need for more insights to guide their strategic decisions? Are stakeholders eager to integrate more data into product development, or does the team prefer to rely on intuition? The extent to which your team values and uses data in decision-making processes is a key measure of their commitment to evidence-based practices.

Another critical factor is the source of evidence generation. When decisions require data, who is responsible for creating it? Is it exclusively the purview of a dedicated research department, or are individuals encouraged to seek out and generate their own insights? This aspect of research democratization is vital for understanding whether employees feel empowered to conduct their own investigations and contribute to the evidence pool.

These elements collectively influence the fourth aspect: the overall culture of evidence-based decision-making within your team. It examines whether product development is predominantly driven by hard data from any available source, or if it leans more toward intuition and the path of least resistance. Such a culture is often closely linked to leadership support, which is essential for transitioning from a mere interest in data-driven practices to fully integrated systems that ensure evidence-based development is the norm at your organization.

The five elements of the culture discussed in Chapter 13 are essential for creating an environment in which the insights created from the FIA are acted upon, and they are pivotal in a company fully embracing the Impact Mindset. However, implementing these elements often necessitates incorporating standard change management practices, with two especially important components.

A well-crafted communication plan is essential. There are entire books written on the topic, offering guidance on crafting messages that effectively promote organizational change, fostering acceptance and enthusiasm for new processes. Recommended titles include *Organizational Change: Creating Change Through Strategic Communication*, by Laurie Lewis, and *Leading Change*, by John Kotter. However, communication alone might not bridge all gaps; targeted education and training are also crucial. This ensures that stakeholders not only are aware of but can adopt the new practices you are implementing. Both are significant supporters in creating a cultural shift, and you should assess the capabilities your company has in place to support you in their development.

Leadership support is integral to both communicating and educating effectively, impacting how these initiatives are resourced and executed. The extent to which executive stakeholders value the Impact Mindset and are prepared to invest in its integration significantly influences its success. Therefore, when evaluating these mechanisms, consider not only the organizational desire for cultural change but also the willingness of leadership to enable various groups, including human resources, to participate actively in these efforts.

Updating the Roadmap

Updating the roadmap to support the cultural transformation essential for adopting an Impact Mindset parallels the systems approach discussed in the previous chapter. Begin by identifying what is necessary for your inaugural FIA to succeed, followed by determining the requirements for effective action based on the results. Since these cultural elements are more abstract than systematic components, clear criteria for success are less obvious. Instead, focus on identifying major areas of resistance and evaluate the potential benefits of overcoming these challenges.

As you transition from conducting an initial FIA to making it a standard process, it becomes critical to pinpoint the primary obstacles hindering the adoption of the key cultural elements necessary for an Impact Mindset. Consider how shifts in personnel attitudes, rather than system adjustments, could facilitate the desired outcomes. The goal is to cultivate a culture of evidence-based decision-making that leverages existing systems effectively. From this foundation, map out all the necessary steps, prioritizing those that offer the most value. This strategic planning not only helps in overcoming initial hurdles but also in maintaining momentum as the new processes become embedded in the organizational culture.

In the spirit of experimentation and agile development, avoid the trap of believing that this cultural shift needs to be done in a single push. Instead, consider this shift a series of small, celebrated steps that reinforce desired behaviors and gradually instill them as habits. You are spearheading a grassroots movement—what may initially feel like an overwhelming effort will soon become second nature.

Generating Buy-In Across Groups

Throughout this book, I've emphasized the necessity of collaborating with various groups to not only complete the FIA but also cultivate an Impact Mindset culture. The support from different groups facilitates the implementation and ensures that the insights generated have a meaningful impact. The cooperation of four primary groups is crucial, each with its own goals and incentives.

Product managers (PMs): Many product managers don't build just for the sake of it—they desire to build something that genuinely satisfies a problem a user brings to the platform. I have been speaking with product managers throughout this book. If you are not one, the way I have phrased the introduction of new topics can be replicated in the conversations that you have with product managers. As the primary stakeholder responsible for a successful product, these individuals are commonly focused on core product metrics such as adoption, retention, and growth.

Most product managers aim to resolve user issues effectively, hoping to create successful features that warrant further investment. The User Outcome Connection can be an invaluable tool for product managers to understand the impact of their features better and to refine them to maximize value. Integrating this with the Impact Mindset provides a fresh perspective on feature development that bases the roadmap on solid evidence.

Designers: As user research has become integral to design, these teams are often pivotal in experimentation efforts. There is a natural connection between the goals of design teams and the principles of the Impact Mindset, as both aim to accurately meet user needs. Convincing these teams of the benefits of focusing on specific user behaviors can streamline their efforts in creating the right solutions. In my experience, these teams become especially interested in research efforts when they can view it as an opportunity to refine their user discovery skills.

Teams focused on design are likely incentivized on metrics like those of the product team, with the inclusion of satisfaction and ease. Highlighting how behavior metrics complement these traditional usability metrics can demonstrate the added value of this approach. As you pitch the Impact Mindset, be sure to highlight the potential for building features based on known connected behaviors, such as suggesting that a fitness application needs to be designed to increase minutes exercised or that a tax application needs to increase the saving of important documents. Doing so highlights the additional value that the design team can bring by ensuring the right solution is chosen.

Data science team/engineers: Whether to assist with the experimentation efforts or in the creation of new metrics, it is likely that you will work with your data science team in some capacity. Not all companies have a dedicated data science team, and it may be the same as the engineering team. Regardless of the team you will be working with, it is common that you will be working with a data engineer or product analyst. These stakeholders generally own the raw data associated with a product and will clarify what is possible.

Engaging them involves illustrating how insights into behaviors and outcomes can lead to useful metrics for the product team. When it comes to experimentation, data scientists themselves are likely to understand the value that comes from testing. If a deeper case needs to be made, it should be connected to the potential for reducing rework that a more nuanced understanding offered by the Impact Mindset can create.

I find engineers to be some of the best supporters of the Impact Mindset; they quickly understand the power of having more metrics available and are excited by the chance to push the technological infrastructure of the organization further. Even if there is not a natural reason to get them involved, I recommend sharing your efforts with this team, as you may generate supporters eager to help see this vision come to life.

Marketing: Though marketing teams might not be directly involved in creating the FIA, they use its outcomes. Effective messaging that leverages insights from the FIA can significantly enhance customer engagement and sales. For this reason, these teams may be able to invest resources to ensure you were able to launch your experiment. Additionally, marketing teams are also keen on reducing customer acquisition costs and increasing lifetime value, making them likely supporters of initiatives that prove the product's efficacy and promote organic growth. This not only helps in reducing marketing spend but also enhances customer retention and upselling opportunities.

Each of these groups brings unique perspectives and resources to the table. By aligning their objectives with the goals of the Impact Mindset, you can foster a collaborative environment that not only supports but also actively participates in the cultural transformation toward evidence-based decision-making.

Creating Sustained Change

The concept of a cultural shift is a recurring theme because it is foundational in establishing processes and organizational norms that prompt changes in employee behavior, aligning with the Impact Mindset. Sustained change involves ingraining new habits and normalizing the development of features focused on behavioral impacts. A successful initial FIA does not automatically guarantee a transformative shift; rather, the shift depends on meticulous planning, effective guidance, and adherence to proven change management principles.

It's critical to keep all stakeholders engaged with the progress of the FIA and related activities. Determine the most effective channels for updates and a frequency that aligns with your company's communication practices. I recommend weekly updates via platforms like Slack to maintain momentum, even if they merely recap the actions taken. Celebrating significant achievements is crucial, as it fosters goodwill and secures ongoing buy-in from all participants.

When communicating with different groups—partners, stakeholders, and executive stakeholders—tailor your messages to ensure involvement without overwhelming them. For executives, provide enough detail to foster a sense of participation, but avoid excessive granularity that might prompt unnecessary requests for information. Striking this balance is key to fostering ownership while ensuring the process remains efficient and not bogged down by excessive individual input.

Celebratory moments and major updates, such as through a newsletter or email blast, should coincide with significant milestones outlined in your roadmap. Besides recognizing these broader achievements, highlight teams and individuals who exemplify the Impact Mindset in action. The goal is to keep everyone informed and celebrate positive developments while establishing new norms and continuously expanding support for the initiative. This approach not only reinforces the desired cultural shift but also solidifies the foundation for sustained organizational change.

Formulating New Processes

In addition to best practices in change management, the implementation of new processes is often essential to catalyze genuine transformation. For these new processes to be embraced naturally, they must either be simpler or offer significantly greater value than the existing ones. Thoughtful design and the use of templates and other supportive materials can help achieve this goal. In some instances, however, it may be necessary to adjust incentives and engage with leadership to ensure that the product team has the necessary time and resources to adopt these new practices.

The rollout of new technology presents a prime opportunity to establish new habits, particularly when stakeholders are already adapting to changes. Explore ways to integrate these tools as part of a broader strategy to enhance value, positioning the adoption of both the technology and the associated behavioral changes as components of a single, unified process.

Experimentation is a central theme of this book and is critical to these cultural change initiatives. I advocate for initiating changes on a small scale, starting with the most engaged individuals and gradually expanding. This approach allows you to see what resonates and then refine your processes based on the feedback received. It's important to involve a diverse range of voices in designing these new processes. This inclusivity ensures that multiple perspectives are considered, which helps in simplifying the processes and maximizing the creation of value.

Upskilling and Support

As your initiatives progress, what starts as a single project will likely expand into a series of projects, increasing the demand for evidence generation. Initially, you may find yourself as the initiator and main orchestrator of these projects, but over time, the goal is for you to become one of many leaders driving this change. As the scale of your involvement grows, it will become impractical for you to single-handedly manage queries and support the creation and launch of each FIA.

Initially, you might not have considered the scalability of these efforts, but it is crucial to plan for how others can start developing their own user outcome connections and FIAs. Leveraging the materials provided in this book might suffice. However, as the need grows, collaborating with teams responsible for developing training and development materials will be vital to facilitate the scaling of this mindset.

Moreover, as more people contribute to the Insights Hub and conduct their own experiments, they will inevitably have questions about executing experiments and using new technologies. Start by identifying and supporting partners who are fully invested in these efforts and can help with troubleshooting. As the scale of these activities increases, coordinate with your internal IT team to establish effective support mechanisms for handling inquiries.

Developing an Impact Mindset within your organization requires the right systems to be in place. However, systems alone are insufficient—it also requires a cultural shift to ensure these systems are used effectively. It begins with understanding the existing norms within your organization and building on them, while also adhering to change management best practices to empower others to build on your initial efforts and sustain the momentum.

CHAPTER RECAP

- **Creating a cultural shift for Impact Mindset adoption:** To realize the full potential of the FIA, it is necessary to create a cultural shift to establish new organizational norms and processes that promote evidence-based decision-making and align employee behaviors with the Impact Mindset.

- **Formulating and implementing new processes:** Intuitive and beneficial new processes that integrate smoothly with existing technologies to replace outdated methods yield easier adoption and greater value.

- **Generating buy-in across groups:** Strategies for securing cooperation across diverse organizational groups are offered, aligning departmental goals with the Impact Mindset through tailored communication and engagement practices.

- **Upskilling and support for scalable change:** As the Impact Mindset culture shift continues, there is tremendous opportunity in building upskilling resources and support networks to ensure that those who want to experiment have the knowledge and ability to begin their own FIAs.

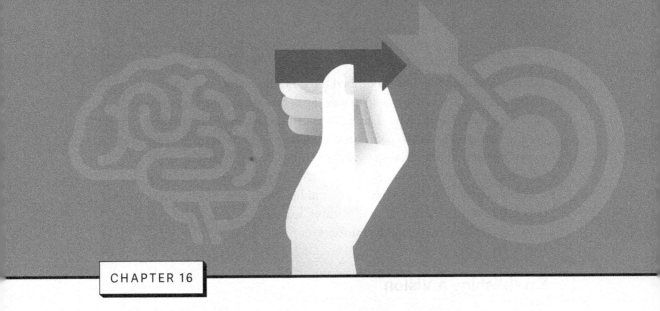

CHAPTER 16

Connecting to a Vision

Judging the success of products based purely on usage and satisfaction leads product teams of all sizes astray. This fixation on these measurements has fostered a product development philosophy that prioritizes growth and retention under the flawed assumption that these metrics alone define an effective feature. Although this strategy may seem like a winning formula, over time, most products begin to experience rising churn rates and escalating customer acquisition costs as users migrate to other solutions in search of something more useful.

In response, companies often double down on design tweaks and product-led growth strategies to boost engagement. Such tactics can generate temporary spikes in usage, but they fail to address the root issue. Without ensuring that the developed solutions truly solve user problems, the cycle continues, pulling the company further away from its original purpose.

Throughout this book, I have outlined the Impact Mindset to counter this flawed paradigm. It starts by expanding the definition of feature success to include measurable behavioral, user, and business outcomes. From there, you need to create more formal definitions of all core features using the User Outcome Connection, which can be validated using the experimental approach known as the Feature Impact Analysis (FIA). All this is aimed at realigning companies with their original purpose, guiding them toward a future in which they can confidently invest in new features, knowing they will deliver positive outcomes for both users and the business.

Establishing a Vision

We previously discussed the concept of a roadmap that guides you and your organization from the present to an ideal future. To provide clarity and direction, the final component of this journey is establishing a vision that will serve as a guiding light for all the roadmap's elements. This vision reminds all stakeholders of the flaws inherent in the current product development paradigm, underscores why the company strives to enhance its operations, and describes the desired future state.

A compelling vision assists in securing the resources needed to build out the systems and people aspects while keeping the team committed to achieving an Impact Mindset, even in the face of inevitable setbacks. Ultimately, a strong vision unifies and motivates your organization, ensuring that everyone remains focused on reaching this impactful future.

Using a Proactive Impact Mindset as a Template Vision

Throughout this book, a vision has been laid out for you, the adoption of an Impact Mindset. Building out the four components—User Outcome Connections for all core features, experimentation infrastructure, an established Insights Hub, and an evidence-based decision-making process—is in itself an ambitious and intricate endeavor and can be a multi-year project. For most, pursuing this outcome provides an ideal starting point for their vision, suggesting that each step brings unique value while moving closer to the significant benefits of a fully developed Impact Mindset.

In my experience, most companies have a solid sense of the gaps in the use of evidence throughout their decision-making process. Caused by neither a lack of desire nor malicious intent, these ineffective practices are driven by broken incentives and the pressure to hit business goals focused on output over outcomes. All of which boils down to a lack of strategy and vision. It's what compels companies to spend millions on strategy consulting. Many of the recommendations are not immediately actionable, but they create a destination to work toward. Pursuing the Impact Mindset can become that vision.

The true Impact Mindset philosophy, as hinted at throughout the book, means creating new features with proactive FIAs (**TABLE 16.1**). Here, the User Outcome Connection starts to be validated during the define and validate phases as the feature is being designed. By encouraging the team to view the new feature through the lens of specific behaviors and outcomes, they will be more inclined to seek existing evidence. This mental shift ensures that the solution provides genuine benefits for users rather than simply responding to desires for growth. As the team validates these connections with existing research, their assumptions will be challenged, highlighting the need for more evidence to confidently declare a feature successful.

TABLE 16.1 Proactive Feature Impact Analysis

DEVELOPMENT PHASE	FIA STEP	DESCRIPTION
Design	1. Define	Create the User Outcome Connection while the feature is being designed.
	2. Validate	Assess the current state of evidence that supports each connection during design.
Development	3. Collect data	Scope out metrics to be collected while the feature is being developed.
Post-Development	4. Experiment and analyze	Begin experimenting with the feature as soon as the team is comfortable getting the feature in front of customers.
	5. Take action	Continue collecting data to help refine the feature and maximize effectiveness.

As the product moves from design to development, the collect data phase begins with the team defining realistic metrics based on how the product is being developed. If new data pipelines or database connections are required, conducting the FIA concurrently with development gives the data team more lead time to build them out. By defining success metrics before launch, the team can establish a clear benchmark based on these new variables.

Once the feature is ready for testing, the fourth stage of the FIA, experiment and analyze, can begin. Instead of waiting for the product to be fully launched, experimenting on early users or a random sample of live customers allows the team to catch issues early, reducing rework costs. Experimenting prior to a full launch also increases the potential for more advanced experimental techniques, such as A/B testing or even testing multiple versions, which is considered a multivariate test. A control group of those who have nothing or a basic version of the feature can also be established, which is highly useful for establishing statistical significance.

In this vision of the Impact Mindset, the take action phase becomes an iterative process on the launched feature. Instead of being a single effort with a readout, actions can be taken on a product that has yet to be fully launched, ensuring the final solution is as effective as possible. With metrics established, they can be continually monitored as the features fully enter the market, all within your Insights Hub, where teams can see the status of the feature and how new features could build on the successful aspects of the launched solution.

Relying on the four core elements of the Impact Mindset is an ideal place to begin when crafting your vision. Depending on the culture of your organization, this could easily be enough, especially for larger enterprises, where getting to this state could take years and significant change. For smaller organizations or those with solid experimentation infrastructures in place already, there is potential for two simple extensions to this vision.

- Highlight the potential to conduct more experimentation before formally launching. The entire FIA could be completed on prototypes or even mock-ups, though the lower the fidelity, the less reliable the evidence for determining whether a solution will effectively change behaviors. In such cases, companies can leverage external research candidate pools like MTurk and Prolific to simplify test deployment.

- Identify opportunities to bring in research earlier in the development cycle. During the validate phase, whenever there is no existing research to support a connection at any stage of the User Outcome Connection, user research can be conducted. Although it may not offer the quantitative value of FIA-aligned experiments, it provides tremendous insight into how users perceive the relationship between behaviors and outcomes and how satisfying those outcomes influences their purchasing decisions. Including this in your vision can help generate buy-in and support from established research teams.

Starting with the standard vision of the Impact Mindset and proactive FIAs to ensure that launched features are maximized for driving desired behaviors and achieving outcomes, you have the components to build your own vision statement. You can choose to emphasize specific aspects, as in the previous two examples. With the template vision in hand, the next step is to craft a more tailored version based on your company's specifics.

Here's an example of a company's vision statement: "Embracing an Impact Mindset where the designing of each feature includes a clear purpose followed by the validation of their effectiveness through proactive FIAs, ensuring every insight is captured and readily accessible to inform data-driven decisions."

Creating Your Tailored Vision

With a standard vision based on the Impact Mindset established, the next step is to refine it further so that it directly resonates with your company's employees. You can achieve this in two primary ways: connect it to your company's mission statement and highlight relevant business factors. By shaping the vision around these characteristics, your direction will be more closely aligned with something your team can rally around.

1. Connecting to your mission and values

Start by tailoring the vision to fit your company's mission. Review the mission statement and any associated values. As it's currently designed, is your product genuinely helping users move closer to fulfilling the mission? It's not uncommon to find that many recently released features cannot be easily linked to user outcomes that would contribute to the company's mission. When intuition or ad-hoc customer requests drive product decisions, the product often evolves in a way that diverges from the original vision.

Regarding values, ask if the team is building products in a manner that aligns with the company's stated values. Many organizations advocate for having an experimental mindset, providing open feedback, and using data in decision-making, yet these values are often more aspirational than practiced.

Don't limit your investigation to leadership's communicated values; ask values-related questions when talking to the product team and observe how new features are created. These insights can help pinpoint precisely how current behaviors misalign with desired ones.

After reviewing the gap between the firm's noble ambitions, as reflected in the mission statement and values, and the realities of actual product development, you can re-create your vision to describe how these gaps will be bridged. The revised vision can specifically focus on building products that more closely align with the company's mission statement by identifying particular behaviors and user outcomes tied to the company's aspirations.

Similarly, address a few behaviors that prevent employees from acting according to their values. It might be that creating a stronger experimental infrastructure will catalyze the democratization of decision-making. Properly defining features could also encourage more data-driven decision-making by the team. Wherever a known void within the development of product exists, adopting the Impact Mindset can serve as a catalyst for continued values-based actions. The result is a more finely tuned vision.

Mission and values vision: "Embracing an Impact Mindset will involve designing features with a clear purpose and validating their effectiveness through proactive Feature Impact Analyses. This will be done by creating the experimentation and insight infrastructure required to allow employees to embrace an experimental mindset and align features with our mission of helping users achieve their fitness goals."

2. Connecting to business metrics

Another essential component in tailoring your vision to connect with your organization is to highlight specific business metrics most relevant to your company and market. All companies compete for customers, and various factors contribute to making a product competitive. In markets with many players and new entrants, building something that effectively retains users is critical. One of the best ways to accomplish this is by increasing the switching costs associated with the product. If switching costs can't be improved, another approach is to decrease customer acquisition costs so new customers can be brought in at a limited expense.

In other markets, particularly those with established players, product effectiveness is especially important in driving business growth. Some companies seek to leverage customer loyalty to increase organic marketing through referrals. Others use the measurable success of a product to create marketing campaigns highlighting the positive outcomes achieved through engagement, focusing on metrics like marketing effectiveness or time to close deals. Your firm's market and specific strategy dictate the approach you take and the metrics to include. By connecting your vision statement to these metrics, you'll increase buy-in from your business stakeholders.

Business metric vision: "Embracing an Impact Mindset will entail designing features with a clear purpose and validating their effectiveness through proactive Feature Impact Analyses. This will be achieved by creating the experimentation and insight infrastructure required to allow employees to embrace an experimental mindset. Building a successful product will position the team to maximize switching costs and organic growth, while capturing every insight to inform data-driven decisions."

With all your thoughts collected, it's time to write down your vision statement and include it in your roadmap document. This vision serves as the future state you and your team are working toward, with all corresponding efforts aligned with the Impact Mindset. In addition to the vision, give the overall project a name that connects to the vision. My first effort in this space was called Project Maximize Outcomes. With the project name and vision in place, make sure they are listed everywhere possible. Ensure that your executive stakeholders are familiar with them so they can easily communicate this effort among themselves and other leaders.

Defining a North Star

Your vision statement provides a singular future state that your team is working toward. This vision may seem so distant that it feels unattainable, but as you get closer it will start to resemble a nearly finished job. Throughout this journey, having an underlying, never-ending pursuit with which to guide your team toward something better is beneficial. I call this a North Star.

The unending pursuit of the Impact Mindset itself serves as a North Star, especially for companies with a limited experimentation culture. Similarly, converting to a truly evidence-based decision-making culture may feel like something that will never be fully realized. However, with a solid roadmap, effective project management, and a strong change management strategy, both can be achieved.

For many teams, having a guiding light beyond a tangible outcome is crucial—something greater that they can continue striving to achieve. A common North Star for most teams is building a best-in-class product. Creating a product that fully solves your users' problems will indeed achieve that goal, but in reality it's rarely attainable. No fitness solution helps everyone pursuing weight loss or muscle gain fulfill that mission. No bank has helped all its customers achieve financial security. No security software makes its customers impenetrable. Striving to develop a product that meets this vision is a North Star.

Even for a product that is the market leader, maintaining best-in-class status requires constant adaptation. It means being agile enough to recognize and respond to shifting user needs. At the same time, it requires understanding environmental forces that could disrupt a solution's effectiveness, such as significant world events, identifying their impact on users before it becomes a widespread problem.

By continually striving to be and remain the best, teams will stay sharp and ready to adapt to the evolving nature of products, aiming to avoid disruption. Teams in 2024 are facing this with the proliferation of generative AI models and their potential for significant product enhancements. New solutions are being created at rapid pace, some of which might achieve better outcomes for users faster. Backed by an evidence-based decision-making culture, teams can stay in step with these seismic changes. It starts with focusing on their well-defined behaviors and user needs, then experimenting with how the new technology can be used to impact them. Doing so keeps the team away from the trap of building for output's sake and steadfast in their pursuit to truly satisfy outcomes.

Being best-in-class is just one example of a North Star. It's up to you to determine what aligns with your company's ethos and compels your team to continue pushing toward a desired future.

Personalization as North Star

As I observe the advances in artificial intelligence, the evolving nature of design, and the value of measuring specific behaviors connected to user outcomes, a natural conclusion for the future begins to emerge: personalization of the product experience. This manifests as products tailored to segments and ultimately to individuals, covering everything from content to layout, from highlighted features to communications, and nudges. At its core, this will require a deep understanding of user needs, behaviors that lead to desired outcomes, and the ability to rapidly experiment to determine the best solution for each user. All this is underpinned by the Impact Mindset. The pursuit of personalization is a North Star in itself and one that I, along with others,[1] recommend for any company seeking what I believe is the inevitable future of product experience.

The desire to personalize is not new. For over a decade, marketing has been pursuing communication tailoring, supported by the belief that targeted messaging is more effective at converting potential buyers into customers. These efforts have led to meeting customers where they are with the most captivating messages, suggesting products they are most likely to desire. Sephora stands out in this category, having been recognized multiple times[2] for its ability to effectively segment customers using predictive analytics and quick surveys. Through this approach, they have simplified the daunting task of choosing from a collection of beauty products by delivering targeted recommendations on the most desired platform, using tested messaging to maximize app opens and subsequent purchases.

More recently, content personalization to increase usage has become a strategy for media and social media companies. TikTok, which saw a meteoric rise in the early 2020s, is commonly considered to have the best personalization algorithm. Their ability to understand and predict people has become a phenomenon, with users suggesting it noticed their pregnancy or emerging mental state before they did. Netflix and other media companies not only suggest content they believe users will enjoy the most, but they are also creating movies and television shows specifically tailored to audience segments. Gaming companies are an emerging group, with major games like *Call of Duty* recommending game modes and Duolingo suggesting content.

Whether it's personalizing marketing to increase conversion or targeting content to increase time spent on a platform, the goal is to persuade users that the

---

1 Generative UI and Outcome-Oriented Design, https://www.nngroup.com/articles/generative-ui/
2 www.sailthru.com/personalization-index/sephora/?utm_source=wwd&utm_medium=
public-relations&utm_campaign=rpi-2019

company understands their needs and can satisfy them. This leads to the next frontier: re-creating the entire product experience based on the unique visitor. Not just communication and content but features and flow. I've seen this first-hand at every company I've worked for; an outstanding opportunity exists to show only what a user needs and might find additional value in using.

For a weight training platform, this would involve showing curated metrics for their established goal, such as "gain muscle," followed by content to help them pursue that goal. If the user is part of a group struggling with follow-through on workouts, a feature to schedule and use a virtual coach to encourage adherence would be prominently displayed. Meanwhile, those who have already achieved consistency would be shown a different feature focused on learning new moves. The aim would be to tailor every aspect of the product experience to the user's segment and ultimately to the individual user.

One company I've enjoyed watching grow in this space is MutinyHQ. They assist B2B companies in building personalized landing pages for their products. By integrating with other marketing and sales platforms, they understand users and place them into segments that receive a landing page with text and content relevant to that audience. From there, they use additional data and learnings from their platform and others to refine content using generative AI for each individual customer. This ensures every customer receives a tailored landing page. This all exists today; now imagine what is possible from here. After purchasing the platform, a customer could be greeted with an onboarding experience showcasing all the most relevant features. Afterward, the homepage and menu could be tailored with the best information architecture for that person. In the long run, new features could be created on the spot for the user, combining solutions from others. The product would be able to truly satisfy each customer's needs.

This is a North Star. Is it possible? Yes, in theory. Is it something for which a company would need to strive for years to accomplish? Also yes. Personalization of the product experience at the scale of this example is only possible if generative AI applications continue to grow at the pace we've witnessed in 2023 and 2024. Yet even if the technology continues to evolve to meet technical needs, it doesn't guarantee companies will be ready to use it. Just as having the data infrastructure doesn't ensure that valuable outcome metrics will be created.

Companies seeking to progress toward this North Star of personalization need to invest in deeply understanding their users. First, their outcomes to understand what they are solving for, then their behaviors to understand how to design targeted solutions, and ultimately how it leads to business impact. They also need an experimental infrastructure and culture to rapidly test solutions tailored to unique customer needs. This is where the Impact Mindset becomes the path to enable this future.

A Never-Ending Process

With a clear vision and North Star encapsulating a fully developed roadmap and a FIA already in motion, you are ready to bring the Impact Mindset to your entire company. Once momentum is built and within your comfort level, distribute the document widely. You'll likely have one of the best-thought-out approaches to grassroots cultural change that most of your colleagues have encountered. The best part is that it will be linked not just to the pursuit of higher profits or maximizing usage but to building something that genuinely satisfies user needs. It is a path to guiding your organization back on and further down the path toward fulfilling its mission in alignment with its values.

Sharing it across the company will undoubtedly generate significant feedback, so it's crucial to establish a system for collecting feedback from all stakeholders. Not all recommendations must be acted upon, but every contributor should feel heard, which will minimize negative opinions about the endeavor. A simple Google Form combined with a public spreadsheet listing comments and actions taken (with justifications) can suffice. Alternatively, the process can be integrated into existing mechanisms your company already has, depending on the maturity of your project management systems. Regardless, the goal is to ensure that feedback mechanisms are in place, and anyone who wants to contribute can feel they had the chance to share their suggestions.

A central theme of the FIA is to remain flexible and adapt to expected and unexpected changes. Implementing the Impact Mindset requires the same. That's where the feedback you collect will be invaluable, serving as a pulse on both the progress being made and the perception of that progress, allowing you to adjust. Your goal is to build out the maturity of all 18 components that were spelled out in Chapter 13 and further elaborated through this chapter and the previous two, though you may need to adjust priorities along the way. Likewise, you might need to spend more time communicating certain aspects or building buy-in for specific projects. You might even need to pivot the mission or North Star, but only if there is significant pressure, as these should be the foundation of your Impact Mindset journey.

Stay strong but agile: build, share, build, share, succeed, build, and share.

Moving Toward Greater Impact

Through the pages of this book, I hope you've connected with the passion I have for this subject. In the introduction, I shared my disillusionment with the current product development trap, which measures success based solely on usage. As a result of it, we are surrounded by products that use behavioral science not to help users bridge the gap from knowledge to action but instead to keep them habitually engaged in ways that offer no real benefit. This has sparked a backlash against technology, which, in my view, is a necessary component for scaling interventions that could be truly helpful.

In response, I've been writing and speaking on this subject for the past five years, culminating in the frameworks and knowledge presented in this book. I've designed this book to be a comprehensive handbook, covering, in varying degrees of detail, all the components needed to progress toward a better way of building and measuring feature success. My goal is to empower you, the reader, to believe you can be the catalyst for this change at your organization because you can. With the knowledge provided in this book, the recommended additional readings, and the accompanying online material, you are ready to kick-start your movement.

In the spirit of the experimentation mindset, I recognize that this is the beginning, not the end. I'm excited to hear feedback from readers as you build out aspects of the Impact Mindset. In turn, I will continue to refine the philosophy and accompanying content. With the launch of this book, the refinement cycle begins, and I'm eager to see what it will grow to become. Until then, see you on the product development playing field.

CHAPTER RECAP

- **Impact Mindset as a North Star:** The Impact Mindset serves as the guiding philosophy for transcending traditional metrics like usage and satisfaction, focusing instead on genuinely satisfying user needs.

- **Creating a tailored vision:** The vision of the Impact Mindset is customized to align with organizational missions and values, ensuring that product development efforts resonate with company goals and employee beliefs.

- **Personalization as a pinnacle goal:** Personalization of the product experience is advocated as a North Star, aiming for a future where product features and interactions are uniquely tailored to individual user needs, behaviors, and outcomes.

- **A never-ending process:** The implementation of the Impact Mindset involves continuous feedback, adaptation, and refinement of strategies to stay aligned with evolving user demands and business objectives.

- **Onward and upward:** Continuous dialogue and feedback are encouraged to refine and adapt the frameworks and philosophies introduced, promoting an experimental mindset that views the book's launch as the beginning of an evolutionary process in product development.

Index

A

A/B tests, 171
academic articles, 88
Acorns financial app, 36
active vs. passive collection, 140–141
adaptive agility, 260
advanced metrics, 126. *See also* metrics; impactful metrics; success metrics
advertisement business model, 11–12. *See also* business philosophies
advertisement spending, 7–8
advertising campaigns, 11
advertising revenue, 6
"aha moment," identifying, 239–240
AI (artificial intelligence), xvi–xvii, 261. *See also* GenAI space
"AI Habit Formation: Future-Proofing Your UX Career," 98
AI-tool development, 98
already collected classification, 154–156
Amplitude tool, 126
analysis. *See* data analysis
ANOVA (Analysis of Variance) tests, inferential technique, 203
anthropology and psychology, 136
Apple Fitness three rings, 63–64, 67, 111
Apple Health app, 66
Apple mouse, 28
Apple Watch
    features, 37, 62
    metrics for charting impact, 65–67
    User Outcome Connection, 65
Apple's products, 89
applied research. *See also* research
    hypotheses, 114
    trade-offs, 193
Arnold, John, 28
Asana project management application, 46
assumptions, determining, 107–109
Atlan, 124
attitudinal data, 149–150, 158
attitudinal vs. behavioral metrics, 140, 157
audit step, data collection, 153–155

B

B2B (business-to-business) entities
    vs. B2C, 45
    and B2C connections, 57
    business customer outcome, 96
    outcomes, 48–49
B2B User Outcome Connection
    framework, 50–51
    Mailchimp, 53–54
B2B vignette, ideal narrative, 137
B2C (business-to-customer) firms
    vs. B2B, 45
    outcomes, 48–49
B2C User Outcome Connection
    framework, 50–51
    Noom, 52–53
B2C vignette, ideal narrative, 137
basic moderated experiments, 187
behavior assumption
    determining, 107–108
    FIA Step 5 (Take Action), 220–221
    Google Tasks, 109
    validating, 109–110
behavior assumption validation, 120
behavioral and user outcomes, 15–18
behavioral assumption and hypothesis, 115–116
behavioral data collection, system aspect, 280
behavioral hypothesis, 117, 119
behavioral outcomes. *See also Design for Behavioral Change: Applying Psychology and Behavioral Economics; Engaged: Designing for Behavior Change*
    Apple Fitness three rings, 67
    Grammarly, 19
    Impact Mindset, 16–18
    Jochi chatbot, 146
    Ninjio, 20
    success level, 16
behavioral outcomes metric, 129–131
behavioral vs. attitudinal metrics, 140, 157
behaviors. *See also* The Hawthorne effect
    Define step, 81–83